C3206   8 00

.52

MY LOVE AFFAIR

WITH THE NAVY

Books by Allan R. Bosworth

NON-FICTION

A Cabin in the Hills
Ginza Go, Papa-San
New Country
The Lovely World of Richi-San
Ozona Country
America's Concentration Camps
My Love Affair with the Navy

NOVELS

Wherever the Grass Grows
Full Crash Dive
Hang and Rattle
Bury Me Not
The Drifters
The Crows of Edwina Hill
Steel to the Sunset

JUVENILES

Sancho of the Long, Long Horns
Ladd of the Lone Star

MY LOVE AFFAIR
WITH THE NAVY

by *Allan R. Bosworth*

CAPTAIN, U.S.N.R. (RETIRED)

Foreword by Rear Admiral Ernest M. Eller

U.S.N. (RETIRED)

NEW YORK  W·W·NORTON & COMPANY·INC·

Library of Congress Catalog Card No. 73-77397. Printed in the United States of America.   SBN 393 07449 8

2 3 4 5 6 7 8 9 0

To All My Shipmates

CONTENTS

FOREWORD

"They that go down to the sea in ships, that do business in great waters; these see the works of the Lord, and his wonders in the deep," sang the psalmist and so sing the hearts of most who sail blue water to this day. As a microcosm of eternity, it brings man into closer understanding that something far bigger than we can conceive awaits over the last horizon.

Some men love the sea for itself alone. Some love it for horizons that ever recede and for the far shores where winds and waves bear them. Some love it for the sun and stars and "the storm clouds blowing down God's wide expanse" that sweep them from the littleness of the world into the vastness of the Divine. Some love it because of its profound meaning to the security of America. Allan Bosworth, "Bos," man of many parts, obviously loves it for all of these as well as other reasons.

In the book that follows he tells much of the history of the Navy that has importantly shaped the destiny of America. He has likewise told in his own inimitable way some of the tall tales that have lightened the hours of sailors at sea over the generations. He has often told them with tongue in cheek "as it was told to me sitting on my ditty box in the old North D."

With typical Bosworthian skill he fashions verse out of hemp, tar, and scud mixed with grog fumes from the "Old Ironsides" yarn that will cause him no end of buffeting when he sails on to the seas where old sailors ever sail. There he will be keelhauled by the shades of veterans of this fighting frigate, whose valor and dedication have become priceless threads of steel in American character.

9

Foreword

Bos has not concentrated on the drama of combat, the valor, the sacrifice even to death that mark the long sea road of dedicated service to America—without which she could not have endured free. However, he has interwoven enough of these to show that the lighthearted side of the Navy only covers the surface, like sunlight on the sea.

The book becomes thus a unique mingling of his own career in the Navy and the influence of the Navy upon the history of our country. It shows the decisive influence of the sea in the United States' destiny, so little understood by most Americans. They understand even less that power at sea has steadily grown. As the United States has expanded into world duties, it has had increasing need for more strength at sea. Ultimately, the man ashore has to win wars but the Navy has to take him there and keep him there. More and more it has to and has gained the ability to clear the way and to overwhelm any land fortification. More and more sea power can reach inland on the wings of planes and missiles.

More and more sea power has become needed by the United States as leader of the free nations that the sea joins or divides depending upon our ability to control it.

As Bos says, there will always be a Navy until the seas run dry—but we must add, whose Navy will it be? The Allies controlled the sea in World War II and won. In the process the United States developed the greatest Navy ever to sail deep water. Yet, immediately afterwards, she began cutting it to the bone. I shall never forget the heartsick dismay experienced in a conference with the British Chiefs of Staffs, while we laid plans for the NATO Military Organization, upon hearing the U.S. spokesman say less than four years after VJ Day:

In the event of war we cannot hold a line in the Mediterranean east of Tunis-Malta.

In those incredible years political leaders sought to do away with the United States Marine Corps; to abolish aircraft carriers, the backbone of sea power; and to reduce the Navy simply to a transport and escort force.

A similar madness caused a reduction in the Army and to a lesser degree the Air Force as we approached the verge of catastrophe.

The Korean War suddenly shattered the illusion of security behind the monster of the atomic bomb. Had the communists waited a few more years, the reduction of United States' power afloat would probably have passed the point of no return. As it was, with veterans still around from World War II and ships called out of reserve, the Navy came through in the crisis. As in the dark days after Pearl Harbor, it followed Admiral King's unflinching order, "Do the best you can with what you have." It did this magnificently in many operations, but never more so than at Inchon where General MacArthur said as the amphibious assault swept over the beach, "The Navy and Marines have never shown more brightly than this morning."

Inchon will long stand in military history as a perfect example of bold maritime strategy. Yet a motley assemblage of ships carried out this overwhelmingly successful assault. Ships of every kind, hastily assembled, had little time to prepare or rehearse. The Marines had less time. The operation succeeded because of will and skill, because of courage and improvisation, and because of the expertise remaining in these sailormen and marines who had just won the greatest amphibious war of history.

I am convinced that the Korean War would not have come had we maintained the strength demanded of us as the world leader of freedom. I am not convinced that we learned this lesson from the war. Let us listen again to Bos's admirable words, "There will always be a Navy until the seas run dry," while asking again the question, almost in despair, "Whose Navy will it be?" Note the equanimity with which during the 1960's the Secretary of Defense, many Congressmen, and most Americans have looked upon the phenomenal rise of Soviet sea power.

Although the communists have not veered from their set course to win the world, we have let our active Merchant Marine decline while the Soviets have surged forward and will soon surpass ours. Our fisheries wither away while Soviet fishing fleets,

11

doubling in intelligence, range the world. Happily, in the past few years we have continued naval construction, but far too slowly as the Soviets close the gap. Only in Polaris submarines and in the aircraft carrier (which, ironically, men wanted to abandon a few years ago) do we have clear-cut superiority.

Perhaps Americans as a whole, immersed in daily duties, can never learn. Certainly their leaders can. Hopefully they can look into the past, swiftly surveyed by Bos in this interesting book, and see the need and their responsibilities stated for them by our first and greatest President. Through the long years of the American Revolution George Washington grew as a military leader, thinker, and strategist. The more his armies struggled, the more he came to know the truth which, generation by generation, has developed even more profound significance to this island continent of ours. In that war, in Washington's words, sea power was "the pivot on which everything turned," or as he wrote at another time:

Without a decisive naval force we can do nothing definitive and with it everything honorable and glorious.

E. M. ELLER
Rear Admiral, U.S.N. (retired),
Director of Naval History

PREFACE

I might be satisfied ashore if I had never seen
The big waves top the foc'sle, and race aft white
*   and green;*
If I had never felt the wind, or heard the
*   lightnings hurled,*
And watched the storm clouds blowing down
*   God's wide expanse of world;*
If I had never served the Flag, or known the big
*   guns' roar,*
Or worn the Navy blue—I might be satisfied
*   ashore.*

EACH MAN HAS his own horizons, and they are what he makes them. Those of the prairie man appear limitless but do not change; those of the sailor look to be changeless, but are ever changing. For music, the prairie dweller has the song of the lonesome wind. The sailor has a full symphony of harp strings in the rigging, the tympany of waves against the hull, and the soft sighing of the bow-wash alongside. No melody was ever sweeter, and the crawling years cannot diminish it in memory . . .

Memories are all I have left now, because I have become what W. S. Gilbert (*The Yarn of the Nancy Bell*) called "an elderly naval man." All men eventually become elderly, except those cut down in the flower of their youth, or the fatness of their forties. Still, the modifying adjective is a relative term, not to be confused with "senile." I suspect one qualifies as elderly when he begins to use the prefatory remark "Now, in the Old Navy . . ." more and more.

13

Preface

At best, this is an inexplicit introduction. It could mean the days of John Paul Jones, or—usually in my case—the battleship Navy of the 1920's. It is a less boastful and much nicer way of informing a younger generation than employing the ancient Navy brag of, "Why, I have passed more lighthouses than you have passed telegraph poles! I have peed more salt water than you ever sailed over!"

By all means, the reference to the Old Navy does not imply that the Navy itself was ever decrepit. Aside from the Boy Scouts, I can think of no other organization, civil or military, which has so consistently preserved its youth and flexibility in all the years from round shot to rockets. The Navy has always adapted to new concepts, new inventions, and changing times.

The first drastic adaptation, of course, was from sail to steam, when steam—like the miniskirt—made wind unnecessary. The next was when man conquered both the air and the undersea depths, and the Navy recognized the potentialities of new weapons. The last big change came when the atom bomb fell on Hiroshima.

Some military experts and armchair strategists felt that this had literally lowered the boom on sea power. Warships would no longer be needed, they thought, because war would become a push-button affair.

They were very wrong. The "police action" in Korea soon proved that unless we are willing to destroy civilization, war in the final analysis, oversimplified, comes down to putting a foot soldier ashore with a rifle, to occupy the enemy's territory. This means amphibious landings. Somebody has to deliver the soldier with the rifle, and that somebody is the Navy . . .

At the same time, the Navy was proving that it had the capability of delivering The Bomb, and then it entered the field of nuclear propulsion, and did so well that it has sent submarines around the world, nonstop, submerged.

So the Navy is still with us, and will still be with us until the seas run dry . . .

Just what is the United States Navy?

Some sizable volumes have been written on mere segments of it: battleships, aircraft carriers, destroyers, submarines, and even the PT's, or Motor Torpedo Boats.

This book will attempt to give the answer in a less technical, but perhaps lighter and more human way. To be sure, the Navy is surface ships and submarines and airplanes. It is battleships in mothballs—not so obsolescent as some people think. It is far-flung shore establishments. It is history and tradition, glory and tragedy, and plain hard work. It is salty humor, and old sea stories told during the dog watch; it is a terrible and shining pride of outfit, and the precise, heart-catching splendor of the Brigade of Midshipmen at Annapolis on dress parade. It is the Marines at Belleau Wood and Iwo Jima, and Arleigh Burke's immortally famed destroyers rocketing down the channel at his signature speed of thirty-one knots. It is a submarine commander, shot in half, gasping his last order: "Take her down!"—while he stayed outside the conning tower. And many more things.

Above all else, however, the Navy is and always has been *people*. Its men—and of late the women in the WAVES—make up a gallant, fighting, seagoing outfit that may have been out-gunned in a few individual engagements, but has never yet lost a war.

A Navy ship is today—as it always has been—a small bit of America upon the sea. It sails everywhere, defending the Flag, or just showing it, building good will for our nation, broadening the horizons and the outlook and understanding of its people. Navy men become wise, traveled, and sophisticated much earlier than do most of their civilian counterparts. Depending upon its size, the ship has everything an American community has: its own police force and fire department, a hospital, a store, a telephone exchange, and even a newspaper. The population may exceed two thousand souls. The commanding officer's authority is an awesome thing. The mayor of a city could hardly lead the nation into war. The commander of a warship can, simply by saying: "Prepare to fire . . . commence firing!"

For myself, I shall say only that I have been an apprentice

seaman, seaman second class, hospital apprentice first class, pharmacist's mate (now called hospitalman) third class, and pharmacist's mate second class in the Regular Navy. Then ensign, junior grade lieutenant, lieutenant, lieutenant commander, commander, and captain in the Naval Reserve. This means that there are only two ratings and two ranks I have never held. I was never a first class petty officer or a chief petty officer, never a warrant officer or an Admiral.

On May 31, 1960, I received the following message:

FM CHINFO

TO USLO SACLANT NORVA

BT

/UNCLASSIFIED/

FOR CAPTAIN A. R. BOSWORTH. AS YOUR DISTINGUISHED CAREER AS AN ENLISTED MAN AND AN OFFICER IN THE NAVY AND NAVAL RESERVE DRAWS TO A CLOSE, ALL HANDS IN THE OFFICE OF INFORMATION JOIN ME IN WISHING YOU AND MRS. BOSWORTH THE BEST OF EVERYTHING IN YOUR WELL EARNED RETIREMENT. YOU WILL BE MISSED BY THE NAVY AND THE PRESS CORPS, BOTH OF WHICH YOU HAVE SERVED SO WELL FOR THESE MANY YEARS AND WHO WILL ALWAYS LOOK UPON YOU WITH RESPECT AND WARM AFFECTION. WELL DONE, GOOD LUCK AND GODSPEED.

BT   C. C. KIRKPATRICK

31/1734 Z   REAR ADMIRAL, U.S. NAVY

TOR: 31 MAY 60 1814Z.

A word, now, about what Admiral Kirkpatrick called my "distinguished career." The Admiral was being characteristically kind, and was leaning over backward to observe naval courtesy. There may have been a number of such congratulatory messages, and, indeed, they may have been what the Navy calls SOP, or Standard Order of Procedure. But I have never seen another, and I treasure the dispatch and have had it enlarged, matted, and framed. The best words in it are "well done." To a Navy man, a "well done" is just short of a medal.

Certainly my Navy career was largely due to fortuitous timing and circumstances. My enlisted peacetime service was in no way spectacular, although I made good quarterly marks on everything from neatness, military bearing, and military conduct to performance of the duties of my rating. We played war games in earnest in those days, and during one session of long-range battle practice the word was passed, "Casualty in Number Two Turret! Casualty in Number Two Turret!"

This turret was my responsibility. A short time before, a man had been killed in it when a 16-inch gun jumped its carriage and cut him in two against the bulkhead.

I took off on the double with a first-aid pouch and four stretcher bearers, not knowing whether the casualty was a drill, or real. When we reached the turret a man was lying on deck. The turret officer, an ensign, was grinning, and I knew then that the casualty was only simulated.

But the game had to go on. I said, "Sir, what has happened to this man?" The ensign said, "His head has been blown off. What will you do with him?"

I said, "Dump him over the side, and sand the bloody deck!" Then I caught the man by a leg and began dragging him to the side. The *Maryland's* stanchions and lifelines were down for the firing. The ensign yelled in sudden alarm, "Belay that!" But I had given the correct answer, and was mentioned at meritorious mast for it.

In 1925 I was given an honorable discharge and had quite a bit of leave coming. I went to work, during the leave, for the old *San Diego Sun,* a Scripps paper and very short-staffed. My main job was covering police, but I also had to cover hotels, schools, and the chamber of commerce.

Jerry MacMullen, who covered police alone for the more affluent *San Diego Union,* suggested that I apply for a commission in the Naval Reserve. He had been given such a commission a few months earlier. I applied with trepidation: Jerry had been to college, I had had only two years of high school.

This is where unplanned timing and luck came into the picture. We did not know it, but the Navy Department had just hit upon the idea of beefing up Naval Intelligence by commissioning sixteen or seventeen young officers—mostly newspapermen—in the Reserve. And I was one of them.

What could a reserve officer do when inactive? Not much, except try to present the Navy in a favorable light in print, and try to do away with such a phrase as "Congress is spending money like a drunken sailor." I will always think the Navy was too sensitive about that one.

But the inactive reserve in San Francisco and the 12th Naval District, in the mid-Thirties, suddenly became very active, indeed.

The Intelligence unit had a monthly luncheon at a place in Chinatown where we could enjoy a couple of drinks and some excellent food, while the District Intelligence Officer gave us the poop on what was happening. One day he read us a dispatch that had just been received from Commander Fourth Naval District, Philadelphia. It said that one Lieutenant Commander Omae of the Imperial Japanese Navy had been enrolled at the University of Pennsylvania as an English-language student, but had dropped out after a couple of weeks, and was believed to be headed west in a 1935 Ford sedan, Pennsylvania license so and so.

"Watch for that car," the Intelligence officer said.

We finished lunch. As I went down the street, Grant Avenue, I—and a couple of others—found the Ford sedan parked in front of the Yamato Hotel.

Intelligence put a "tail" on the car immediately. Omae was living in an apartment on Fillmore Street, with a very attractive Nisei girl from Hawaii.

We watched him closely for about two years. I spent so many evenings watching him, and feeling I could not tell my wife what I was doing, that I was nearly threatened with divorce. We decided that Omae was living it up, and selling his country short. I parked near him one day at Land's End, and we watched battleships steam into the Golden Gate. He made sketches of their fighting tops, but all of that was in Jane's *Fighting Ships*.

He and the Nisei girl would go out to eat in a Japanese restaurant on Fillmore Street. Then, with a pass key we had made, we would enter his apartment, take all his papers—they were not filed in any orderly fashion—and rush them to Navy Headquarters for photostats.

Such visits to the apartment were necessarily brief: we had only about a half hour in which we could safely photostat the papers and return them. Meanwhile, the Navy attached so much importance to our work that it provided funds. We first rented another apartment across the street, and kept Omae under surveillance. Then we took an apartment across the hall from him. Finally, we went into his apartment and bugged it for sound. Most of the things we heard were of a very intimate nature and had nothing to do with naval information.

One evening we went in and found Omae's brief case open on the bed, with more than $600 in crisp new $20 bills carelessly exposed. Another time we were elated when we found what at first glance appeared to be a semaphore code of the alphabet. But when we had time to examine the photostat later, it turned out to be a cartograph illustrating twenty-six different sexual positions.

This, it seemed, was Omae's real career, and some of us considered going on a rice and fish diet. The Nisei girl was built like a Shetland pony, and was very easy to shadow. I could follow her and Omae down Fillmore Street, a teeming thoroughfare, keep thirty paces astern, and still look out from under my snap-brim hat (a must for secret agents of the day) and see her derriere twinkling like a flashing light.

[*ii*] We had enough on Omae, after the first few weeks, that we could have had the FBI pick him up at any time. I was in favor of this, but cooler heads and wiser judgment fortunately prevailed. Gene Kerrigan, a Reserve lieutenant commander and the best private investigator I have ever known, pointed out that Omae wasn't getting anything as a spy, but that one day he would be relieved, and his successor might be an entirely different type. It was important to know who that successor was.

Preface

We had an excellent translator, a young law student who had been raised in Japan, the son of an American missionary. When Omae's orders came, we were able to read them, and we watched him when he booked passage in a Japanese luxury liner.

Then even Gene Kerrigan got worried. Omae had nothing—or was he more clever than we thought? What was he taking back to Japan in the lining of his suitcases?

There was only one thing to do. The evening before Omae was to sail, I followed him and the Nisei girl to the restaurant and saw them seated. Then I sprinted back to the apartment. We went into Omae's apartment and stole everything he had, including a fine camera and a pair of binoculars.

It helped that the chief of police was a Naval Reserve Intelligence officer. The suitcases yielded nothing. The binoculars and camera were pawned, and arrangements made for Omae to recover them; the whole thing looked like a sneak burglary—although I am sure Omae knew the truth. He had the nerve to report the theft promptly, and the police assured him his property would be restored.

Next morning, a few hours before sailing time, we saw a car pull up in front of the apartment, and a Japanese get out with his luggage. He and Omae shook hands. Omae gave him the keys to the Ford sedan.

It was a complete takeover. Omae took a cab to the Embarcadero, his recovered luggage now intact. And his successor took the Nisei girl into the apartment.

It was all very exciting, playing Secret Agent 'enry 'yde, but things were building up on a larger scale, and a short time later I received orders to active duty. I never learned what happened to Omae's relief except that he was seized when Pearl Harbor was attacked, along with many others.

Now my classification as an Intelligence officer was changed to Public Relations. This, at first, was a blow. The Admiral to whom I reported said, "You have been sent here to handle my public relations. I do not desire any public relations. Should I desire any public relations, I am quite capable of handling them for myself."

It did me no good to say, "Admiral, whether you desire them or not, you will always have them."

I went first on duty at headquarters in San Francisco, then to the Fourth Naval District in Philadelphia. I rented an apartment and ordered a telephone installed. It was 7 December, 1941.

Next morning I slept late. No telephone, no radio. When I finally started down for breakfast, newspapers were stacked in the elevator a yard high.

Headlines shouted *U.S. LOSS HEAVY* and things like that. The time differential was such that Philadelphia papers—there were none on Sunday afternoon—did not get the story until Monday morning. I did a quick backtrack to the apartment and read the news. Then I went to Navy headquarters and pretended I had known it all along. I was not alone in this, because many of the officers had been in the country all day Sunday and had not heard.

What a way for war to come to a man who sincerely thought he had been preparing for war all his life!

I wanted, now, to get to the Pacific, and began submitting requests asking for duty with the fleet in a combatant ship. It must be admitted that this was not realistic. I was not a gunnery officer or a navigator; I could not "hand, reef, or steer, or ship a selvagee." But I got back to San Francisco, and then wangled my way into the Armed Guard—an outfit that manned guns aboard merchant ships. I would have command of such a shipboard unit, but first I had to go to gunnery school.

I did this for some six weeks and became fairly expert at calling the range and directing shore batteries on the beach, firing at sleeve targets being towed by planes. In fact, I passed the final test and was awaiting orders to my first ship. Two days later, and I would have been gone.

Then the District Personnel office sent for me and showed me a copy of a dispatch. Admiral "Bull" Halsey, in the South Pacific, had requested me by name.

"It will do no good to send you out aboard ship," the personnel officer said. "What Halsey wants, Halsey gets. We may as well cancel the other orders."

I was flattered, of course, but I knew what had happened. An old friend, Jim Bassett, was due to come back Stateside after a long tour in the Pacific and the South Pacific. He had simply recommended to Halsey that I replace him on Halsey's staff.

So I went to Noumea and Guadalcanal, and saw a brief bit of fighting on Bougainville—but my main job was still taking care of the press, and for all time afterward I could never get away from that. I can see, now, that it made sense.

Later I worked for Admiral Nimitz, and returned to civilian life. The Navy called me up to active duty for six months a short time later. After that, it called me up for active duty for a year. At that point, I made a difficult choice. I was doing pretty well writing for the *Saturday Evening Post, Liberty, Collier's* and other late lamented magazines, but I felt I had too much time in the Navy to throw the service away. I wrote to Don Varian, then a Captain, and asked what assurance I could have of staying in uniform.

Varian telephoned me aboard U.S.S. *Yosemite* at Newport. "Doctor," he said (a gag title), "I am glad to tell you that you stand number one on the list of reserve officers for retention on active duty."

There you have it. Followed nearly six years in Japan and Korea, and once again (only the second time) I heard shots fired in anger. But I neither fired them nor directed their firing. I did not con the ship or pilot a plane. This still rankles, until I tell myself to knock off the Rover Boy attitude and be damned glad that I had some thirty-eight years of association with the Navy, twenty of them on active duty, before age put me on the beach.

To be sure, this service in itself in no way qualifies me to write a book about the Navy. But I have old friends and shipmates who are wonderfully willing to pool their memories with my own. Some of the book's content will cause Navy personnel to frown and say, "I knew that, before." Residents of Navy towns such as Newport, Norfolk, San Pedro, Long Beach, and Seattle may say the same.

I ask their indulgence. There is a large portion of the inland America which does not know much about the Navy, even though it supplies most of the Navy's manpower. A few years ago, while still on active duty, I went through my old home country of West Texas. This is the range of the hard-butted cavalryman, and the Mexican border wars. My lovely niece, Bess, asked, "Uncle Al, what are you in the Navy now?"

"Captain," I said in a modest, lower-case tone.

"That's wonderful!" she enthused. "You just keep on, and you'll be a Major some day!"

To write this kind of book, I think you have to go far inland, away from the seductive sounds of the sea, and then sit down and look back.

A Navy ship is christened, launched, and commissioned.

A book usually is commissioned, christened, and launched.

The warship slides gracefully down the ways, makes a lovely splash, and then floats proudly.

A book may make no splash at all, and may sink without a trace.

In spite of all this, stand by to launch!

ALLAN R. BOSWORTH

Roanoke, Virginia
20 April 1969

ACKNOWLEDGMENTS

THIS BOOK owes much to many. Some of the people I have listed below in alphabetical order are old friends and shipmates; some I have never met. Without exception, all were most courteous and kind in sharing their memories with me, or in giving me permission to draw upon their own writings.

I owe very special thanks to Captain James Bassett, U.S.N.R. (ret.), to Captain E. L. Castillo, U.S.N (ret.) and to Rear Admiral Ernest M. Eller, U.S.N. (ret.). To an old boss of mine, Admiral Roscoe F. Good, U.S.N. (ret.). Thanks are due to Mrs. A. Gilbert, Frank Graham, George E. "Rojo" Hickman, Donald Jackson, Captain Charles L. Kessler, U.S.N., Professor Harold D. Langley, Captain F. Kent Loomis, U.S.N., Howard P. Nash, and Editor Merrill Pollack.

I am very grateful to Mrs. Inez Reidenbach, Lisa Rideout, and Rear Admiral J. A. Robbins, U.S.N. (ret.).

Thanks are due to Marie Rodell, who guides me on the literary path and has never yet been wrong. Some Smiths helped here: Rear Admiral D. F. Smith, U.S.N., Captain Roy Campbell Smith, III, U.S.N.R. (ret.) and Ruby Smith, typist. Warwick Tompkins, an old Navy hand. Luther G. Whittier, a Maine man who knew the fabulous Griffith Price Owen. Rear Admiral Donald C. Varian, U.S.N. (ret.), old shipmate, good friend, and drinking companion.

I thank them all, and hope I have not failed them. If I have failed to name anyone, I apologize for my poor bookkeeping.

ALLAN R. BOSWORTH
Captain, U.S.N.R. (retired)

MY LOVE AFFAIR

WITH THE NAVY

1. HOW IT ALL
BEGAN

Head Quarters, Cambridge,
July 15, 1775
    The Commanding Officers of each Regiment
to report the names of such Men in their respective Corps, as are most expert in the management
of whaleboats.
—*General Orders of George Washington*

THE ABOVE EXTRACT from Washington's General Orders was
written on the very day he was sworn in as Commander in Chief
of the Army of the United Colonies. One of his first official acts in
that capacity was to charter a number of small but fast merchant
ships and fishing schooners. He put guns aboard these vessels and
supplied Army gun crews. He encouraged the captains of other
ships to become privateers, and to raid and capture English merchantmen. Very soon the American colonies were chopping, with
great success, at the supply lines for the British forces in Boston
and other Atlantic ports.

The first such vessel was the schooner *Hannah*, with Nicholas
Broughton as her captain. The *Hannah* had a most lively career,
retaking the American ship *Unity*, which had been captured by
the British.

Out of this small but auspicious beginning, the most powerful
fighting force in the world—the United States Navy—was born.
George Washington was not only the Father of his Country, but
also the founder of the Navy.

29

At first glance, this is truly remarkable, considering Washington's background. A Virginia planter. An Army man from way back in the French and Indian wars. He did not know the first thing about seamanship, or shiphandling, and the Navy has laughed for many years because (according to the painting) he stood up in the boat when crossing the Delaware. But his concepts were broad, and he was second to none in his understanding of the importance of sea power, and its use in the Revolution. In 1781, he wrote to Lafayette:

"It follows then as certain as the Night succeeds the day, that without a decisive Naval force we can do nothing definitive—and with it everything honourable and glorious."

Let's take another look at the school history texts. As I remember them, they made much of Bunker Hill, Brandywine and other land battles, none of them decisive in the least. I do not recall that they mentioned sea fights except perhaps to refer to one or two of John Paul Jones's heroic engagements. As for the single *decisive* battle that ended the Revolutionary War, the fleet engagement off Chesapeake Bay, I do not think that the school texts referred to it at all. They simply said that Washington bottled up the forces of General Cornwallis on the Yorktown Peninsula . . .

Historians agree now, however, that the American Revolution was as much a naval war as it was a land war. And they say that Washington as much deserved the title "Admiral" as he did "General."

Our infant sea service first consisted of a few chartered ships, under the Army, and hundreds of others acting as privateers and seizing British vessels and their cargoes for prize money. If this is little short of piracy on the high seas, at least it was practiced by all nations in the eighteenth century, and it was very effective.

The newly established Navy was naturally patterned after the Royal Navy, a great and glorious establishment in that day, and our Marine Corps—founded just four months after Washington took command—also copied the British. But the success of the early chartered ships showed that the concept of having seamen sail the ships and soldiers man the guns made good sense.

30

It still does. In the era of the modern battleships, sailors manned the turret guns while marines stood by to service the five-inch batteries and perform most of the amphibious landings. The amphibious ships did not come into their own until World War II, when there were not enough marines, and Army troops had to be put ashore to secure beach heads. Then came the Navy's Sea-Bees, the famed Construction Battalions who fight for what they build. They were a wonderful, bastardly outfit, half horse and half alligator, part Navy, part Army, and part Marines, with a *Gung ho!* attitude that could be heard from Guadalcanal to Tokyo.

I once flew home from the South Pacific with an Army Major General who had just become a lifelong admirer of the SeaBees. He had taken command of an island base that they had built under fire. On his arrival there, everything was complete, even to a private head for the General, appropriately marked with two star-shaped ventilators on each side, as the insignia of his rank.

A few evenings later, the General was strolling about the compound. A middle-aged SeaBee, cap askew, was lounging on the seat of a bulldozer. He did not rise. He waved casually—it was not a salute—and called, "Hi-ya, General?"

The General halted. "Do I know you?" he inquired.

"Why, hell yes, General, you know me! I'm the man who built your—house!"

A bon mot, the General said.

[*ii*] We have always had Big Navy Presidents and Little Navy Presidents, the first kind keeping an eye to national defense and to working the shipyards; the second with an eye to cutting appropriations, pleasing the taxpayer, and perpetuating themselves in office. Unfortunately, the affairs of the world are not always geared to these maneuvers. It has ever been the policy, after we have won a war, to reduce our armed forces and to scrap the hulls of future warships that are on the ways. This is not only a false economy, but it puts the Navy (and the other Armed Services) in the position of being able to

fight the last war, but not the next one.

Washington, fortunately, was a Big Navy President.

Naval gunnery was just beginning to be something of a science in the Revolutionary War. The maneuvers required to fire a shot were so formidable that it is remarkable that we got off as many as we did. The shipboard guns, mounted on wooden wheels, had to be run in and out of the gunports by rope tackles. (In the Navy, you pronounce "tackle" not as a football player does, but with a long *a*.) Most of them were nine- or eighteen-pounders—the weight of the shot fired. The gunner of each piece had to check such things as the rammer, the sponge, the tub of water, the powderhorn, crow, spike, wedge, and bed before he gave the order, "Cast loose your guns." Then it was "Level your guns." "Take out your tompions." "Load with cartridge!" It wasn't a cartridge at all, but a bag of powder rammed in at the muzzle, followed by a wad. Then "Shot your guns!" and the cannon ball went in at the muzzle. "Run out your guns!" "Prime!" "Point your guns!"

And, finally, "Fire!" The firing was done when the roll of the ship brought the guns to their topmost elevation. After firing, the guns had to be hauled inboard and sponged to remove any burning fragments.

It was an exercise more muscular than scientific, but our Navy's gunnery in the Revolution was far better than that of the British. With the preponderance of tonnage and gunpower on the part of the enemy, we needed this desperately.

Fortunately for the American Colonies, England even then was a "nation of shopkeepers" far more interested in their lucrative trade with the islands of the West Indies than in the doings of a handful of ragged rebels in America. The bulk of her overseas fleet was usually found in the Caribbean, except during the hurricane season, when almost no ships stayed there. And it seems that even God was on our side. Because of the prevailing westerly winds, a ship could sail from America to Europe in a month or less; the crossing from Europe took two months.

The conflict was decided in a naval battle off the Virginia

Capes, after two and a half hours of gunfire. This fight has been known by several names: Michael Lewis, in *The History of the British Navy,* said, "The Battle of Chesapeake Bay was one of the decisive battles of the world. Before it, the creation of the United States of America was possible; after it, it was certain." A European historian, Emil Reich, called it "the British naval Waterloo off Cape Henry."

Although it was the only decisive battle of the war, in itself it was most indecisive. Not one ship was captured or sunk by either side, although the British had to burn one afterward. Neither Admiral was driven off, or had to strike his flag. The fight has been called a "drawn battle," a "lively skirmish," and so on. George Washington referred to it as a "partial engagement."

Nevertheless, it denied the use of Chesapeake Bay to the British, and without control of Chesapeake Bay there was no hope of saving the seven thousand troops of General Cornwallis on the Yorktown Peninsula. George Washington had engineered the junction of fleet and army at the crucial time—another proof of his naval genius.

And things, as Alice said, got curiouser and curiouser. Perhaps one reason the history texts say so little about the Battle of Chesapeake Bay is that it was not an American battle at all. Not one American ship fired a shot there.

It was fought and won against the British by a French fleet under the command of Count de Grasse. But history and diplomatic correspondence show with what consummate skill the naval genius of George Washington was used to persuade the French to send their fleet up from the West Indies in time to strike. His timing was perfect. It must have taken into account the fact that it was the hurricane season in the Caribbean.

[*iii*] We should regard the Revolutionary War as a spawning ground for the leaders of the War of 1812, and the same has largely been true of our other conflicts.

Consider the career of Joshua Barney, born in Maryland in 1759. He went to sea at the age of twelve, and remained at sea constantly. Three years later he was in the merchant ship *Sidney,* commanded by Thomas Drysdale.

The *Sidney* left Baltimore on 22 Dec., 1774, with a cargo of wheat destined for Nice—not Nice, France, but a port on the island of Sardinia by the same name. Joshua Barney was Drysdale's brother-in-law. Nepotism apparently had reared its head, because at the age of fifteen Joshua was the second mate.

After passing the Virginia Capes, the *Sidney* sprung a leak, and because of the perishable nature of her cargo had to put back into Norfolk Harbor for repairs. The cargo had to be off-loaded. Here the first mate and the master had some sort of altercation. Records do not show whether or not this came to fisticuffs, marlinespikes, or knives—but the first mate left the ship in a huff. And Joshua Barney became first mate.

The crew of the *Sidney* certainly included old, bearded, salty, tough, and tattooed men, often drunk. There were few else in the ships of those days, where the hammocks were slung fourteen inches apart in the hold, above sloshing bilge water that stank with the carcasses of drowned rats; where a man had no means of taking a bath and seldom changed his clothes, and had fleas and was lousy. What with the certainty of scurvy and the chance of being drowned, it was a hell of a way to make a living, and could not have attracted the most desirable characters.

The *Sidney* cleared from Norfolk after juggling the wheat back aboard. Drysdale took sick. We are not told the nature of his ailment, but he died several days later.

And then First Mate Joshua Barney, fifteen, took command of the ship. He not only handled the crew and kept them in line— which must have been a job—but he navigated by star and compass, and took the *Sidney* across the Atlantic. A heavy gale at the mouth of the Mediterranean so badly damaged the ship that Barney had to take her into Gibraltar for repairs that required three months. Once more the cargo of wheat had to be off-loaded.

He had to make a considerable bond, here, to take care of the "bottomry"—the repairs. He had some trouble doing this, because of his minority. Joshua Barney and another man walked a long way to reach the proper authorities and convince them that his bond was good.

All of this was training for what was to come. At fifteen, Joshua Barney must have stood tall; perhaps a frontier conspires with the biological processes to speed manhood. At any rate, he did a man's job in the *Sidney*. He went on to become Captain of a privateer in the Revolution, while still in his teens, and then served as Commodore of the Navy in the War of 1812. He was one of the shining heroes of that conflict.

2. SHOVE OFF, SAILOR!

Service in the Navy can be whatever you make it. It takes some time to understand and become adapted to the ways of the Navy, for going to sea in ships and aircraft is a tough, serious business, particularly in these troubled times. If you must work hard and at times miss a leave period or a few liberties in your home port, remember that you chose a man's job when you joined the Navy.

—*W. R. Smedberg, III, Vice Admiral, U.S. Navy, recently Chief of Naval Personnel, in an official Navy brochure*

IT USUALLY BEGINS with a Navy recruiter, most likely a first class or chief petty officer. He is a trained and dedicated man who aims to enlist the top people in high school graduating classes before his competitors—the Army, Air Force, and Marine Corps—can lay hands upon them. Usually he has a number of hashmarks on his sleeve denoting years of service, looks sharp in his uniform, and knows his subject thoroughly; often he understands the uses of applied psychology.

Not long ago, a Navy chief and a Marine Corps sergeant were invited to address a high school senior class. The globe-and-anchor man spoke first, and turned out to be quite an orator. He made a very dramatic talk about the traditions and honors of the Marines, and ended on a high note by thumping the table and saying, "Remember this! The Marine Corps builds *men!*"

The Navy CPO rose, and studied his audience for a full minute without opening his mouth. Finally, in a perfectly flat tone, he said: "If you aren't already a man, the Navy doesn't want you." Then he sat down.

This spiked the Marine Corps' guns—a thing that has seldom happened—and the Navy got all the lads who were eligible and and could pass the physical examination.

These boys became "boots." A boot in the Navy is a fresh-caught Seaman Recruit (they used to be called Apprentice Seamen) with the ink hardly dry on his enlistment papers. He is sent to a Training Center, unofficially known as a boot camp, and both he and the camp got their names from the leggins trainees wear during the several weeks they spend doing "Hup! Two, Three, Four!" and learning the school of the squad, the manual of arms, and more advanced infantry drills. They also perform sentry duty over such things as garbage cans and clothes lines—with empty rifles.

George "Rojo" Hickman, now of Roswell, New Mexico, is retired from both the Navy and the State Department, as a radioman and a communications expert. He got his boot training at the Newport Training Station in 1925. He remembers a recruit from Fall River, named Barbarou, who was handed an ancient and empty Springfield and ordered to guard the clotheslines. Barbarou was what the Navy calls "duty-struck," and marched up and down as militarily as if he had been guarding the U.S. Mint, challenging anyone who came near. His Four-point-Oh or hundred-per cent attitude attracted the attention of Lieutenant Commander Frederick G. Reinicke, former Annapolis football star, who thought he would have some fun. Reinicke had an Irish setter that followed him all the time. One night he approached the clotheslines, and Barbarou sang out: "Halt! Who goes there?"

Reinicke answered, "Lieutenant Commander Reinicke, and his dog."

Quick as a flash, Barbarou said, "Advance, Lieutenant Commander Reinicke, and be recognized. Dog, mark time!"

Most Navy men still come from inland, from the farm belt. Many go back there to retire. During the Korean War, one destroyer collided slightly with another during maneuvers. The Task Force Commander, an Admiral, gigged the skipper of the offending destroyer with a personal message: "What do you propose to do now?" The reply was immediate: "Go back and buy a small farm . . ."

[*ii*] Hillaire Belloc once said, "To sail the sea is an occupation at once repulsive and attractive." The good old Doctor Samuel Johnson told Boswell, "No man will be a sailor who has contrivance enough to get himself into a jail; for being in a ship is being in a jail, with the chance of being drowned. . . . A man in a jail has more room, better food and commonly better company."

The Navy has always had an answer to such calumnies. One of them goes, "In a ship, you may die like a dog, but you live like a gentleman. On land [i.e., in the Army], you live like a dog, and may die like one." Many occupants of muddy foxholes in World War II agree.

Of course the term "gentleman" must be used advisedly. After the expansion of the Navy in the last war, and the great influx of officers who were Reserves or "Ninety-day Wonders," an old Annapolis man was heard to remark: "Any girl of today who marries an officer and a gentleman may have to commit bigamy."

When Admiral Robley D. (Fighting Bob) Evans commanded the Asiatic Station in 1902, he ordered officers to wear evening dress or mess jackets for dinner. There is always a rebel. One officer doubted that Evans had the authority to compel him to appear for his meals in any specified uniform, and took dinner in his room for several days. Then, becoming lonely, he complied. Soon after, when the flagship was taking on coal, the word was passed that officers would not dress for dinner that day. Whereupon the same rebel said, "I can't see why coaling ship should prevent me from dressing like a gentleman for my dinner!"

A ship being coaled was far dirtier than trench or foxhole.

However, even a foxhole may have some semblance of privacy if it is deep enough—and the Navy has never had privacy. From the moment a Navy man arrives at boot camp and is paraded naked for several hours along with other recruits, to get a second severe physical examination and his first shots, he is never alone. At chow, a shipmate's elbow is in his ribs, and the cry of "Rig in your boom!" is frequent. Showers are taken *en masse*. No illusions are left after periodic "short arm" inspections for venereal disease.

There is no privacy whatsoever. The crew's head even in a battleship had no stalls with or without doors. A model of sanitary engineering, it consisted of a long trough that seated a dozen or more men at a time, and was flushed continuously by a stream of salt water pumped in and flowing out the scuppers.

No privacy. But there is the word "shipmate," which is about as indefinable as the wonderful word *simpatico*—and the two have much the same meaning. The Marines use "shipmate," too. Recruit training at Parris Island is so rugged that only strong men can take it, and those who finish the course have bought something precious—membership in a priceless brotherhood. Although Marines may be scattered all over the world a few weeks later, those who went through "boots" together are shipmates forever.

The Navy may seem to treat the term a little more lightly. When someone says, "Be a shipmate, and lend me ten bucks until pay day," the response is likely to be, "Don't you know that all the shipmates went down with the *Maine?*" But if the solicited sailor has it, the ten bucks likely will be forthcoming. There is an old Navy saying: "Messmate before shipmate, shipmate before stranger, stranger before a dog." (This is from *The Sailor's Word Book*, by W. H. Smyth. I do not agree. I will put my dog before a stranger, any day.)

Were he extant now, Dr. Johnson would be forced to amend his comparison of ships and jails. In his time, most seamen were impressed—many from jail cells. Even later, the majority of American Navy men were foreigners, and little better than mercenaries. But today, the mere fact of having had a jail record is enough to keep a man out of the Navy forever.

Not just anyone can join the Navy. The recruit must have references. In a recent survey, the Navy found that more than half of its 663,831 enlisted men and women were between nineteen and twenty-two years old. When 2,340 new sailors were asked why they chose the Navy, the answers were both revealing and reassuring. Eighty-nine per cent said that love of country— patriotism—was a strong factor in their enlistments. Less than 57 per cent conceded that selective service had anything at all to do with their joining up, and 44 per cent flatly stated that the draft played no part in their decision. All but one per cent of this group had attended high school, 81 per cent were high school graduates, and some had enjoyed a year or two of college. Ninety-four percent were attracted by the training opportunities offered by the Navy, and 91 per cent wanted to travel.

This latter statistic upheld the effectiveness of the old Navy recruiting slogan, "Join the Navy and See the World." Nearly twenty years ago, while on duty with the Navy's Recruiting Service, I ran a survey of my own to find why men enlisted. It was my contention that no slogan had the appeal of "Join the Navy and See the World," which had just been discarded.

The desire to travel won hands down. The answer which came nearest to proving my theory was a succinct: "For to get away from Danville, Virginia."

In 1922, when I tried to enlist, the Navy's attitude toward recruits was almost that of "Repel boarders!" There had been economy cuts, and personnel was being drastically reduced. I went to the recruiting office in Houston.

"Son," said the CPO with his feet on the desk, "the Navy isn't taking anybody. I don't even know what they are going to do with *me!*"

I turned to the Marine Corps, an outfit for which I have always had a vast and affectionate respect. It was a Navy lieutenant-commander medical officer, a tobacco chewer, who gave me my physical. He did not find my slight inguinal hernia when we went through the "Now turn your head and cough!" routine. But after he had me jog around the floor, the hernia descended visibly.

"What are you trying to put over on us?" Dr. McDonald asked.

It pays to level under such circumstances. I said, "Sir, I have no money for an operation. I thought if the Marines sent me to Parris Island, I would jump down from the train, clutch my groin, and cry out with pain. Then the Marine Corps would have to operate on me."

McDonald spat tobacco juice and laughed heartily. "They'd send you back so fast it would make your head swim! But because you have tried so hard to enlist, I'll tell you what to do. Go to the County Hospital Clinic. Tell them you have lived here for years . . ."

I went to the Clinic, and to the County Hospital, which was then in some old wooden Army buildings a mile from the end of a shuttle-car line. I was turned in between two elderly men. Next morning, I saw that the man on my right was dead. I rang for the orderly, who put a screen around that bed. I turned over on my left side—and that man was dead, too. Just then the crew came from the operating room with the wheeled stretcher. They said, cheerily, "Well, you're next!"

In those days, you lay flat on your back for twenty-one days after such an operation. There was nothing to read, but there was a beautiful little night nurse from Mexico City, my own age. She held my hand. Something could have come of this, except that I was bound to join the Navy.

I lost weight on the horrible hospital chow, and had to gain it back by drinking buttermilk until it ran out of my ears. The Navy began sending out all of four recruits a week from all of Texas. Eight weeks after the surgery, I was sworn in as an Apprentice Seaman at $21 per month, and went to Goat Island, San Francisco, for my boot training. There had been goats on it in the early days, and I had the feeling that I was one of them.

Drill was incessant. I wanted to become a gunner, a quarter-master, or a radioman, in that order. Only the Yeoman's school and the Hospital Corps school were open. I took the latter. It was just building up, with four or five men reporting weekly from Detention Camp. After we had fifty or more men, the warrant officer —a pharmacist called "Tubby" Lansdowne—paraded us and sang out "Bosworth, front and center!"

I advanced with trepidation. But Tubby faced the entire company and said, "Bosworth will be the adjutant of the senior class. I do not wish to inspect the adjutant; I shall expect him to set an example for the class."

And then he took off on a tour of inspection, with me following. I stepped high, and saw some resentful looks . . . and there had to be a few grudge fights, later. But I never put a man on the report. I never knew why I was chosen as the leading acting petty officer of the school.

We got advance word that Captain Stitt, Surgeon General of the Navy, was coming to inspect the Hospital Corps school. Tubby Lansdowne and I entered into a delightful conspiracy. On a hill that overlooked the parade ground was a huge, flat-topped reservoir that supplied water to the entire island. We planted a man on this, out of sight from the parade ground, in a Stokes wire basket litter. He was swathed from head to foot in every kind of surgical bandage known to medical science and the Boy Scouts. He had a Barton head bandage fitting like a skull cap; he had the shoulder Velpeau, and spiral bandages on both legs. There were even bandages on all his fingers.

The ship's company passed in review before Captain Stitt, and did right well. We came back to company front, and Stitt was about to say a few complimentary words. Just then a man showed at the rim of the reservoir, lying down and dangling his arms over the side as he shouted, "Help! Help!"

I called, "Away, fire and rescue party! Away, stretcher bearers!"

Four sailors manned a Stokes stretcher, and I carried a first-aid pouch. We dashed dramatically to the foot of the reservoir, made a human pyramid, and reached the top. The empty basket stretcher was hoisted. I began unreeling gauze bandage at a great rate, and at the same time we pulled the supposedly injured man back out of sight. We gave him a boot in the sternsheets and sent him off the rear end of the reservoir. Then we pulled the other stretcher forward, lowered it down the face of the reservoir, and did double time back to the parade ground.

Elapsed time, perhaps three minutes.

Captain Stitt's face was a study. He could not believe, and yet he had seen. He looked at the bandaged man more closely.

"Remarkable!" he said. "Incredible! I don't see how it could have been done so quickly!"

Commander Dollard, the skipper of the school, had not been let in on the plot, and was just as mystified. But he swelled with pride, and said, "Sir, as you can see, we have some mighty fine men here!"

[iii] After finishing the school and becoming a Hospital Apprentice first class, I was sent to the Naval Hospital at San Diego for duty. Having now been in the Navy eight months, I had learned the nomenclature, and had escaped many things that happen to boot seamen when they first go aboard ship. Nobody ever sent me to get the key to the anchor watch, or green oil for the starboard lamp, or a can of striped paint; nobody ever mentioned the "dead Marine" in the double-bottoms. I had already learned that a "dead Marine" was an empty bottle . . .

Correct designations and succinct language are very necessary to the Navy. Consider the range covered by the terse order, "When in all respects ready for sea, proceed on duty assigned." Years ago, the Navy changed from *starboard* and *larboard* to *starboard* and *port*—when winds were howling around the bridge, the two older terms were easily confused. Tradition requires that a messenger be sent to the Captain each evening, with the word: "Eight o'clock, and chronometers wound." On one occasion, a boot seaman rendered this as, "Eight o'clock, and chow gone down."

Some people—especially those who have never been to sea—
are inclined to get a bit too salty in their speech. The Navy
expression of "How's for," or "How's to," always precedes a request. I was up at mast (or on the report) at the San Diego
Naval Hospital, for missing muster, and I heard a nurse testify
against another corpsman.

"Miss Blank," said the executive officer, "you have charged
this man with insolence. Just what was the nature of his insolence?"

"Well, Commander, he had been to the ship's store, and he
came into the ward with several candy bars. I said to him,
'How's for a piece of that candy?' And he said to me, 'Just what
would you do for a piece of this candy?' "

The executive officer drummed a pencil on his desk for a long
and judicial minute, considering the fact that the nurse—a commissioned officer—had been the first to break the bounds of pro-
priety between an officer and an enlisted man.

"Well, Miss Blank," the Commander said, "just what *would*
you have done for a piece of candy? *Case dismissed!*"

The Naval Hospital was the setting for both comedy and
tragedy. One morning my shipmates Barney and Thacker returned from a night on the town, not too sober, just in time to
accompany the Ward E doctor on his tour of the ward, and to
write down his orders in the medication and treatment book.

Ward E contained some supernumeraries, who were not Navy
people—they were a mixture of veterans of World War I and
civil service employees. Two of these were bunked side by side.
One was suffering that morning from a terrible itch caused by his
reaction to shots for a staphylococcic infection; the other was terribly flatulent and had a case of old-fashioned bellyache.

The medical officer was efficient, and brisk. Of the itching
man, he said, "Give him a sodium bicarbonate bath." For the gas-
eous patient, he ordered a soapsuds enema.

After the doctor had departed, Barney and Thacker repaired

to the linen locker, and had another shot or two of medical department alcohol.

They decided that they had written the doctor's instructions wrong. Obviously, a man with the itch needed a bath with castile soap, while one with flatulence required a sodium bicarbonate enema. On this premise, they proceeded.

Both patients had heard and understood the doctor's orders. Both protested that the hospital corpsmen were not carrying them out properly. But both were equally helpless.

One man got the enema, and the other got his bath. The latter itched terribly, the first was heard all over the ward. But neither reported the two corpsmen. Such things are the fortunes of war, and its aftermaths . . .

3. HALF SEAS OVER

Some are fond of red wine, and some are fond
of white,
And some are all for dancing by the pale
moon light,
But rum alone's the tipple and the heart's
delight
Of the old bold mate of Henry Morgan.
—John Masefield, "Captain Stratton's Fancy,"
from *Poems*

Prince Rupert Bay (18 March 1799)—
Employ'd clearing ship for sea Wind at E.N.E.
Saild the U.S. Ship (George) Washington &
Brigt. Pickering with a Convoy of Americans
Broach'd a Cask Rum Contents 44 Gallons sent
an officer & 12 men to cut brooms Saild the U.S.
Ship Herald and an Armed Schooner.
—*Journal of James Pity, U.S. Frigate* Constitution

Sunday, 20 April, 1800. The First part Fresh
Breezes and flying Clouds at 6 P M Carrayd away
the fore Top sail Tye . . . this Day the Steward
Broachd one Hogshead of Brandy and did not
Acquaint me Joseph Whitmore Sailing Master nor
Mates nor the Capt of the Warren he broached it
in presance of James Keasy the Capt of the Hold
and the Steward has Broachd other Cask of pro-
visions in the same line Michael Keatan was pres-
ant when the Hogshead of Brandy was Broachd
—*Log book of Sailing Master Joseph Whitmore,*
U.S.S. Warren

46

IN A LATER NAVY ERA, they would have said that Sailing Master Whitmore "had the ship on his shoulders." His rank was much more lowly than the title suggests; when the grade was finally abolished in 1882, the few holding it became very elderly lieutenants, junior grade. However, one of the duties of the Sailing Master was to inspect stores and provisions.

A lot of people were broaching casks of brandy or rum, contents 44 gallons, in those early days, and the Navy was steering for rocks and shoals. The rum ration was one of many customs inherited from the British Navy.

It was legal, however. An Act of Congress of 27 March, 1794, provided that every man in the Navy should have a daily half-pint of rum, to be issued between 10 and 12 A.M., and between 4 and 6 P.M. Eleven years later the custom had caught on very well: in 1805, Secretary of the Navy Robert Smith reported that the annual consumption of rum in the Navy was 45,000 gallons.

(In 1805, the Navy had 24 ships, 574 guns, and 6,600 men—despite a British propaganda report that said it had 66,000 men.)

Secretary Smith was not criticizing the Navy's drinking habits, but was trying to save the taxpayer some money. He believed that whiskey was better and cheaper than rum, and in 1806 he ordered 20,000 gallons of rye for the Navy's use.

This was served mixed with equal parts of water in a wooden tub that was guarded by an armed sentry and supervised by an officer. When all hands were piped forward to splice the main brace (the modern British command is "Up spirits!") each man stepped forward as his name was called, and had his cup filled. Many drank their ration on the spot—and then tried, often successfully, to fall into the line again. This was known as "doubling the tub."

Others carried their cups below and swapped the spirit ration for food or favors, or sold it for cash. Thus it was possible for thirsty old-timers to get much more than their allotted share—and in a day when "salt horse" and other salt-preserved foods were the mainstay of Navy diet, the thirsty ones were legion.

The law provided that "boys" should not participate. But no one had a birth certificate, and many a lad of fourteen swore upon enlisting that he was eighteen or more, and got away with it. These attained a legal status of manhood when they were only about seventeen, and quite naturally tossed off their rum mixed with an equal part of bravado, to prove they were men. As a result, some of them were addicts by the time they actually had reached twenty-one.

All this had begun in the British Navy with Admiral Sir David Vernon, an old sea dog of parts. He insisted that men doing hard work aboard ship needed to drink. He wore habitually a foul-weather cloak of coarse blue woolen material called "grogram," and was known as "Old Grog." His issue of rum and water took on the same name, and the modern usage of "grog" and "groggy" comes from the Navy.

Before long, there was a song:

> *For grog is our starboard, our larboard,*
> *Our mainmast, our mizzen, our log—*
> *At sea, or ashore, or when harbor'd*
> *The mariner's compass is grog.*

There is no record of any Navy ship's being unable to sail or fight because of intoxication in the crew. Nor has there even been an actual mutiny in the U.S. Navy—as against England's Great Mutiny of 1797—although several incipient plots were nipped in the bud.

The first, aboard the frigate *Congress*, ended with several men getting thoroughly flogged and kicked out of the Navy. The second was in 1842 aboard the brig *Somers*, and the alleged ringleader was Midshipman Philip Spencer, son of the then Secretary of War, who supposedly plotted with two seamen to murder the officers, seize the brig, and enter her in the pirate trade. Whether drinking played a part in this is not known, and historians disagree—not so much on the guilt of Spencer as on the doubtful guilt of the two seamen. At any rate, Commander Alexander Slidell Mackenzie seized the trio and promptly hanged all three from the yardarm—observing all the amenities, such as half-masting the Flag, firing a gun, and reading the burial service for the dead. He was tried for what seemed a high-handed action, but was acquitted.

We will deal, in a later chapter, with the *Somers* incident.

We moved on into the steamship era, and a new expression was coined for drunks returning aboard from liberty. A "smokestack jag" referred to that state of intoxication in which a man could still ascend the ladder, tell fore from aft, salute the quarterdeck and the officer of the deck, say "I report my return from liberty, sir,"—and then turn forward and collapse behind the after smokestack. Let us charitably believe that the warmth from the stack contributed to this denouement.

Grog probably warded off colds and pneumonia in winter weathers, but it had its evil aspects. One was flogging for the enlisted men, a cruel corporal punishment meted out more often for drunkenness than for any other offense. The other was pistols at twenty paces for officers, on the field of honor. An incredible number of duels were fought, too many of them as result of disputes and challenges when the principals were "warm with wine."

[*ii*] The Navy's grog ration became the center of a dispute that lasted sixty years, reverberated in the halls of Congress, and came near to putting the later efforts of Carrie Nation and the W.C.T.U. in the shade. Grog was a Navy tradition, and if Navy traditions die at all, they die hard. Some commanding officers believed that the grog ration was beneficial; others condemned it. After all, the custom went back to Nelson, and earlier. And everybody had heard the scandalous story—not necessarily true—about Nelson:

> *Oh, Nelson fell in Trafalgar's fray,*
> *Yo ho, me lads, yo ho!*
> *And tenderly was borne away,*
> *Yo ho, me lads, yo ho!*
> *Where a mightly cask stood full of booze*

To last the flagship for its cruise—
But Admirals must have their dues,
Yo ho, me lads, yo ho!

They hoisted Nelson by a leg,
Yo ho, me lads, yo ho!
To the rim of the Victory's *liquor keg,*
Yo ho, me lads, yo ho!
And they turned him loose and let him fall
To pickle him well in alcohol—
But the plan, it didn't work at all,
Yo ho, me lads, yo ho!

For heroes go, and heroes come,
Yo ho, me lads, yo ho!
But sailormen must have their rum,
Yo ho, me lads, yo ho!
There were tears in many a manly eye,
But they fought them back with sob and sigh—
And then they drank the barrel dry!
Yo ho, me lads, yo ho!

Among those concerned about the grog problem was the famous Captain Thomas Truxtun. On 9 May, 1801, he wrote the Acting Secretary of the Navy:

SIR I have examined the Act of Congress for providing the Naval Peace establishment. the Allowance of half a pint of rum pr day is too much for Seamen, it requires great attention to prevent their being continually in a state of intoxication from this great allowance of spirits, for they will in addition to their allowance find landsmen & Boys, who will privately Barter their rum to them for Butter Cheese &c &c or sell it, on this Account I have been obliged to prohibit from the commencement of the Navy the boys having any grog, and have made the stopping of grog to Seamen & others a principal punishment for crimes & Misdemeanors committed on board, which in the *President* has been a saving to the U S in addition to the provisions short served on Account of their not being able to consume it, of several thousand dollars, the reduced ration by the last Act of Congress is therefore a good thing, but I am of opinion that on account of health & other considerations it would have been better to have allowed the Seamen but one Jill of rum pr. day & in lieu of the other Jill, Molasses & Tea Coffee & Sugar.

There was no middle ground. If Truxtun punished drinking men by stopping their grog, he could only punish non-drinkers by having them flogged. Some of the latter only pretended to drink their rations, and then if they were had up at mast, stoppage of rum did not disturb them in the least. But the old-timers who came back to the ship to be logged as "D & D" (drunk and dirty) instead of "C & S" (clean and sober) were flogged again and again.

Meanwhile, some devilishly clever means were being devised to bring strong drink aboard ship, to augment the official supply . . .

The bluejacket's uniform was always notably devoid of pockets. An officer at the gangway could run his hands over any suspicious bulges under the men's blouses, and speedily detect a hidden bottle. The sailors resorted to what they called "snakes." These were the intestines of cattle or sheep, filled with liquor, and then coiled around a man's lower legs, under his bell-bottomed trousers.

Commissarymen and ship's cooks used fowl tactics—they secreted pints in the bodies of dressed chickens, buried quarts in bushels of potatoes, hid "snakes" of rum in barrels of water that were being taken aboard, and even brought a whole barrel of liquor aboard one ship disguised as paint. Chaplain Charles Rockwell in 1842 told about an enlisted crew that came up with an ingenious blend of white paint, olive oil, and whiskey. The oil rose to the top, the paint settled to the bottom, and the men used straws to drink the liquor in between. Such "make-do" cleverness has always been in evidence toward things "out of bounds"—the Navy's word for "off limits." During World War II one of the first detachments of WAVES reported at a Navy shore station. The commanding officer had many things on his mind, but now, being a gentleman, he had to listen to the WAVE officer in charge of the group.

"Captain," she said, "I want to set one thing straight. I want it strictly understood that there will be no fraternization between your men and my girls."

"Very well," said the Captain. "No fraternization."

"I want you to know," said the WAVE officer, "that my girls

are very high class girls."

"I don't doubt it," said the Captain. He looked at the paper work piled high on his desk, and wished that she would go away.

"My girls," the WAVE officer persisted—and now she tapped her forehead—"have got it, *up here!*"

At this point, the Captain's patience broke down. He said, "I don't care where your girls have got it, *my* men will get it!"

That terminated the interview. But in the history of the Navy, the same has always been true of liquor.

[*iii*] Perhaps the consumption of 45,000 gallons of rum in a year was stunting the Navy's growth. In 1820, the highest rank was post captain, and the total appropriations fell short of six million dollars for pay and ship upkeep. Bureaucracy was barely beginning: the salary of the Secretary of the Navy was $6000 per year, and there were less than ten people in the Navy Department, including a messenger who earned a dollar every day.

Except for a brief burgeoning during the Civil War, the outfit remained small. By the 1880's, it had settled down to 8500 men—and was reporting more than a thousand desertions a year. Grog and flogging both had been abolished by then, but Navy life was still hard—and so were many of its people. The latter were becoming even more expert in how to smuggle liquor aboard ship.

The executive offier in one vessel triumphantly told the Captain that he had discovered how a jug of rum was coming into the ship every day. The Captain's own gig, he said, brought it from ashore, and it was being smuggled through a porthole of the Captain's own cabin.

A Captain does not like to hear criticism of his personal staff, since it reflects on his judgment of men. This one doubted the charges. The gig crew was part of his official family.

The exec had the master-at-arms run down the gangway ladder and seize a bucket of iced liquid from the Captain's gig. Things looked pretty bad, and the cox'n of the gig was required to report aboard immediately. He looked the picture of innocence.

"It's swanky," the cox'n said.

None of the officers had heard that term. The ship's doctor was summoned. He sniffed and sipped, and said that it was not alcohol. The cox'n then explained that "swanky" was a mixture of vinegar, water, and sugar; it was very good for the stomach, and helped prevent scurvy.

All the officers apologized to the cox'n for their unfounded suspicions: any anti-scorbutic in those days was given gangway. A few hours later, however, the cox'n and his mates were enjoying their usual strong rum punch. Somebody had tipped off the cox'n that he and the gig were suspect, and he had made the temporary substitution of "swanky," which ordinarily he would not have touched with a boat hook . . .

This, of course, was another example of the lack of privacy aboard a warship. A wardroom steward probably had heard officers discussing the suspected gig. Navy "scuttlebutt" spreads just as fast as what the Army calls "latrine rumors."

In at least one instance, the foc'sle people did not actually broach a cask of rum, but simply bored into one through the adjoining bulkhead and inserted a pipe. By the time this ruse had been discovered, the contents of the cask had been siphoned away, and its staves were beginning to fall in on themselves.

It was none other than Abraham Lincoln who did away with the grog ration by an official order that said, ". . . from and after the first day of September, 1862, the spirit ration in the Navy of the United States shall forever cease, and thereafter no distilled spirituous liquor shall be admitted on board vessels of war, except as medical stores."

Whether any old salts and tipplers deserted to the Confederacy as the result of this order cannot be determined. That qualifying phrase "except as medical stores," has been important ever since. But was Honest Abe a consistent man? When he was told that U. S. Grant was drunk, he reportedly suggested that barrels of Grant's favorite brand be sent to other Union generals. He said nothing about sending whiskey to Union Navy captains—not even after the battle of Mobile Bay.

There is a legend that U.S.S. *Constitution*—"Old Ironsides"—sailed from Boston on 23 August, 1779, under orders to sink and destroy British shipping. She had aboard 475 officers and men, 48,600 gallons of fresh water, 7,400 cannon shot, 11,600 pounds of black powder—and 79,400 gallons of rum.

She raised Jamaica on 6 October, and took aboard 826 pounds of flour—and 68,300 gallons of rum.

She reached the Azores on 12 November, and provisioned with 550 pounds of beef—and 64,300 gallons of Portuguese wine.

She sailed for England on 18 November, and scuttled twelve British merchant ships—salvaging their rum. On 27 January, her munitions were exhausted, but she raided the Firth of Clyde, captured a distillery—and took 40,000 gallons of whiskey aboard.

She arrived in Boston on 20 February, 1780, with no shot or powder, no provisions, no rum or whiskey—but with 48,600 gallons of stagnant water . . .

This is one of the tallest of sea stories, and proof of the old adage that figures don't lie, but liars can figure. Just for fun, I have gone to considerable research to find out what actually happened to Old Ironsides on that cruise. It is true that she did run dry on the high seas, and her log tells about it. On 9 January, 1800, "Moderate Breezes and cloudy . . . Served half allowance of Spirits to the Ships company the Rum being Totally expended."

But the next day she received from the U.S. ship *Boston* thirty gallons of Rum, and served out full allowance of Spirits to the ship's company. On 14 January, off Cape Francois, she fell in with the U.S. ship *General Greene*, and scrounged the following Articles:

Viz one pipe and 16 keggs of Brandy containing 283 Gallons
Fifteen small Keggs of Gin ditto   153 ditto
Nine Hhds of Mollasses
Four cask of Vinegar
One cask of oil.

On the China station, many years later, the Navy learned to call this sort of thing "cumshaw," a word which probably originally derived from the Chinese pronunciation of "commission." At any rate, the *Constitution* was proficient at the practice. On 15 January, she took aboard from *General Greene* and /or Boston:

Viz 3 Pipes of Brandy
2 puncheons of Rum . . .
and some Hogsheads of Mollasses, a Cask of Vinegar, 1 Box of candles, and two live oxen for Ships use.

Now Old Ironsides had both meat and drink, and it appears from the log that she got by for five weeks. But on Friday, 28 February, she took aboard "Viz 26 Cask of Brandy."

An official example of how to be afloat and awash at the same time had been set the year before. The frigate *United States,* commanded by Captain John Barry, was ordered on 18 October, 1779, to carry two U.S. Ministers—each accompanied by a secretary and a servant—to their diplomatic posts in Europe. Six men, all told.

The Secretary of the Navy advised Navy agents Gibbs & Channing, of Newport , R.I., as follows:

I have imagined that 12 dozen Porter, 12 dozen Cyder (a very agreeable Liquor on board of Ship) and 12 doz good Wine & 15 Gallons of good spirit or French Brandy would be a sufficient stock of Liquor in addition to which there should be a sufficient quantity of Live Stock, the best Mess Beef, good Butter, Flour, Tea, Coffee, Sugar &c to enable them to enjoy at least the Comforts of good living . . .

Divide the stock of liquor by six, and assume that the voyage took as much as thirty days. Four hundred and thirty-two bottles of wine and fifteen gallons of brandy should have kept the diplomats pleasantly plastered for the entire cruise.

[iv] Concerning the *Constitution* —Old Ironsides—a colorful and touching bit of ceremony still prevails at Boston. Every August 19th, at five minutes past six P.M., a 15-starred and 15-striped flag is hoisted in commemoration of the victory of Captain Isaac Hull over the British frigate

Guerriere, on 19 August, 1812. It is flown for forty minutes—the duration of that battle. Then it is carefully stowed away until the next year.

The British have always preferred Greek names for their warships. A few years after the War of 1812, some British naval officers were inspecting the *Constitution.* They saw her name plaque, and said, "That's an 'ell of a name for a warship, the Old I-ronsides!"

They also thought that while the whole ship was beautiful, her wheel was one of the ugliest they had ever seen. And they were very embarrassed when told that that wheel had come out of their own frigate, *Java* . . .

Although Lincoln's edict of 1862 made shipboard drinking unofficial, clandestine, and admittedly more difficult, the Navy would find ways and means. In tropical ports, rum could be brought aboard in coconuts that had been drained of their milk, and this transmitted a marvelous flavor to the coconut meat. But in tropical ports, many young sailors were exposed to the more exotic liquors for the first time. They ran down the list, trying out daiquiris and other things unfamiliar, and mixing them, with dire results. One man who returned aboard in a very foggy state reported that he had drunk "two bottles of that Spanish beer they call cognac . . ."

In Panama City in the old days—the 1920's, that is—liberty was very wisely terminated on the dock at sundown. The housing, and even the cat-housing accommodations, would not take care of the floating population. Even so, the late afternoon sun on white hats, after a few beers, made men higher than a kite, and sometimes a whole sprawling boat load had to be hoisted aboard ship in a cargo net.

The shore patrols on the dock were alert. Any bulge under the uniform was suspect. A shore patrolman said, "What have you got there, sailor?" and slammed his club against a lump at the man's midriff.

Glass shattered, and the duty-free French perfume the man had bought for his girl ran down his legs. He danced, shaking broken glass out of his bell bottoms, and swearing eloquently. He shed a feminine scent upon the tropical air, and other sailors cavorted around him, waving and calling, "Yoo-hoo!"

We in the Hospital Corps had means which were not available to everybody. We had hot water bottles. A hot water bottle tied around the waist with gauze bandage could be worn ashore empty, and brought back containing nearly a quart of rum. It made little bulge at all, and if a shore patrolman struck it, his club bounced and he only concluded that beer produces flatulence.

But back in the States, these were Volsteadian days, and it was time for a change. Instead of trying to smuggle inferior bootleg aboard ship, the problem now was how to smuggle Navy alcohol *ashore*.

Alcohol, both denatured and pure grain, had many uses aboard ship. It supplied the fuel for torpedoes. It floated the spirit compass. The sick bay had both rubbing alcohol (denatured) and pure grain alcohol to sterilize surgical instruments and to use on surgical dressings. The torpedo alcohol required further distillation, and any quartermaster who drank compass alcohol was likely to take off in all directions at once.

In the 1920's a large number of the old four-stack, flush-deck destroyers, out of commission, were being maintained at the San Diego Destroyer Base. (They figured prominently, fifteen years later, in the Lend-Lease program.) Upkeep and maintenance meant that one was always on the marine railway for hull inspection and painting. The others, nested to buoys, had to have their decks red-leaded, their double bottoms painted, and everything preserved from rust.

Maintenance crews of dungaree-clad enlisted men went out in small boats to do these jobs, which were lonely and dirty duties. The warheads had been removed from the torpedoes, but some of them, at least, still contained fuel. I was a third class pharmacist's mate in U.S.S. *Rigel,* the Destroyer Base tender: I recall several occasions when fire and rescue parties had to be called away because stills had exploded in the double bottoms of the destroyers.

Torpedo alcohol, "pink lady" or denatured alcohol, and even the rubbing alcohol from the sick bay (which contained soap liniment) could be refined by a very simple but somewhat slow process. Every compartment and every office aboard ship had its own "jamoke pot" for making coffee, and its own hot plate. But hot coffee could always be obtained in unlimited quantity from the galley, and when hot plates burned far into the night, we were not just brewing jamoke.

You took an ordinary one-gallon, enameled coffeepot, and wrenched the lid off its hinges. You poured some four inches of pink lady into the pot, and placed a heavy Navy tumbler in the exact center of the liquid. Then you turned the conical lid upside down, filled it with ice, and began cooking.

The denatured alcohol boiled quickly. Steam rose to the inverted lid, and condensed because of the ice. The resultant liquid, all its impurities gone, dripped into the tumbler.

Science is truly wonderful.

It took half an hour to distill a single shot, and it took most of the night for four or five men to get a little high. But, what the hell? We were broke. We didn't rate liberty. And this was forbidden fruit.

4. IN ALL RESPECTS
READY FOR SEA...

Oh, the enlisted men sleep in their hammocks,
The Captain, he sleeps in a bed;
He don't sleep a doggoned bit better,
But he's twenty feet nearer the head . . .
  Sing tooral-a-tooral, a-tooral-aye,
  A-tooral, a-tooral aye-A;
  A-tooral, a-tooral, a-tooral,
  A-tooral, a-tooral aye-A!
—Old Navy Song

IN SOME WAYS it saddens me to report that Navy hammocks
are no more, and that bunks have been installed in warships
along with such things as "gedunk bars," or soda fountains. But
then I can remember hitting the deck and running to my battle
station at night clad only in skivvy shorts—and hanging my chin
over a vacated hammock with force enough to break my
neck . . .

The reconditioned (and air-conditioned) battleship *New Jersey* went for her sea trials in 1968 with bunks for 2,500 men—and
each bunk has its individual lighting. Progress has reared its head
to improve comforts and a rather indefinable thing known as
"morale." And many an old-timer growls, "Yeah, what used to be
a *privilege* is now a *right* . . . and you mark what I say: they'll
make the kids too soft!"

This is not necessarily true. Good morale and pride of ship
can produce a fighting spirit just as much—and perhaps more—

than hardships ever did.

But in its day the hammock was very practical. There was a time when a bluejacket, leaving boot camp or a training school, literally heeded the Biblical admonition from St. John: "Rise, take up thy bed, and walk."

His hammock was lashed with a regulation seven half hitches, and bent around the seabag that contained all his clothing and other possessions. Both seabag and hammock were thoroughly scrubbed with saltwater soap every Friday. The bluejacket thus was assured of having a clean bed—his very own—to sleep in, wherever he might be. It was better than any hotel bed, because no one else had ever slept in it.

And the hammock became a very strong part of the Navy tradition. Kipling immortalized it in his poem about the Royal Regiment of Marines, "Soldier an' Sailor Too," with:

> *'E sleeps in a 'ammick instead of a cot, an' 'e drills*
> *with the deck on a slew,*
> *An' 'e sweats like a Jolly—'Er Majesty's Jolly—*
> *soldier an' sailor too!*

For nearly a quarter of a century, the U.S. Air Force has been very actively engaged in building itself a tradition from scratch— and more power to it. Certainly it has had the required number of heroes and accomplishments; certainly the Navy accords it respect and honors. But in officers' clubs around the world, the Navy—inordinately fond of kidding—is inclined to take an avuncular attitude toward the upstart Air Force, just as it maintains that "the Coast Guard is our Rowing Club, and the Marine Corps is our Shooting Club." (This often makes Coast Guardsmen and Marines fighting mad.)

But . . . did the Air Force ever sleep in hammocks?

No. Well, the Navy did. Never mind that the Navy never had to hit the silk at 5,000 feet. Some of its aviators did, but not to the extent of the Air Force.

"Well, what was so wonderful about sleeping in hammocks?"

Nothing. It was not wonderful at all. It was difficult.

"What was so hard about it?"

The deck. And the humorous pictures of hammocks in Navy magazines, captioned "Advertisement for kidney pills." And the way they said it was strange that a Navy man griped about hammocks, and then went ashore and sat in one for hours with a girl. This was very feeble humor. It overlooked the fact that a bluejacket will sit with a girl anywhere.

"Would a girl have made that much difference in a hammock?"

In a lawn hammock, yes. In a Navy hammock, no. Both the strategic and tactical situation would be different. Let me illustrate:

On 27 January, 1949, the Army's Special Regulation No. 625-10-5 was promulgated by General Omar Bradley. It referred to the "Women's Army Corps, Administrative and Training Positions for Officers . . ." and paragraph *two* read:

The nine officers designated as Women's Army Corps Staff Advisors for the six armies, the military district of Washington, and the overseas commands may be used by the commanding general concerned in any other positions which he deems necessary, in addition to this primary duty.
—*Omar Bradley*
The Chief of Staff

Whereupon General Bradley promptly received a signal from the office of the Chief of Naval Operations. (Admiral Louis E. Denfeld was CNO at the time.) It referred to Bradley's message, and asked: "How about standing up in a canoe?"

I remember the hammock fondly. It was called a "dream sack," and worse, but I was young and supple, and sleep in a hammock came easily to me. No slumber was ever sweeter than that in a Navy hammock that swayed gently with the roll of the ship, and sometimes showed moonbeams slanting through a porthole.

Such sleep was rudely interrupted in those days by an unholy trinity who really hoisted the sun toward the yardarm and made the day begin. These were the bugler, the bosun's mate, and the master-at-arms (pronounced "jimmy-legs"). It was "Up a-a-all hammicks!" and "Hit the deck, sailors! Rise and shine! Lash and stow! Up a-a-all hammicks!"

For some years, the bugler's rating was abolished by the Navy, and his duties taken over by recorded tape and the Public Address system to save manpower. Today's master-at-arms would find it right difficult to wallop the undersides of bunks with a basebell bat or a sawed-off billiard cue, as he used to wallop hammocks. Nor can he tilt bunks and dump their occupants on the deck. However, with the recommissioning of the battleship *New Jersey* in 1968, two buglers were rated. They are Seaman Robert Boling, and Seaman Bertrand R. Trottier, Jr., and they are the only buglers in the Navy.

Hammocks or not, there is no evidence that the outfit has gone soft, and a medical survey possibly would show that the incidence of backache and kidney trouble in the Navy, caused by sleeping slightly doubled up, has decreased.

In the old British Navy there was only one hammock for every two men, half of the crew always being on watch. The cry "Show a leg!", still used in our own Navy, goes back to a time when women were allowed aboard Royal Navy warships. These seagoing sweeties could sleep in if they exhibited a sufficiently hairless and feminine leg over the side of the hammock. But remember this: no Navy hammock was ever, like the fabled bicycle, built for two . . .

In the U.S. Navy, nobody ever had to share a hammock or a bunk. But I remember a time in U.S.S. *Maryland* when one of my shipmates was blithely coming out of the sick bay shower, wearing only a loose towel. It was Sunday afternoon—visitors' day—and two elderly ladies, unescorted, were just entering the sick bay. My shipmate made a dive for the nearest bunk, which already had a patient in it. He got under the cover in time to be quite decent. But one of the old ladies sniffed, "Tchk! Tchk! You'd think the Navy could provide a bunk for every sick man!"

Insofar as women aboard ship are concerned, we had several back in Revolutionary days, when there was very little physical examination. It seems that they served well, and one, at least, distinguished herself as a gunner. Her messmates later were surprised to find they had been shipmates with a woman in disguise. I doubt, however, that they were disappointed at not having made the discovery earlier. A woman who was man enough to climb the rigging, or swing a cutlass to repel boarders, would not have been woman enough to have to repel advances.

Away back on 2 April, 1803 Midshipman Henry Wadsworth of the U.S.S *Chesapeake* made an entry in his Journal:

> On the 22^d Feb^{ry} it being the day after we left Algiers: Mrs. Low (wife to James Low Captain of the Forecastle) bore a Son, in the Boatswain's Store Room: on the 31st inst. (March)—the babe was baptiz'd in the Midshipmen's apartment: The Contriver of this business was Melancthon Taylor Wolsey a Mid: who stood Godfather on the occasion & provided a handsome collation of Wine & Fruit: Mrs. Low being unwell Mrs. Hays the Gunner's Lady officiated: Divine Service by Rev. Alex McFarlan: —All was conducted with due decorum & decency no doubt to the great satisfaction of the parents, as Mr. Woolsey's attention to them must in some measure have ameliorated the unhappy situation of the Lady who was so unfortunate as to conceive & bare on the Salt Sea. NB. The other Ladies of the Bay *
> —* The Forward Most part of the Birth Deck—viz. Mrs. Watson: the Boatswain's wife, Mrs. Myres the Carpenter's Lady—with Mrs. Crosby the Corporal's Lady: got drunk in their own Quarters out of pure spite—not being invited to celebrate the Christening of Melancthon Woolsey Low.

It would appear from his spelling of "bare" and "Birth" that young Mr. Wadsworth had a sly and roguish sense of humor. It would have been wonderful to hear more from him through the Journal he was keeping . . . but he was destined to die a heroic death not long after he made this entry.

He did not mention that a broadside was fired when Melancthon Woolsey Low was born, and by this we may assume that Mrs. Low had an easy delivery. Firing all the guns broadside was sometimes done, not as a salute to the newly-arrived infant, but to hasten his arrival. The shock from such gunfire helped difficult births.

And of course such births were where we got the term "son-of-a-gun," which originally was more than just an expletive. It meant illegitimacy. Listen to the brag of an old-timer, a century

63

and more ago:

"Begotten in the galley and born under a gun. Every hair a rope yarn, every tooth a marlinespike; every finger a fish hook, and in my blood right good Stockholm tar."

For a long time, more than a century and a half, the Navy has been sharply opposed to any coeducational advantages aboard ship, and I remember a case in which such opposition was extended to a beach camp that was dedicated to—of all things—recreation. The San Diego Naval Hospital, at the behest of the chaplain, had set up two tents on Coronado's Silver Strand, about a mile below Tent City, a public resort. One of the big tents was for cooking; the other was for sleeping. Eight men were sent there for a week at a time, to get sun and surf: they were hospital corpsmen, and not patients.

I went to the camp the second week. A chief petty officer was in charge of this group, but being married, he did not spend nights in camp. I was going with the girl who later became my wife, so I did not stick around evenings, either. After three or four days of surf and sun, the other sailors wandered up to Tent City one evening, and met six—count 'em—girls who were stenographers and beauty parlor operators . . .

When I returned to the camp about midnight, I raised the flap of the sleeping tent, and found every bunk doubly occupied. I took my hammock out on the sand and slept there. Just after sunrise, I heard a car.

It was the chaplain, who lived farther down the Strand, and was stopping by to see how the camp was going. I watched him raise the tent flap, and saw him turn back to his car, his shoulders despondent. He had not spoken a word to arouse the sleepers.

I got dressed and went to the tent. "All right, men!" I said. "Stand by to break up camp! You might as well strike the tents now—it will save time."

They were about to take their girl friends to breakfast, and they wanted to know what the hell I meant. I chose to remain mysterious, and simply told them that the camp would be decommissioned, that day. Sure enough, about ten o'clock two pickup trucks came for the gear, and two cars to take us back to the

Naval Hospital.

"Recreation" can be a very loose word.

I remember a cruise, *circa* 1923, when the entire Fleet was a couple of days out of New York, bound for the Caribbean. The battleship *Arizona* wisely made a visual—not audio—signal. (Things were always happening to the *Arizona*.) She reported that two girl stowaways, wearing undress blue uniforms, had been found in her blower room—and that they said four other women were stowed away somewhere in the Fleet.

All gunnery drills were immediately halted. More visual signals, this time from the battleship *California,* which was the Fleet flagship. There would be an immediate physical inspection of all hands, done by divisions.

The *Maryland*'s medical officer, a Commander, stuck his head in the sick bay, and surveyed H Division's twelve or fourteen men with a slight, bemused grin. Then he said, "I am quite sure that all of you are men. I shall report that fact. It will not be necessary for you to fall in topside."

But the bigger divisions such as the deck force and the black gang (engine room people) did not get off so easily. The word was already being passed over the PA system, and it was very strange:

"Now hear this! Now hear this! All hands lay topside on the double! All hands fall in on the foc'sle with pants at half mast! All hands, short arm inspection on the foc'sle! This is no drill!"

Ships were close enough in formation that in *Maryland* we could look across stretches of bright blue water and see the crews of other battleships falling in by the numbers to prove their maleness.

P.S. No other women were found. As for the two in the *Arizona,* the Navy was very close-mouthed. Scuttlebutt had it that they were beached in—of all places—the Virgin Islands, and had to work their passage back to New York.

Commander Edward Whitehead, late of the Royal Navy and later president of Schweppes, U.S.A., is known as The Beard, because of his magnificent pink brush. He also has a fund of sea stories.

A British cruiser, fighting heavy seas in a Fleet exercise, received a signal: "Inform Ordinary Seaman James T. Russell that his father has died."

The Officer of the Watch passed this to the signal bosun to handle. To his horror, the signal bosun walked to the voice pipe of the ship's intercom, and roared, "Attention, Ordinary Seaman James T. Russell. Your father's dead—end of message."

The officer chewed out the signal bosun, or, as the British say, "tore him off a strip." Two days later, a similar signal came from the Admiralty, and the same officer was on the bridge. The message said, "Inform Leading Stoker Abernathy his mother died yesterday."

The officer was about to pass this to the same signal bosun, when he remembered. "Not again, Bosun!" he said. "I'll handle this myself."

"Oh, sir," the bosun pleaded. "I've learned my lesson. I took to heart what you said the other day. I can promise you I will handle it differently, this time!"

So, the O.O.W. relented. The bosun thought a bit, then went to the voice pipe and called, "Attention, Leading Stokers! All Leading Stokers fall in aft on the quarterdeck, in five minutes!"

The bosun went aft himself, and found half a dozen men standing at ease, waiting for him. He called them to attention, and said:

"All Leading Stokers whose mothers are alive, step one pace forward! Not so fast, Abernathy—not so fast!"

[*ii*] Naval officers have at times been hoist by their own petard, as the saying goes. In 1918 Lieutenant Commander (later Rear Admiral) Ridley McLean had just written a new edition of the *Bluejacket's Manual*—the Bible for enlisted men—in which he laid great stress upon new lifesaving drills and procedures.

McLean was the executive officer of the old U.S.S. *Columbia*.

Rear Admiral Albert Weston Grant, Annapolis 1877, had his flag in that ship. McLean was a perfectionist; Grant was a kibitzer. While the Admiral was a Force commander, the handling of *Columbia* and the training of her crew was the responsibility of her captain.

McLean had written in the Manual:

Q. What is the first principle of discipline?
A. A prompt obedience to the orders of superiors.
Q. How is this obtained and enforced?
A. . . . Discipline is obtained . . . by requiring an absolute compliance with the details of all drills and evolutions . . .
Q. What language is always improper aboard ship?
A. Profane, abusive, obscene, loud, boisterous language; and noises, disturbances, or confusion of any kind.

McLean sallied forth to morning quarters one day, wanting to put his new lifeboat drill to an actual test. Admiral Grant, as usual, was on deck kibitzing. McLean paid no attention to him, and, instead of going to his post to receive the morning reports, proceeded to the upper platform of the starboard gangway. There, he yelled, "Man overboard!" and jumped.

His newly prescribed procedures went into effect with neatness and despatch—with one exception. Admiral Grant walked to the rail, spat at the spot where the Exec had splashed (and spat to *windward*, at that, which is a cardinal sin in the Navy).

Then he said in a loud voice: "Let the son-of-a-bitch drown!"

At least Admiral Grant remained in character, and practiced what he preached. Not long afterward, *Columbia* went to Manhattan, and anchored in the North River, off Ninety-sixth Street. Returning to the ship, Grant kibitzed again and stood up in the stern sheets of his barge to give the coxswain the most explicit directions for making the starboard gangway.

The cox'n knew his job, and was fed up. He was conning the barge, and did not look astern. But with precision timing he flipped the barge under the *Columbia*'s quarter boom, which picked off the Old Man as neatly as ever a low tree limb unhorsed any cowboy.

The tidal current was running at full ebb. The horrified officer of the deck, a young ensign, shucked his white gloves and hat, laid his long glass carefully on the deck, and dived to the Admiral's assistance. He surfaced right in front of the Old Man's ancient but strong breast stroke just in time to take one on the chin and hear a wet snarl: "Get out of my way, you young whippersnapper! You'll get no medal for saving *my* life!"

Grant beat the ensign to the gangway, but sent for him when they were both dried out. What followed probably confused the lad for weeks. Grant complimented him on his quick reaction, gave him holy hell for leaving his post without having been properly relieved, and then thanked him by asking the skipper to give him three days of special liberty. The cox'n? He probably grew a long white beard in the brig.

It may be that "R.H.I.P." stands not only for "Rank Has Its Privileges," but also "Rank Has Its Perils." Things were always happening to Admirals . . .

In World War I, the battleship *Texas* went aground off Block Island, with Admiral H. A. Wiley embarked. Admiral Wiley immediately issued a command seldom heard in the modern Navy— to "sally ship." This is accomplished by having the whole crew rush fore and aft in a body, to help shake the ship free.

Admiral Wiley led the way, and literally threw his weight around by jumping up and down on the foc'sle. Then he slipped, and fell down the hawsepipe.

The bosun's mate quickly piped "Man overboard!" and then looked over the side. One anchor was down. Admiral Wiley was sitting on the other one.

Then the bosun's mate really tore it. He bellowed, "Belay that—it's only the Admiral!"

5. ROOM TO SWING A CAT

(Captain) JAMES SEVER Esqr

SIR, the Charge respecting Partrick (sic) Brown, (ordinary seaman), of which I enter'd a Complaint—is as follows—when calling him to account for his Quarrell with (Hugh, ordinary seaman) Dunbar—he attempted to colar me the first attempt I clear'd myself, by knocking him down—the second attempt he accomplish'd—which obliged me to call for my side arms—and soon disingaged myself—the men surrounding me where supporting me as much as possible—

The Insult receiv'd from him Obligates me to request of you a Court Martial—
Frig^t *Congress*

> I am Sir
> With Respect
> Your Ob^t Servt
> J B CORDIS
> Frig^t *Congress*
> April 9th, 1800

Saturday, 3 August 1805 This day a Marine was flogged through the fleet. 18 of the *Philadelphia*'s crew went on board the *Syren*.
—*Journal of Hezekiah Loomis, Steward, USN, U.S. Brig* Vixen

A LOT OF THINGS were happening aboard the frigate *Congress* in that year of 1800, and none of them good. She was well on her way toward becoming known as a jinx ship, and the enlisted men were not the only ones who were quarreling. Some

69

official correspondence had been written about "a lack of harmony" among her officers. This was a rather mild expression, considering the fact that two of the *Congress* midshipmen had just fought a duel in which one was killed. Official letters were being written about Lieutenant Cordis, too.

Cordis might well have handled the affair with Patrick Brown along lines of tact and persuasion, if he had not been so distraught and jumpy himself. The enlisted men didn't know it, but Cordis was in very hot water, with the threat of court martial hanging over his own head. He had been court martialed once before, and—in the words of Secretary of the Navy Benjamin Stoddert—had escaped, but "not with honor."

His current trouble went back to a stormy night four months before, when the *Congress* "lost her sticks," a Navy expression for being dismasted. At the same time Cordis was asking for a trial of Patrick Brown, he was very unwisely and improperly writing directly to the Secretary of the Navy about the dismasting, and not sending the letters through channels, or via his commanding officer.

He told the Secretary that on the evening before the mishap, he had warned Captain Sever that the rigging was slack, and that Sever said, "I Sir am the best judge," and did nothing about it. Cordis took over the deck at 4 A.M., and "immediately employed the watch in swiftering the lower rigging," to make it taut.

Perhaps Capain Sever was indeed "the best judge." While the swiftering was being done in the blow, the mainmast suddenly became unseated, and was sprung fifteen feet above the deck. Somebody must have put a strain on the wrong line. Now, to save the mainmast, they had to cut away the main topmast.

Fourth Lieutenant Nathaniel Bosworth, of Bristol, R.I., laid aloft in the raging gale with four men to accomplish this task. The mainmast broke from its original spring and carried away the head of the mizzen mast, putting it over the side with the five people. The four seamen were saved, fortunately, but Lieutenant Bosworth was drowned.

If the dismasting was not enough of a headache for Captain

James Sever, it was shortly supplemented by the alarming discovery that mutiny was being actively plotted aboard *Congress*.

In 1800, the very whisper of the word "mutiny" sent cold chills along the spine of every commanding officer. The U.S. Navy had never been subjected to one, but only three years before the British Navy's "Great Mutiny" had taken place at Portsmouth and Spithead. Fifty thousand men in 113 ships refused orders, and threw out their officers. This was a protest against failure to draw pay for more than a year, against wretched living conditions, short rations, and brutal punishment. The Great Mutiny shook the Royal Navy from stem to stern, and American commanders wondered if it could happen here.

It never did. Aboard the *Congress*, Captain Sever quickly convened a court martial. Benjamin Davis was acquitted on a charge of plotting mutiny. Andrew Robb, William Brown, John Davis, and John Wilson were sentenced to receive seventy-two lashes. Ansel Robinson and John Carter, accused as the ringleaders, were sentenced to be hanged by their necks from the fore yardarm of the *Congress* until dead.

The Commander in Chief of the Fleet, Captain Thomas Truxtun, as the reviewing authority, reversed the two death sentences. Robinson and Carter each got 100 lashes with the cat-o'-nine-tails, were cashiered of any pay they might have had on the books, and were kicked out of the Navy forever.

Truxtun strongly suspected that a ship was only as good as her commanding officer, and thought that conditions aboard the *Congress* might have stemmed from Captain Sever. The frigate became short-handed while her masts were being replaced, and Truxtun wrote the Secretary of the Navy, "I fear some difficulty in manning her—the prejudices against Captain Sever—are very great—indeed I fear his Idea of discipline is not correct—Discipline is to be effected by a particular deportment, much easier than by great Severity."

At any rate, whether the *Congress* was a jinx ship or not, Patrick Brown could shortly feel that he had been somewhat vindicated. Just about a month after Lieutenant John B. Cordis had put Brown up for a court martial, Cordis was dropped from the rolls of the Navy—by the Secretary, himself.

[*ii*] The *Congress* fired a single gun as a signal that a General Court Martial was convened, and the trial began. Patrick Brown was scared to death that he would be punished by the stopping of his grog. But the findings were as follows:

> On Examination of the Evidence &c the Court are Unanimouslly of the opinion that the Prisoner is guilty of both charges, of quarreling with his Messmates & Laying Violent hands, on his Superior officer, and that he has been guilty of a great Violation of the Laws & Discipline of the Navy of the United States, but the court taking into consideration the contrition of the Prisoner since, desist from inflicting that punishment which in other circumstances that case wou'd require, and do therefore Award & order that the said Patrick Brown, shall on the 14 day of the Month on board the U.S. Frigate *Congress* receive 48 Lashes with a cat of Nine Tails at the Gangway—the Court was adjourned untill 7 Oclock the 13th inst
> —*Samuel Barron, President*

Patrick Brown was in irons. They marched him up from the dark and narrow brig, which smelled of urine and vomit; they took him topside to the gangway, and removed the irons and his blouse. They laid a grating flat on the deck, and lashed his feet to it. They raised his hands so high above his head that he was standing on tiptoe, and all his back muscles were suitably taut. Then they tied his hands on high to the futtock shrouds.

Below decks and all through the ship the bosun's pipe was shrilling; the bosun's mate's voice was roaring for all hands to fall in topside to witness punishment. This happened every few days. Many an old-timer who had never quailed at the sight of blood in battle flinched and averted his eyes when he stood by for a flogging. Many another, flogged so many times that his back was a mass of scar tissue, knew well what Patrick Brown would be feeling, but philosophized that the cat was not as bad as losing his daily grog. One honest old-timer who had been severely lectured said, "Talkin' to is worse'n floggin'!" And a few youngsters, seeing it for the first time, got sick.

It was not a pretty sight. The master-at-arms took a fresh cat-o'-nine-tails out of a bag. When there were several men to be punished, they always used a fresh cat for each culprit. This was probably very fortunate in that syphilis could have been transmitted otherwise, but the spirochete had not yet been isolated, and no such thoughtful clinical motives were involved: it was simply that a cat that had been saturated with blood would not bite nearly so hard as a dry one.

The cat-o'-nine-tails was made of nine hard-twisted cords of twine, some eighteen inches long, affixed to a wooden handle like a whipstock. Each strand of twine ended in either a hard knot, or a small leaden pellet. There was a lesser instrument of punishment known as the "colt," which was a finger-sized rope, three feet long. Deck officers carried "colts" coiled in their caps, and used them as a "starter"—they laid them on the backs of seamen when the crew had to hoist, heave around, or otherwise haul on a line. The "colt" was always applied through clothing.

There is a curious bit of psychology here. The colt could well have smarted as much as the cat, but it was less dreaded. Apparently there is something about naked punishment, about blows on the bare skin.

Patrick Brown was getting the cat on his bare back.

An officer read the charges, and the sentence of the court. Patrick Brown stood extended and tense, waiting. The bosun's mate blew his whistle and raised a brawny arm . . .

Whack!

"One!" intoned the master-at-arms, who had to keep count.

Patrick Brown did not cry out, but the muscles of his back crawled, and some blood showed.

Whack!

"Two!"

More blood, and a second stripe across the first one.

Whack!

The Captain and other officers were required to watch. The bosun's mate dared not hold back the strength of his arm. He was graded as much on his ability to wield the lash as on anything else . . .

Whack!

Now the blood was running freely, incarnadining Patrick Brown's waist; now a crimson mist sprayed from the cat each time it rose and fell. The wind caught this; the nearest spectators felt it on their cheeks. Some of the ship's boys were crying.

Patrick Brown began to sag, no longer putting any weight on his toes, but hanging by his wrists. He moaned softly after each measured blow, and his eyes were closed. Those watching could see his toes jerk upward each time the lash fell.

The next time you hear someone say, "Room enough to swing a cat," think back to where the English language acquired that little piece of whimsy.

[*iii*] Patrick Brown's forty-eight lashes were quite a few, but many men endured much more. The mutiny plotters got a hundred. The unidentified marine who was "flogged through the fleet" was taken in an open boat, and whipped alongside every ship present, so that all hands could witness his punishment. At Portsmouth, England, on 20 February, 1807, George Melvin—a seaman who had deserted from HMS *Antelope*—was rowed through the fleet and given 300 lashes.

That many blows with the cat could be fatal. Another fight, similar to the one waged against grog, began to simmer in Congress. When a protest first came up, legislators from the Southern slave states were horrified. They could hardly understand a Yankee's objections to slavery when he countenanced such cruelty in the Navy.

There was a difference of economics, here, hardly discernible. The Southerner regarded a Negro slave as a valuable piece of property; the bluejacket was just a hired man whose term of servitude was limited to a few years. The Southerners were not seagoing people to any extent: they did not know that the laws of the sea had always been hard. A little later, two enduring pieces of literature gave a tremendous impetus to the drive to abolish flogging. These were Richard Henry Dana's *Two Years Before the Mast,* and Herman Melville's *White Jacket; Life Aboard a Man-o-War.* Melville, especially, devoted a number of pages to a sermon against flogging.

It is curious that nobody delved into history to ask how the practice ever started, in the first place. Nobody ever related it to some rather cruel customs that came over in the *Mayflower.* I seem to remember that a witch or two got burned at Salem, and that we had the ducking-stool, and pilloried a few people in stocks.

The evidence seems to indicate that our Anglo-Saxon heritage included a bent toward violent punishment exceeding that of any other civilized people. Catherine the Great abolished capital punishment in Russia in 1767; Joseph II ended it in Austria in 1781, and the Grand Duke of Tuscany followed suit in 1786. Even the French, in 1791, cut their list of capital crimes from 115 to 32.

But in England, under the Georgian kings, the "Bloody Code" prescribed death for any one of more than 350 offenses—including such things as the cutting down of a squire's tree, or theft of a bun in a London street. Just before 1800, at least, people in England were still being drawn and quartered.

And the American Navy, showing a lamentable lack of originality in its formative years, was strictly molded after the Royal Navy.

Congress finally demanded statistics, which were forthcoming. In the years 1846 and 1847, with sixty ships reporting, we had the amazing total of 5,936 floggings.

No action had been taken yet, but the Navy apparently was sensitive to Congressional debate and inquiry. In 1848, only 424 men were reported flogged.

In one earlier instance, the flogging of a man might easily have brought on war.

It was aboard U.S.S. *Enterprise,* in Gibraltar Bay, on 25 July, 1806. These were parlous times, and troubled waters. A man came alongside and was very insolent to an *Enterprise* officer.

Master Commandant David Porter had him lay aboard, and demanded an apology, which was refused. Porter promptly gave him a dozen lashes on the bare back, and then ordered him back into his boat.

Next day, Porter received a letter from the British transport *Arethusa.* It said that Thomas Grant, an *Arethusa* seaman, had been punished with "one Dozen lashes on his bare back on board the Vessel which you Command," and it requested particulars.

All honor to Porter. He was in British waters, and outnumbered and out-gunned, but he did not back down. He admitted flogging the man, and said,

> The indignity offered to the Flag under which I sail was of such a nature as I was convinced would not be overlooked under similar circumstances by one of his Britanic Majesties Officers, and as no other means of redress presented themselves, I was compel'd to use the same that they would have used, and in so doing I have confined myself strictly to the Twenty-eight article of the Act for the better Government of the Navy of the United States.

Porter heard no more about the incident.

Other times, other customs—or rather, other orders to the Navy's commanding officers. Contrast Porter's action in bearding the British lion with what happened, not very long ago, to U.S.S. *Pueblo,* off North Korea.

I doubt that the U.S. Navy ever keel-hauled a man, except in the modern sense of the phrase, which means a very stern reprimand. But there was a time when sailors were actually keel-hauled. They were put into the water at the starboard gangway, and hauled all the way under the ship from starboard to port, scraping and bumping and grinding en route. This punishment could be given by the Captain, or by court martial. Of course this was an excellent drill for the time when they might have to work a collision mat into place over a hole in the bottom, but it had little else to recommend it as a drill. The severity of the punishment did not depend upon the enormity of the man's offense, but upon the draught of the ship: in a small vessel it amounted to little more than a ducking, but in a larger one, they might well haul up a corpse.

Just as in the matter of the spirit ration, legislators who had a humanitarian streak or a bent for reform tried again and again to get flogging abolished in the Navy. They finally succeeded on 28 September, 1850, by a very close Senate vote of 26 to 24. Thus they anticipated the abolition of grog by a dozen years.

The cat-o'-nine-tails became a museum piece, along with the rack and other devices of the Spanish Inquisition. Naval officers were now at a loss as to what punishment to use to enforce discipline. But not for long. They struck at culprits through their stomachs—Brig, Bread and Water, with a full ration every third day.

Ten, twenty, or thirty days of Brig, Bread and Water brings around the most recalcitrant.

There was a cry of "Man overboard!" and the whole ship went to action stations. Boats were lowered, and a search was made. Later, the entire ship's company was mustered, and nobody was missing.

Everybody from the officer of the deck to the skipper thought this was very strange. Then a scared seaman second stepped forward.

"I guess the man overboard must have been me, sir. I went over the side, all right, but I managed to grab the anchor chain and climb back on deck."

"Then why in hell didn't you report it?" demanded the O.D.

"Well, I am very sorry, sir, but you see, sir, I am in the lifeboat crew . . . and I had to go into the boat to look for a man overboard . . ."

An excellent example of the Navy's rigid law of "obey the last order first."

6. PISTOLS
AT HOW MANY
PACES?

Saturday, 27 March 1802
  Commences clear Weather & strong Easterly winds.
  At ½ past 5 PM was returning from Algeziras, when I rec a note from L Decatur informing that M Higinbothom & M Swartwout Midshipmen with several others had permission to go on shore & that the above named Gentlemen had fought without his knowledge & M Swartwout was brought on board dead. Immediately on my getting aboard I arrested M Higginbothom. At 5 AM sent a boat to Gibraltar to procure boards to make a Coffin & wrote to our Consul to obtain permission to bury him there, he sent for answer that it was not admissible.
—*Journal of U.S.S.* Essex, *Captain William Bainbridge, U.S. Navy, commanding*

THE YEARS covering more than a century and a half have dissolved what young Mr. Higginbothom and Mr. Swartwout wrote in blood. Ships' logs and journals are tantalizing things: they hint at epic novels, but never write them. Aside from being young and hot-blooded, why did the two midshipmen fight? Was their dispute over some sultry-eyed Mediterranean maiden? Were they at odds over political beliefs, or did they resort to pistols as a result of insults fanciful or real?

78

There was no privacy, in the wardroom or anywhere else. In the wardroom, it was considered bad manners to discuss women, politics, or religion. The conversation thus was stilted. But the spirit of knighthood still flowered a little. Maybe one of the midshipmen was late in relieving the other of the watch, and words were exchanged . . . and the words led to a challenge. They were both fighting men by profession, and a challenge could not go unheeded.

And so they met on a foreign shore, which became "the field of honor," and one of them died. It was a tragic waste.

The *code duello* was plainly an inheritance from the days when champions, each representing a whole army, went to the lists and saved a lot of lives by fighting it out with lance or broadsword. In medieval times, the bigger and stronger man usually triumphed. But firearms changed that drastically—the bigger the man, the better the target.

Dueling was always the business of "gentlemen," and according to the code, you did not have to fight me if I happened to be your social inferior. In the Navy, therefore, duels were fought only by officers. The enlisted men acted much more sensibly. They did not overrate honor, or take insults too seriously; when they quarreled, they simply laid topside and endeavored to beat the hell out of each other with their fists. This spared a great deal of formality and inconvenience, as well as a large number of lives. It also developed the tradition of Navy "grudge fights," which became refereed and supervised on most occasions, with participants encouraged to shake hands and forget the grudge afterward.

During the first half of the nineteenth century, the Navy lost in duels some two-thirds as many officers as it lost in combat action. The jinxed frigate *Congress,* with its flogging troubles under Captain James Sever, had other problems. On 18 April, 1800, Midshipman John Dubose attempted to resign his commission because of difficulties with the Captain. The Secretary of the Navy rejected this, and mailed Dubose's warrant back to him on 25 April. But that day Dubose killed Midshipman Samuel W. Cushing in a duel at Norfolk, and resigned in another way. An officer's log said, "Dubose has, I believe, made his Entire Elopement . . ."

Or, as the Navy used to say later, Dubose had "joined the birds."

Most duels occurred on foreign stations. It is my amateur guess that the locale was significant. There was most likely a lack of social contacts ashore. Warships were small and crowded: the other guy's elbow was always in your ribs. Nobody in those days had ever heard of athletic contests, and the only way to let off steam was to go ashore and drink—and here was the same guy, nudging you at the bar, and eyeing the same chick. Also, in the early 1800's there were many tensions, due to half-wars and undeclared wars, that put nerves on edge.

In March 1801, off Cape Francois Lieutenant Van Renselaer and Lieutenant Turner, both of the U.S.S. *Adams,* fought a duel. Van Renselaer was killed.

In Leghorn, Italy, on 14 October, 1802, Marine Corps Captain James McKnight was killed by Navy Lieutenant R. H. L. Lawson, of the U.S.S. *Constellation.* This was an exciting affair, because McKnight had the reputation of being a famous duelist. He issued the challenge in writing, and Lawson replied in kind. Lawson accepted, on condition that the distance be *three paces.*

This, of course, was suicidal. McKnight's second would not agree, and called Lawson an "assassin" for proposing so short a distance. He also branded Lawson a coward, which seemed unlikely.

Events hung in the balance. Lawson retorted in writing that he had proved the famous duelist a coward. McKnight consulted his superior officer, Captain Daniel Carmick, of the Marine Corps. It was Carmick's opinion that neither contestant would be remembered as a coward.

And so the duel was fought. Seconds and principals agreed to double the proposed interval, and make it six paces. They would fire a brace of pistols, then advance, and have it out with cutlasses.

Even in the days of cap-and-ball pistols, it was pretty hard to miss a man at six paces. "Capt. McKnight," Carmick reported to the Commandant of the Marine Corps, "received the ball directly through the center of his heart—he had but time to say he was shot and expired."

Carmick was then subjected to a horrible ordeal. The laws in Leghorn required an inquest; it happened that the Italian coroner also taught a class of future surgeons. He said the ball would have to be removed so it could be exhibited at the coroner's court —so he began cutting McKnight's heart out of his body.

Daniel Carmick suspected, however, that the coroner was doing this for the edification of his students, and threatened to kill the official. The situation could have brought on war. But the coroner proved that such was indeed the law, and Carmick had to abide by it. Later he raised money to erect a monument over McKnight's grave.

Captain Alexander Murray, commanding the *Constellation*, wrote the Secretary of the Navy on 7 November, 1802:

> The unhappy catastrophy, of Capt McKnight, who was a very deserving officer, tho rather irritable, induces me to wish that an article might be incerted in the regulations for the Navy, rendering every Officer liable to heavy penalties, & even to loss of his Commission, for giving or receiving a Challange, & also the seconds, for aiding & abetting in such unwarrantable acts, especially upon Foreign Service. I would even extend it further, & make every Officer Amenable to such penalties, if they did not make their Commander acquainted with events of that serious nature . . .

Captain Murray had thought, he added, that his officers lived in perfect harmony together. But Carmick reported that Murray was rather deaf. Therefore a lot of the hissed and muttered imprecations in the *Constellation's* wardroom could have escaped him.

[*ii*] Midshipman Henry Wadsworth of the *Chesapeake,* who so ably reported the christening of Melancthon Woolsey Low, also was good at reporting duels. In his Journal for 31 January, 1803, he noted that on the previous

day a duel had been fought at Valetta between Lieutenant Henry Vandyke of the U.S.S. *New York,* and Lieutenant William S. Osborn, Marine Corps, also of the *New York.* Vandyke was killed. (Note the prevalence of duels between officers attached to the same ship, and also that of duels between the Navy and the Marine Corps. Pride of outfit was carried a little too far.)

Fourteen days later, Wadsworth wrote that Midshipman Joseph Bainbridge of the *New York* fought a duel at four paces with a Mr. Cochran, an Englishman residing at Valetta. Each man got off two shots. Cochran was hit in the head, and killed.

Midshipmen and Lieutenants who dueled were engaging in a sort of internecine strife that was partially understandable. But when our Navy officers started knocking off foreign nationals who were civilians, the Navy Department felt that things were going too far. It decided to charge the next Navy survivor of a duel with murder.

One can imagine that defense attorneys of the day were well prepared to shoot such indictments full of holes. It was hardly murder in the first degree if you and I met by mutual consent, each bent upon wounding or killing one another, because a strong element of self-defense entered into the case. Still, the awful authority of Naval Regulations had to be reckoned with: a Navy man can be cleared in civil court, and still lose his entire career by court martial. He faces double jeopardy.

The first case of a proposed murder trial for dueling came about on 18 September, 1804, when Midshipman William R. Nicholson was killed in a duel at Syracuse by Midshipman F. Cornelius de Krafft. Their seconds were arrested the next day aboard the brig *Siren.* De Krafft was transferred to Norfolk in a U.S. brig appropriately named *Scourge,* and he waited and waited there. Then he was ordered to report to the office of the Secretary of the Navy, where he had a hearing. Followed more weeks of waiting, which could have reduced the young man to a nervous wreck.

Every indication was that the Navy was going to make an example of him. Then a very generous and humane thing happened. The Honorable Joseph Hopper Nicholson, member of Congress from Maryland, wrote a letter to the Secretary of the Navy on 28 February, 1805.

Congressman Nicholson was a relative—most likely an uncle —of the midshipman slain in the duel. He told the Secretary:

To you I need not say that however reprehensible the Practice of duelling may be, yet the wisest Legislators and the most able Magistrates, have for some hundred years, in vain endeavoured to check it—It is one of those Evils which is consequent upon Society. It and [sic] most frequently proceeds from the noblest feeling of the Heart. Before it can be stopped, the State of Society itself must change, and till then, human Laws and human Punishments will be vain.

But if the Executive should think differently from me in this particular, permit me to ask if the first Instance of severe Punishment should be directed to a Boy, who may have been led to the Commission of his offence by the too prevalent Example of older, wiser and more exalted men than himself, and who perhaps at the Moment conceived his own Life or that of his adversary a necessary sacrifice to his Reputation. . . .

Congressman Nicholson actually did not know de Krafft's name, and referred to him in the letter as "Mr. Dehart." But he had learned from another midshipman that the duel was fair. Because of his letter, Midshipman de Krafft was restored to duty, and sent back to the Mediterranean to report aboard U.S. Frigate *President.* The first test case attempting to link a dueling fatality to murder had failed.

The Navy Department was quite understandably confused, and got no help from any other governmental authority. Next there was a duel on the New York station, between Midshipmen Joseph Henry Barrymore and David Redick, of U.S. Gunboat No. 2. The Secretary of the Navy wrote a letter, confessing that there was no regulation to prevent duels. He said, though, that there was one regarding quarreling, and urged that officers be punished under that clause.

This was feeble, because it was most often after the fact. Before anybody could be had up for quarreling, somebody was dead.

[*iii*] The most famous and most tragic of all Navy duels took place between James Barron and Stephen Decatur, on 22 March, 1820. It was not a hasty or ill-tempered thing. The quarrel had fermented and festered for a dozen years.

"Decatur the Younger" (son of a naval officer by the same name) was a veteran of the wars with the Barbary pirates, a hero only slightly second to John Paul Jones. He had had some experience, administratively, with dueling. The Secretary of the Navy had written him on 26 October, 1807, regretting the death of Lieutenant Benjamin Smith in a duel. Said the Secretary: "I hear with great pain of duels between Officers of the Navy and *Citizens*. It exposes the Officers, especially those of the *Chesapeak,* to very unpleasant circumstances. . . ."

By "especially those of the *Chesapeak,*" the Secretary did not mean to refer to previous duels. Earlier in the year of 1807, the 36-gun frigate *Chesapeake* had just put to sea under command of James Barron. In Virginia's Lynnhaven Bay, she was stopped and boarded by His Majesty's Ship *Leopard,* of 50 guns, and was searched for British deserters.

Barron did not fight. He refused to give up the alleged deserters, but he did not clear his cluttered decks for action or man his guns until too late. *Leopard* fired several broadsides into *Chesapeake,* killing three men and wounding eighteen. Barron was hit seven times.

Barron struck his colors and offered the *Chesapeake* to the British vessel as a prize. The British captain took the suspected deserters, but refused the ship. Barron was shortly court-martialed on charges that he had not struck all the gear below decks when he sailed, and consequently was unable to fire.

Stephen Decatur, eleven years Barron's junior, succeeded him as captain of the *Chesapeake,* and was ordered to sit on Barron's court martial. Decatur wrote an official letter requesting that he be excused from this duty, and making it plain that he had already formed his own opinions of the *Chesapeake-Leopard* incident. But there was a shortage of captains with enough seniority to try Barron, and Decatur had to serve.

Barron was suspended from the Navy's active duty list for five years, and became a most embittered man. He blamed Decatur most of all, and so the feud began.

It simmered and stewed for a dozen years, and has long been debated by naval historians. Barron's hate did not diminish, although certainly he knew Decatur had served the court martial board with great reluctance. The real trouble was that he knew Decatur would have fought the *Leopard* at the drop of a hat.

The duel finally took place at Bladensburg, Maryland, on 22 March, 1820. Decatur was fatally wounded. Barron never had another active command at sea, but headed up shore establishments and lived out a long life.

[*iv*] According to the old records, it would seem that as long as dueling was confined to midshipmen and junior officers, a sort of "Well, boys will be boys!" attitude prevailed in the Navy. But Stephen Decatur was forty-one, and that was something else. He had been the youngest Captain ever to command an American ship, and his career was completely glorious. The Navy and the nation were shocked by his death.

From that time on, the practice of dueling in the Navy began to decline. But some four years before Decatur's death a duel was fought that was the first (and probably the only one) to stem from religious discrimination. Sailing Master Uriah Phillips Levy, serving in 1816 aboard U.S.S. *Franklin,* was a Jew. He was handsome, athletic, and intelligent; he had fought honorably in the War of 1812 and spent time in England's dank Dartmoor Prison.

At a dance in Philadelphia, Navy Lieutenant William Potter bumped into Levy, who was doing a polka with a pretty girl. Levy begged Potter's pardon. Potter said he trusted that Levy could navigate better at sea than he did on the dance floor. Levy danced away, trying to avoid trouble.

Potter was drunk. When he rammed Levy for the third time, Levy slapped his face.

"You damned Jew!" Potter spat, and Levy answered calmly,

"That I am a Jew, I neither deny nor regret."

Potter was removed from the ballroom, and next day a young officer came to Levy with a challenge. Levy accepted, but advised the young man to warn Potter that he was a very good pistol shot.

They fought at twenty paces, in a New Jersey meadow. When asked if he had anything to say, Levy uttered a Hebrew prayer, and then announced that he would not aim at his opponent. Potter called him a coward; he called Potter a fool. The duel began.

Potter shot quickly and missed. Levy fired in the air.

Potter reloaded, fired, and again went wide of the mark. Again Levy shot in the air. This went on four times. The seconds tried to stop the duel, but Potter would not stop. His fifth shot pinked the lobe of Levy's ear.

Then Levy brought his pistol down level, and fired. Potter was dead.

Levy was tried in civil court and acquitted. He was later given a lieutenant's commission, and went on through a long and stormy but distinguished career. He was Commodore of the Mediterranean Squadron when that grade was the highest rank in the Navy.

[*v*]　What likely was the last actual duel in the Navy took place shortly after the turn of the century, and was in the best tradition of Richard Harding Davis.

Two men, revolvers in hand, faced each other in a clearing on the jungle island of Maranduke, in the Philippines. One was Captain Emilio Alapap of the Philippine Army, so smartly uniformed that he might have been mistaken, at least, for a Brigadier General. He was the cousin of Emilio Aguinaldo, the hero of the Insurrection.

The other was a U.S. Navy bluejacket, wearing a faded and tattered uniform. His name was Griffith Price Owen—but because of the duel he was about to change that name for one that would become more famous. He was somewhere in his thirties, and hailed from Lewiston, Maine.

Alapap had reportedly tied a U.S. sailor to a tree, and then blasted him to death at close range with a Krag rifle. Owen sought out Alapap, slapped his face, and challenged him to a duel.

Now the two principals stood apart at the prescribed distance, and so did the two groups of spectators. The Americans were outnumbered five to one, and were sadly outclassed both in the matter of weapons and in that of physical fitness. They had been doing undercover work in the jungle for a long time, and had all suffered from malarial fevers.

The referee was a Filipino. Some of the Navy men thought that he made a peculiar movement with his right hand and twitched his shoulder before he dropped the hat as a signal to fire. At any rate, Alapap fired before the hat fell, and before the referee shouted "Fuego!"

Owen clapped his hand to his head, where he was nicked by the bullet, and then got off four shots. The first one missed. The other three—any one of which would have been fatal—put three holes in Alapap's forehead, so close together that all could have been covered by a devaluated Spanish *peso*.

Such was the marksmanship of Griffith Price Owen. Later, he was given a General Court Martial, not on a charge of killing Alapap, but on having violated Article 8 of the *Articles for the government of the United States Navy*, Paragraph 5: ". . . or sends or accepts a challenge to fight a duel, or acts as a second in a duel . . . shall be punished by death or such other punishment as court-martial shall direct."

After something like a hundred years, the Navy had finally lowered the boom on the practice of dueling.

The Navy must have been secretly proud of Owen. But rules were rules, and he was kicked out of the Service. Just how long he stayed a civilian is not known, but it may have been only a short time before he was back in uniform under the name of "Jack Golden." In later years he was given a certificate of "continuous service."

My Love Affair with the Navy

Griffith Price Owen—or Jack Golden—was right out of the story books. He was born October 3, 1863; he died aged seventy-seven at the end of 1939, retired from the Navy. Upon his retirement, he had a great deal of trouble getting his true name restored to the records.

According to relatives, he retired in the rank of lieutenant, and yet he never wore anything but the bluejacket's uniform. This can be explained by the fact that most of his career was spent in Naval Intelligence. In World War I, the French awarded him the medal of the *Legion de Honneur*—and he complained that this cost him a kiss on both cheeks. He had other medals, including one for lifesaving, but he never wore them.

He was a long-time friend of Lillian Russell, a year his junior. She appeared at Navy benefits, and Jack Golden—who fought hard and sometimes drank the same way—said that she got him out of jail on a few occasions. "I'd go to hell for that old gal!" he told friends.

There was always something dramatic about the man. In France, wearing mufti, he turned up in bad shape, nearly unconscious and coughing blood. Doctors found he had literally followed the orders to couriers—if there was danger of capture and the message could not be burned, the courier had to swallow it.

The doctors gave him medicine, along with a glass of brandy. He felt better. A doctor said, "Well, my man, if we have to cut into your stomach, do you care which side we enter?"

"Not a damn bit," Golden said. "But before you do that, I wish you'd try out a scheme I just thought of. Give me another dose of that damned oil, but stir a couple of special delivery stamps into it first. Then shove the bottle of brandy over here where I can reach it."

Golden's act sounds melodramatic, but his condition was no joking matter. After another spasm of pain, he told the doctor (a Canadian Expeditionary Force officer): "If I start to go nutty, dope me with something so I won't speak out of turn. Now, send this SOS by wire, or by a French courier, to — (a code word). *Your man Friday says grab your bonnet.*"

The doctors chuckled about this. But soon after the message was sent, they recalled, a high-powered car shot into the village and out of it very mysteriously. What was happening was unknown, but Golden's code message must have been important.

Golden, always the showman, was eminently suited to the cloak-and-dagger role. After having been given the French medal, he was invited to attend a banquet of the *Legion de Honneur.* Later, there was dancing. Golden witnessed what he thought was a deliberate snubbing of a British nurse and her American escort by an actress, whom he identified only as "an Italian woman who thought she was the whole works." The fact that he was rather high at the time did not in the least impair his aim. He whipped out his automatic and neatly shot both high heels out from under the woman.

All hell broke loose on the dance floor. Golden later said that he was saved by a little redheaded English nurse. "She grabbed a damp towel from a refreshment table," he told Colonel Ned Rea, of the Canadian Expeditionary Force. "She snapped it around the gun and my hand, hooked my feet out from under me, sat on my tummy, and bounced up and down like a Canuck cavalryman. But when the French cops swarmed in, she had shoved the gun down her—had concealed it on her person. Haw, haw!

"When we arrived at the calaboose the cops had one big argument. They had brought along a splinter from the dance floor, and one of the three-inch high heels, but as they couldn't produce the gun or the bullets, they couldn't make the charge 'with a deadly weapon' stick.

"When they were trying to make the charge 'drunkenness,' I got mad and told the interpreter that no drunk could shoot as well as I had. Well, they called me 'one veree damn Sauvage,' and slammed me into the cooler. But when they found that little red rosette I had hidden in my tobacco pouch they threw all kinds of fits and spasms. A major named Dreyfus came, and they turned me loose."

(The red rosette, of course, showed that Jack Golden had been awarded the French *Legion de Honneur.*)

My Love Affair with the Navy

Many years after the duel in the jungle, lawmakers decided that "The encounter [with Alapap] occurred during and under war conditions, and therefore peacetime regulations did not obtain." This made it possible for "Jack Golden" to obtain credit for unbroken service in the Navy, and to become Griffith Price Owen again.

[vi] Griffith Price Owen was too remarkable to be called typical of the Navy, and yet he embodied all the things the Navy stands for. After the duel with Alapap, he went on serving the Navy for more than forty years, except for one short hitch in the Army's Signal Corps. Aviation lured him into this, and he became a flier.

He was dreamer and doer, wit and philosopher, fighter and artist and inventor. Being in Naval Intelligence, he was intimately associated with such great Admirals as Fighting Bob Evans, George Dewey, William Sowden Sims, and William A. Moffett. He studied the cameras of more than sixty years ago, and found a way to correct their tendency to produce light streaks on film. Then he built a number of cameras, and records indicate that he built the first stereopticon. None of his inventions was ever patented: after Owen had designed or perfected anything, he lost interest in it and went on to something new.

He has been credited with producing the first range finder that would enable planes to drop bombs with any reasonable accuracy, but he did not profit financially from this.

He loved children and animals, and often appeared on the streets of his home town of Lewiston in the traditional pose of a sailor with a monkey on his shoulder. But there was a difference here: the monkey could talk, because Owen was an expert ventriloquist. His three little nieces, Lisa, Wini, and Neva, still remember that he made their dolls talk . . . and then when he had gone back to sea they spanked the dolls because they were no longer vocal.

His Navy record, while entirely distinguished, was not spotless. Thirst overcame him on occasion, and aside from winning nearly every commendation America and her Allies had to offer, he spent a few periods in the brig.

Once he went ashore with only two bits in his pocket, but this was in a day when a dime would buy a large and foaming schooner of beer. He was very thirsty. Before he got to the nearest bar, he saw a bony, half-starved dog on the sidewalk in front of a butcher shop, and was lost. He went into the butcher shop and bought ten cents' worth of dog meat.

The dog ate this and still was hungry. Owen went back in and ordered another ten cents' worth of dog meat. The butcher said his dog meat was all gone, but he had some liver. Owen was feeding this to the dog when a man came by and was interested in the proceedings. Owen asked, "Who owns this dog, anyway?" The man said, "Why he belongs to the butcher."

Only the fact that the meat market man had the protection of his counter, with cleavers handy, prevented him from getting beaten up by Griffith Price Owen.

7. WHEN THE OLD BATTLESHIP WAS NEW

The shell a 16-inch gun fires [from the battleship *New Jersey*] is as tall as an average man, weighs between 2000 and 2700 pounds, and can penetrate 30 feet of concrete reinforced by steel beams. In 3½ minutes these nine guns can fire seven broadsides, or a total of 63 shells. This is equivalent to the bomb load of approximately 60 aircraft of the types used in Vietnam.
—*The National Observer*, April 1, 1968

THE RECOMMISSIONING of the battleship *New Jersey*, in 1968, did my heart a lot of good. I knew about the 16-inch shells, and just how tall they are. I saw a man killed by one during battle practice. The shell slipped from the ammunition hoist in a turret, and knocked over another shell which fell across the man's body with all its weight of more than a ton, practically cutting him in two.

The word, "Casualty in Number Two Turret!" was sometimes only for drill, but this time it was real. I helped carry the man to the sick bay, and he was put on the operating table. The senior medical officer examined him and found he was fearfully crushed in the abdominal region. He apparently felt no pain, but was terribly thirsty.

"What do you want me to write your mother, son?" the doctor

asked.

"Oh, I'll write her myself in a day or two," the sailor replied.

He died less than an hour later, gallantly joking until the last.

My kinship with the *New Jersey* goes a long way back. In 1923, as a gangling and guileless hospital apprentice first class, I reported aboard the 16-inch gun battleship *Maryland* in San Francisco Bay, along with a dozen other enlisted men. We went out from the Embarcadero at Pier 14, in an officers' motorboat that was resplendent with mahogany and brightwork and *macrame* lace. (It was years before I discovered the true name and correct French spelling of this cockpit ornament, because someone in the Navy, Irish, no doubt, had corrupted it to "McNamara lace.")

We all carried seabags and hammocks on our shoulders. Thus encumbered, the man just ahead of me leaped for the accommodation ladder and fell into the running tide. He may well have contributed to a Navy song that says:

> *Of all the funny feelings,*
> *There is nothing to compare*
> *With jumping for the ladder*
> *When the ladder isn't there . . .*

At any rate, he has fished out with a boathook, along with his gear, and had to stand shivering on the quarterdeck while we were mustered and assigned to our respective divisions. The officer of the deck had not been long out of the Naval Academy, but he knew his Navy. As he regarded the dripping sailor, he said sternly: "Always remember this: you have one hand for the Government, and the other hand for yourself!"

It was a new world, but we were proud. The dreadnoughts were still supreme. No newsreel of the day was complete unless it showed them plunging through the sea in majestic column formation, taking white water over their bows and being ever ready to cross the enemy's T in the classical naval fashion.

Perhaps this needs explaining. In the Navy, "crossing the enemy's T" has nothing to do with the T formation in football. It means simply this: The enemy fleet is approaching in column formation. If your ships can cross the T, they can bring broadside guns to bear on the column, and theoretically sink each ship in line. Meanwhile, the enemy cannot fire guns except from the leading ship—since they would be shooting through all the other ships in the line.

It was true that during Force exercises we could look out and see an especially unlovely ship, a converted collier renamed U.S.S. *Langley* and nicknamed "The Covered Wagon," horsing around to launch and recover a handful of biplanes on her perilous flight deck. But we thought very little of these experimental efforts. Nobody I knew even dreamed that a time would come when the *Langley*'s grandchildren would reduce all battleships— our own and even later types—to what the Navy morbidly describes as a "state of obsolescence."

I call this the Old Navy. At that time, many a bluejacket had H-O-L-D F-A-S-T tattooed on the backs of his fingers.

Enlisted people in the *Maryland* had no time to read prophetic writings on the bulkheads, and would have been horrified to find any there. We were much too busy standing four-hour watches, running to action stations in the loud confusion of General Quarters, swabbing decks, shining brightwork, and painting bulkheads, angle-irons, and overheads for the Saturday inspections when the Captain reached into nooks and crannies and expected to find his white gloves unsullied when he had done. Destroyers might be a dungaree Navy, but battleships, above all others, were spit-and-polish. It was a common saying that you could eat your meals, at any time, off any deck in the ship. Nobody leaned against anything; nobody dared put a hand on the paintwork.

Life aboard was all the more difficult and strange to me because I could seldom understand the word being passed over the PA system. I was not long out of Texas, where we-all spoke to you-all in a slow but intelligible drawl. The *Maryland* had been commissioned on the East Coast, and was manned almost entirely by people from Brooklyn, Boston, the Bronx, and the East Side. Bosun's mates went on the horn with things like this: "Now hear dis! Now hear dis! Sweepers, starcher brooms . . . giver a good sweepdown fore'n aft!" Or, "Now lay up tudy starboard side of de squatterdeck, all de wuxtry duty squad!"

I also had to learn about cumshaw and scrounging. These were allied arts, and I doubt now that without their application any battleship could have been maintained in a condition of readiness. Certainly it could not have passed the white glove inspections.

Under the system, the crew of more than a thousand men managed to cut interdepartmental red tape, and to feed each off the other in goods and services to an astonishing degree. It was a feudalistic system. Non-rated men could not contribute much in the way of cumshaw, but they could be active agents in the art of scrounging. If a petty officer said, "Smitty, lay down to the sail locker and scrounge me a yard of canvas," he expected Smitty to cadge the material through powers of persuasion if the sail locker were attended, and to pilfer it if it were not. That sort of pilfering, in the battleships days, was called "midnight small stores."

Any senior petty officer had it made, and was well on his way to being a career man. The chief petty officers lived like kings: their mess, in any big ship, served "shipping-over chow"—much better food than the wardroom.

I happened, most fortunately, to be rated pharmacist's mate third class soon after reporting aboard, and the "crow" on my left sleeve was not as good as a right-arm (command) rating, but it still opened wide new horizons. I had been thirteen months in the Navy. I knew how to give anesthetics, apply surgical dressings, sterilize instruments, take sutures, open boils, roll certain pills, compound Brown's Mixture and elixir of terpin hydrate, and give hypodermics. In short, I was a living example of the axiom that a little knowledge is a dangerous thing. This is especially true in the field of medicine.

I was put in charge of the ship's operating room. It had the usual operating table, sterilizers, and a locked cabinet for ether, alcohol, and narcotics. It also had a formidable expanse of tiled deck, bulkhead, and overhead that had to be virginal white for Saturday inspection.

[ii]   The *Maryland* was at sea one Friday evening when I was still new aboard, and the decks topside were darkened for Battle Condition Two. I had the battle ports dogged down so no light would show, and was painting the operating room when George Burton entered from the sick bay. He was our pharmacist's mate first class—the Navy had not yet begun calling them "hospitalmen"—and he looked shocked.

"Knock it off!" George said in a tone that was both advice and command. "You don't have to paint this joint."

"Captain's inspection tomorrow," I said. "White gloves."

"Knock it off, I said. Ski will handle it for you."

"Ski?" I asked. Practically every man in the Navy with a Polish name was called "Ski," just as those with Italian names became "Wop." No offense was intended, and none was suspected. My shipmates had already begun calling me "Bozo," as short for Bosworth.

"I mean Walter Kerzwicki, painter first class—in charge of the paint locker," George said. "He's got some strikers working for him." George vanished into the sick bay for a minute, and sent a non-rated man to bring Kerzwicki. "Get smart!" he told me. "You can get this painting done cumshaw."

"How?"

George lighted a cigarette and perched in a very unsterile fashion on the operating table. "Look," he said. "You've got two pints of alky in that locker. One's open for sterilizing instruments, and for surgical dressings—the minute you open it, that pint is expended. The full bottle is for emergencies, operations. Now, who's going to ask you how many surgical dressings you handle? Man falls down a ladder and cuts his knee, *you* fix him up, not the doctor. How about Morgan, the ship's cook first? You know him?"

I said yes. Morgan was the butcher, and had cut his hand slicing meat. I took stitches.

"Morgan likes a little shot of alky, now and then. You fix him up with that, and then when the chow in the mess don't look good, Morgan will fix you up with a steak. See what I mean? Cumshaw."

I began to see what he meant, but it worried me. I believed in the sanctity of the United States Navy, and in the good of the country before the good of the individual. *Pro patria,* et cetera. (I still do.) This was a long time before the mess of deep freezes and fur coats in Washington, a long time before television and payola . . .

"Take Johnny Carroll," George went on. "Storekeeper second, with nine years in this man's Navy. Likes alky, too. You need salt-water soap, brightwork polish, or any other cleaning gear, you don't go through all that red tape of getting a chit from the First Lieutenant. You just tell Johnny what you want." He shook his head. "It has always been like that aboard this packet, so don't try to change things. See what I mean?"

Just then Walter Kerzwicki appeared, a lean, dark man of about thirty. He shook hands with me, but addressed himself to George Burton. He pointed to his Adam's apple.

"Doc, that silver tube in me t'roat—it's rustin'!"

"Give me the key to the alcohol locker," George said.

He poured an ounce of pure grain alcohol into a medicine glass. Ski tossed it off. It must have burned fearfully, but Ski sauntered leisurely to the sink and, talking all the while, drank a medicinal ounce of water for a chaser.

"Been on short rations," he said. "You know them five-gallon cans of shellac, down in the paint locker? You leave them stand, and the alky rises to the top, so you can skim it off. But them dumb strikers of mine, they ain't got enough to do, see? So they decide to crumb up the joint for inspection, and when they move the shellac to paint, they turn all the cans upside down, the stupid jerks. Say, Doc—that silver tube in me t'roat . . ."

George reached for the expendable bottle again, and then suggested there was something Ski's stupid strikers could do. I finished the painting that week, but on the following Friday, three of his non-rated men painted the operating room from stem to stern, and left no brushmarks. I lifted no hand, except to pour Ski a couple of shots when he came to inspect their work.

That same Friday was also fish day in the mess. "It ain't very good fish, either," Ship's Cook Morgan told me as I treated him both externally and internally. "Come up to the galley. How do you like your steak?"

[*iii*] Lacking the soda fountains that later came to big ships, we discovered that a very palatable drink could be made from cocoa, evaporated milk, vanilla extract, sugar, water, and ice. We called the beverage "billiards" and it became popular. The ship's best boxer took to spending much of his time in the operating room, drinking billiards.

His name was Ritchie King, and he was known as "the *Maryland's* Blond Tiger." He was already bantamweight champion of the Pacific Battle Force, and when we got to the Caribbean he would fight the Atlantic Scouting Force champion for the All Navy bantamweight belt.

Ritchie was young, and very good-looking. Nobody in the ship expected him to do a thing except to train for the task ahead, so he had nothing but time and boxing gloves on his hands. But he was growing to maturity, and after a few weeks on the billiards diet, his manager, Chief Warrant Officer Gus Kupbens, was horrified to discover that he had passed the bantamweight limit . . .

It was my fault. Fortunately, at this time, it was discovered that bedbugs were rife in the wardroom country, and all the officers' bedding would have to be run through the big steam sterilizer in the ship's laundry. I was given this job.

It took a couple of weeks, and down off Panama the temperature in the ship's laundry exceeded 120 degrees. While I sweated the bedding through the sterilizer, the Tiger lay moaning on the deck, swathed in blankets, drinking hot beef tea, and sweating off some ten pounds.

I was afraid he didn't have a chance. He looked weak and

ghostly pale when he stepped into the ring on the island of Culebra a few days later.

The fighters touched gloves. And then Ritchie King brought one up from down around his knees, and won the All-Navy championship with a single punch.

[*iv*] The Navy was doing things all over the world around this time. The destroyer *Bainbridge* had just saved 482 lives in the Sea of Marmora, where a French military transport burned; there was a rebellion in the Philippines, and marines from U.S.S. *Sacramento* landed and seized a town; marines and seamen were also protecting property during a revolution in Honduras.

But there was no action big enough to call for the battleships. The only time *Maryland* was under fire while I was aboard was when we were towing a target for two other sixteen-inch battlewagons, the *West Virginia* and *Colorado,* after we had finished our own long-range firing.

The rattan target was a full cable length astern of *Maryland*— 120 fathoms, or 720 feet. But the range was twelve miles. The firing ships were hull down on the horizon, and at that distance the interval between *Maryland* and the target looked like the space between two teeth of a pocket comb. Several hundred men were topside on the *Maryland,* watching the practice, which was very dramatic. First there was a burst of flame on the skyline, then a cloud of black smoke, and then the shells could be heard approaching with a roar like an express train, to explode and rip huge holes in the rattan screen.

But something happened. A sixteen-inch shell fell short by a mile or two, struck the water with a clap of thunder, and then veered straight for the *Maryland,* skipping the surface just like a flat rock that had been skimmed across a pond.

All hands topside rushed to go below and get behind the ship's armor belt. The shell fortunately expended itself and sank a few hundred yards away. A large number of the *Maryland's* crew came back topside just in time to see the same thing happen again. Sailors frantically rushing below collided with sailors coming topside, and the sick-bay staff was very busy treating cracked craniums, skinned knees, and bruises.

It went to show that even in peacetime, life in the Navy is never dull.

But for two weeks on this cruise, the *Maryland* and other battleships swung like fat cats from their anchor chains in the North River, and enjoyed New York. Jack Dempsey graced a big municipal banquet given for Navy personnel. I stood as best man for a shipmate who married a Bronx girl with the storybook name of Gabriella O'Hearn. She had been reared by her Aunt Kate, who had four sons on the New York City police force, and a fifth who was a priest in Oklahoma. Aunt Kate was terribly worried about her son in Oklahoma. Indians, she said.

Ship's Cook Morgan, who said he knew Brooklyn like he knew the palm of his hand or the cut of a T-bone steak, wanted to take me for a "speed run" on the beach. We went by subway on a March night when chunks of ice were bumping the battleships, and Morgan was not long in finding a bootlegger. This was my first taste of hard liquor. We tilted the bottle in a dark alley, because Sands Street and environs had been put out of bounds by Admiral Plunkett, commandant of the Third Naval District. Two shore patrolmen sighted us and chased us up darker alleys, but Morgan knew the town indeed, and we got away. We returned to the ship after midnight.

I was quite sure that I was drunk, but the intoxication was not all from the inferior bootleg whiskey. I was drunk with the adventure and romance of youth and a new liberty port; I felt that all the world's seaports lay before me, like beads on a necklace to be counted and restrung and enjoyed. I had to wake all hands in the sick bay and recount the evening. Morgan, laughing tolerantly, moved to the dressing table and helped himself to some eye drops for a mild conjunctivitis . . . only he picked up iodine instead of argyrol. The whole sick-bay staff had to turn out and hold his head under a water tap.

The *Maryland* and the other battleships weighed their anchors the next morning. And when we got to sea again, things began to happen.

[*v*] On a Friday evening, the senior medical officer, Dr. Hailey, paid a surprise visit to the operating room, and ordered me to shine the nickel-plated sterilizers for the Saturday inspection. I was out of brightwork polish, and sent a man for Johnny Carroll, the storekeeper. I poured Johnny a shot or two of alcohol, and he said, "Sure, Doc—anything you want."

A battle exercise was on, and all watertight doors were secured and guarded. Johnny had to go through one to get to his storeroom. He had been in the Navy long enough to know that you should never argue with a marine, but he was warm with alcohol. He pushed the marine aside and went on to get my brightwork polish—and got put on the report by the corporal of the guard, whose name was Buck Ogilvie.

Johnny promptly challenged Ogilvie to a grudge fight. The time agreed upon was a Sunday morning, on the foc'sle.

George Burton and I were alarmed. Johnny was slightly built and obviously out of shape. The marine outweighed him by at least thirty pounds, and was ten years younger.

"Hell with that noise!" said Johnny. He went into a crouch, and did some fancy footwork around the operating table. Then he held out his glass for another shot. "Once I stayed four rounds with Johnny Buff," he told us. "I'll beat his ears off!"

Scuttlebutt took care of publicizing the grudge fight. On Sunday morning, at least six hundred men assembled on the foc'sle, under the eyes of officers on the bridge. No one did anything.

A chief petty officer stepped forward to act as referee, and to appoint a timekeeper. He asked the principals if they wanted to use gloves: they said they would fight bare-handed. He pointed out that both wore heavy rings; they said that made it equal. They stripped to the waist, and the fight began.

It was as much of a duel as any duel the Navy ever fought. There was more in it than the infraction of ship's regulations. It personified the ancient rivalry between the Navy and the Marine Corps.

At this embattled moment, the ship's chaplain was just beginning divine services, far aft under the awning that covered the quarterdeck, and out of hearing of the shouts that punctuated the fight. On an average Sunday, the chaplain could expect a congregation of perhaps three hundred people, some of whom were moved by the Holy Spirit, and some who simply had nothing else to do. This morning, nobody was on hand except the lad who played the portable organ, and a scattering of Filipino stewards from the wardroom.

The good *padre* ran through a few hymns while waiting for his flock, and valiantly took his text from Psalms CVII, 10: *They that go down to the sea in ships, that do business in great waters . . .*

Then he pronounced a hasty benediction, and went forward to see what was going on. The fight was approaching its tenth round, and should have been stopped at half that number. Johnny Carroll, who in another time and place could have been a Golden Gloves champion, was coldly and methodically cutting Ogilvie's face to pieces. The marine, able only to hammer at Johnny's ribs, refused to allow his second to throw in the sponge.

Horrified, the chaplain stopped the fight, and stormed off to report to the Captain that the Holy Sabbath had been violated. Johnny Carroll, already on the report and a prisoner-at-large, now was thrown into the brig to face more serious charges.

Everybody in the sick bay felt that Johnny was a victim of the cumshaw system. I felt it most of all.

Brig prisoners had to have their temperatures taken twice daily. I took care of this for Johnny, and marked him up a couple of degrees, and told him to practice coughing. On the fourth day, his chart was shown to Dr. Hailey, who immediately ordered him to bed in the sick bay. This was vastly more cheerful and comfortable than the brig, although a marine guard still had to be posted over Johnny day and night.

Having been coached, he coughed, and complained of aches

and vapors. The junior medical officer held sick call, and accepted the temperatures recorded on Johnny's chart. He prescribed elixir of terpin hydrate, which Johnny loved because it had a high alcoholic content.

We probably could have kept Johnny in the sick bay indefinitely. But one evening when a corpsman went to fake his temperature, he found Johnny snoring blissfully. An empty bottle of my alcohol was under his pillow.

"The thieving son-of-a-bitch!" exclaimed George Burton. "If he had asked for a shot, we'd have given him one. But no, he had to steal it." He looked at me. "You leave the alky locker open?"

"No, but I left a half pint out for some dressings. Johnny must have snitched it while the marine was in the passageway for a smoke."

"Okay," George decided. "We won't let him enjoy it. Fix me a hypodermic of apomorphine."

I had seen apomorphine used in cases of suspected poisoning. It acted upon a brain center, and turned the stomach inside out before you could count to fifteen.

I prepared the hypodermic. George took the syringe, and I rolled up Johnny's pajama sleeve to swab his arm. His reaction to the cold alcohol was delayed, but when the needle jabbed him he came upright in his bunk, swearing and lashing out with his fists. The needle broke off in his arm, and the drug was wasted. He sank back, muttering, and then began snoring as before.

"We've got to get that needle out of his arm!" I told George.

"How?" he demanded angrily. "Give him ether and operate? Hell, no—that's a doctor's job. And we can's tell the doctor. The son-of-a-bitch—we can't tell him, either! If it don't travel, he'll be all right . . ."

After that, the sick bay corpsmen stopped faking Johnny's temperature, and he became a prisoner-at-large aboard ship. He could not go ashore in Panama, but he had friends who did go, and somebody brought him a large coconut filled with the famous and potent Three Dagger rum. Two days out of the Canal, and Johnny got drunk in some other part of the ship, where his Hos-

pital Corps friends could not protect him. His forthcoming summary court martial was upped to a general, and all of us knew
that his naval career was over.

He was kicked out of the Service. I heard later that he was
bootlegging to Navy personnel on the ferries between Bremerton
and Seattle. This was still a form of scrounging, and I wished him
well.

In World War II, the *Maryland*—grown old, but still packing
a punch—was among the battleships in Admiral Jesse Oldendorf's
task force at the battle of Surigao Straits, when the enemy's T
was crossed for probably the last time in history.

But quite awhile before that, I had a letter from Johnny Carroll. A little more than a year before Pearl Harbor, I was called to
active duty as a Naval Reserve Lieutenant. That same week, *The
Saturday Evening Post* began running a serial story of mine.
Johnny read the first installment, and wrote me from a veterans'
hospital in the Midwest.

There was, he said, some undefined and undiagnosed trouble
with his back. I answered the letter in a friendly but guarded
fashion, and did not hear from him again.

I still wonder if the needle got into a blood vessel and moved
to his back.

[*vi*] When I was aboard the
Maryland in 1923 and 1924, it was the time—if ever—for a tattoo
to identify me as a Fleet sailor, and seagoing. But I never had the
"Hold Fast" on my fingers, the star and anchor on the backs of
my hands, or the full-rigged ship done on my chest—as Bull
Halsey did.

In my youth, I thought that perhaps one day I would want to
hold up the Southern Pacific or the Santa Fe, and there was no
use providing positive identification—presumably I could do this
without leaving fingerprints, and I could always grow a beard.

And there was another reason. As a hospital corpsman, I had
treated a few patients who swore that they had contracted syphilis from a tattoo artist's needle. The doctors received this word

with much skepticism, but I knew of a couple of cases who had suffered a minor infection as the result of tattooes, and syphilis was certainly a possibility.

Then I also knew sailors who had been tattooed with the traditional dagger and heart, and a girl's name. Later, they had to have "Ann" changed to "Sue," and that kind of stuff. It didn't pay.

One of the greatest of all needle and ink designers was an Englishman, who tattooed the King of Denmark. But he rose to his full heights when he tattooed a full course meal on the belly of a French chef. This was in several courses, and in color. It even included mashed potatoes and brown gravy!

But my friend George "Rojo" (Red) Hickman, who is always able to top my Navy stories, tops this one easily. He was a radioman in the Virgin Islands in the 1920's. One of his shipmates, Paul F. Fulks, moonlighted by operating the Chefoo Tattooing Parlor at St. Thomas in his spare time. Fulks, who retired as a lieutenant, was an accomplished artist, and his establishment was surgically clean. He ran it, as Rojo says, with a flair.

Rojo was young and impressionable at the time, and of course the first elephant a youngster sees will forever be the biggest elephant of all. Looking back now, Rojo remembers the brown island women as being magnificently endowed. He swears (on the *Bluejacket's Manual,* not the Bible,) that it took two men to lift their breasts, but when this was done it nearly always revealed the very tasteful tattoo work of Paul Fulks. In beautiful Old English print, under one breast was tattooed "Sweet," and under the other one, "Sour."

It took a flair, indeed, to do things like that.

8. THE SUNG AND THE UNSUNG

Pluck takes us into a difficulty, nerve brings us
out of it. Both are comprised in the noble quality
we call valor.
—*George John Whyte-Melville*

MRS. JONES is running off a vacation movie for Mrs. Smith and
Mrs. Brown, making them hate her guts. She says, "Now . . .
here we are in San Francisco, at the Top of the Mark. We got the
waiter to take this shot. As you can see, I am wearing my vacation cruise ensemble from I. Magnin, and Murgatroyd has on a
yachting suit from Brooks Brothers. We were just about to take
the boat to Honolulu . . ."

Murgatroyd and Ermintrude Jones were not just about to do
anything of the kind, unless they were actually embarking in a
rowboat, a canoe, an outrigger, a torpedo patrol-boat, or—oddly
enough—a submarine.

Mrs. Jones, along with many other landlubbers, was frac-
turing naval and seagoing nomenclature. The determining factor
between "ships" and "boats" is easy enough to remember. Ships
carry boats. Obviously even a big nuclear submarine cannot carry
boats suspended from davits when submerged, and this fact
helped put submarines into the "boat" category. (A submariner
may refer to his vessel as a "pigboat," but you call it such at your
own peril.)

Navy slang is full of affectionate extremes. Battleships become "wagons," or "battle wagons"; aircraft carriers are "flat-tops," and destroyers are "tin cans." Then you have the "spitkids," or even smaller craft. The command structure follows a similar pattern, from the admiral in the flagship down to the second class seaman in the fleet.

It is the seamen and the petty officers who man the guns and do the real fighting; it is the Admiral or Captain who gets the glory. The seamen remain largely unsung.

This is a fact of life, and nobody can be blamed for it. In time of action, a ship becomes a person. The *Olympia* was Dewey. The *Missouri* was Halsey. The whole Pacific Fleet in World War II was Nimitz.

Without any intention at all of detracting from the honors of these great Navy leaders, let me point out that they were all pretty well—and wisely—protected. To kill Halsey, the Japanese would have had to get through a guard of planes, destroyers, and submarines. But they could—and did—knock off planes, destroyers, and submarines on the fringes of the fleet.

Heroism comes pretty close to being the responsibility and the right of youth, when muscles are still firm and the blood is hot. In the Spanish-American war, Admiral George Dewey and "Fighting Bob" Evans were rightfully acclaimed, but the public is likely to confuse leadership with heroism. The real hero of that conflict was a junior naval officer named Richmond Pearson Hobson.

Hobson was a naval constructor who had been graduated from the Naval Academy in 1889, when he was nineteen years old. He was not quite twenty-eight when he accomplished his daring feat of blowing up the American collier *Merrimac* in the mouth of the harbor at Santiago de Cuba, thus bottling up the Spanish fleet inside.

Doing this had been the idea of Admiral Sampson, but Sampson gave command of the *Merrimac* to Hobson. It was June 3, 1898. Hobson picked a crew of six men—Osborn Deignan, George F. Phillips, Francis Kelly, George Charette, Daniel Montague and J. C. Murphy. After the ship was under weigh, another seaman who had been working aboard and had hidden himself reported for duty. His name was Randolph Clausen.

The *Merrimac* and her skeleton crew came under heavy fire almost immediately. The Spanish ships *Viscaya* and *Almirante Oquendo* opened up on her, and so did the enemy shore batteries. There were also explosions in the water from submarine mines and torpedoes.

Hobson kept going. He had planned to drop the forward anchor as soon as he was in the mouth of the harbor, then let the ship swing broadside, and drop the after anchor. But now the *Merrimac's* rudder was shot away and she became virtually uncontrollable. Hobson fought desperately to get her into position, and now he made a desperate choice: instead of opening the sea cocks and scuttling the collier, he would have to blow her up.

The men aboard had very poor chances of survival, but no one flinched. *Merrimac* carried a catamaran on deck. It was put over the side, and the enlisted men boarded it. Then Hobson set off the explosives, and jumped. *Merrimac* went down squarely across the narrow channel.

Hobson and his men were in the water, clinging to the sides of the catamaran, for an hour. Then they were captured and picked up by a boat from the Spanish *Reina Mercedes*, which was being used as a hospital ship. On July 6 they were exchanged for a Spanish lieutenant and fourteen enlisted men.

Hobson was advanced a great many numbers on the Navy's promotion list, and became a rather senior lieutenant commander. He resigned his commission a few years later, and went on to distinguish himself in another field as a member of Congress.

(Incidentally, the term "Hobson's choice" has nothing to do with the decision Lieutenant Hobson made, but is some three hundred years older. It comes from a Tobias Hobson, an Englishman who rented out riding horses, and always made certain that each customer took the horse nearest the stable door.)

Nine times out of ten, the story of a hero will put him aboard an airplane, a destroyer, a submarine, or in one of the small craft the Navy calls a "spitkid." A spitkid, aboard ship, is a small receptacle filled with sand, to receive cigarette butts or tobacco juice.

Years ago, during an argument with a shipmate, a sailor named Johnson had a spitkid hung over his head after the manner of a watch cap. He was not really injured, but for the rest of his twenty or thirty years in the Navy, he was known as "Spitkid" Johnson . . .

Heroism began early in the Navy, in the days when war was a more personal thing, when enemy ships were boarded and men fought hand-to-hand, hacking at each other with cutlasses. Midshipman Henry Wadsworth, who chronicled the christening of Melancthon Woosley Low aboard U.S.S. *Chesapeake*, became a hero a short time later, and tried to become one even sooner. He volunteered to go with Stephen Decatur when Decatur took the captured ketch *Intrepid* into Tripoli harbor, and burned the captured U.S. Frigate *Philadelphia*. Wadsworth's Journal does not tell us why he didn't go . . . but the log of the *Chesapeake*'s medical officer does. It seems that he was on the sick list with an ailment contracted in an engagement of an entirely different nature.

He had just been promoted to Lieutenant. On 4 September, 1803, he went aboard the same ketch *Intrepid*, as second in command, for an expedition even more daring than Decatur's. The *Intrepid* had been converted into a fire ship. She had a total of thirteen men aboard (apparently they were not superstitious), and was loaded with more than a thousand pounds of powder and hundreds of shells with fixed fuses. Her mission was to blow up the entire town of Tripoli, along with the shipping in the harbor.

Ironically enough, Navy slang of that day gave the name "fire ship" to the kind of woman who had but recently put Henry Wadsworth on the sick list.

The *Intrepid* was scarcely in the harbor before it was boarded by several hundred Algerians. Somebody put a match to the magazine, and Algerians and Americans were blown up together.

[*ii*] Many a Navy ship is so small that it barely escapes being called a boat. Indeed, the minecraft and others, named after birds, are popularly called the "bird

boats," although they are ships with names of their own. Down the years, these tiny craft apparently have felt exactly as do the smallest boys on a football team—they have to distinguish themselves, or they will never be noticed. Some have been extremely successful.

It all adds up. The spitkids have very junior officers, or even chief petty officers as skippers. These can afford to take greater risks than an Admiral, who commits a task force or an entire fleet to action. And they can get away with it out of sheer, reckless audacity.

But in most cases, nobody is on board to tell the world about the exploit. It has always been the practice to embark newspaper and radio correspondents in the flagship, where they have access to the admiral, and can get quotes. Here, also, they were more comfortable than in a pitching destroyer, and had better communication facilities for transmitting their copy.

But they missed a lot. Ernie Pyle, of sacred memory, showed what could be done by associating not with officers, but with the G.I.'s. The Navy found it could profit, too, from accounts of destroyers, submarines, submarine rescue vessels, and the like.

During the piping times of peace of the Twenties and Thirties, some quietly dramatic things were going on, mostly aboard the spitkids of the dungaree Navy. There had been too many tragic submarine disasters, and now young Charles B. Momsen, Annapolis 1920, was dedicated to proving that men trapped in a sunken sub need not die. He had invented and designed an underwater lung which enabled survivors to breathe as they went slowly up an ascending line to the surface—if they went up too fast without breathing out the pressure, their lungs would explode like an over-inflated toy balloon.

At the same time, certain small ships designated as ASR (Auxiliary Submarine Rescue) were learning how to "ping" for submarines on the bottom, and how to locate them by echo. At this point, sonar was not much better than a cumbersome hearing aid, but the pinging worked. A couple of the ASR's had huge metal diving chambers mounted on their fantails. This device weighed nine tons; it could be lowered to a submarine and secured to the conning tower with an air and water-tight seal, so that the conning tower hatch could be opened. Then it could take off eight or nine men at a time, without subjecting them to the pressures of the sea or even getting them wet.

But deep-sea divers had to go down first, to secure a cable to the conning tower. The Navy had a number of men rated as Master Divers, and around 1935 there was almost as much interest in deep-sea diving as there is in skin diving today.

In that year, as a junior grade lieutenant in the Naval Reserve, briefly on active training duty, and as a reporter for the *San Francisco Chronicle*, I took the course.

The deep-sea dive was first, and the result was pure slapstick comedy—not without certain built-in perils. When I went down to some sixty or seventy feet, I had no sooner touched bottom than I inadvertently valved too much air into my suit, and went rocketing to the surface. I thought the boat crew was hoisting me, and tried to tell them via the helmet telephone that I did not wish to come up yet. The telephone was not working. The boat crew had just thrown some fishing lines over the side when I surprised them by breaking water like a released cork: I shot into the air, and then fell back with enough force to rock battleships at their moorings in Pearl Harbor.

Fortunately, I was able to shut off the compressed air before my diving suit extended to the point where I would have been spreadeagled, and unable to reach the valve—in which case the suit would have exploded, and my fifty-pound diving shoes and fifty-pound belt would have taken me back to the bottom to drown. But I learned about deep-sea diving.

It was a good lesson about the perils of inflation, in the era of Franklin Delano Roosevelt.

Then I made a simulated escape from a submarine, sunk at 100 feet. This was done at the submarine escape tank at Pearl Harbor, and I later repeated the training at New London, and felt qualified to escape from a sunken submarine anywhere. The

Momsen lung is like a hot-water bag strapped to the chest; it supplies oxygen, and gives the user a sense of well-being that amounts almost to intoxication. You slide up the line, and take a number of prescribed breaths at certain stops, to get rid of the pressure. In my case, a sailor ahead of me kept freezing on the line, and instructors had to swim down into the tank to pry him loose. Garland Suggs was one of these; he was a master diver who swam like a fish, and had helped to raise the ill-fated S-4 and the S-51, and had spent more than 2000 hours under water. Suggs retired in 1949 as a lieutenant commander.

Some time later, I went into a submarine rescue chamber after the ASR had pinged for a number of hours for a submarine that was lying doggo on the bottom, simulating disability. We finally found her, established the correct location, and lowered the rescue chamber. We latched it on to the conning tower, and opened the hatch. A few gallons of water fell into the submarine, and a voice rose. It said, "What took you so goddamned long?"

With that, I felt that my education in submarine rescue was complete.

[*iii*] The Melanesian name *Kolombangara* rings like a cymbal, and denotes "King of the Waters." Around the island, the air is always soft and humid, and often heavy with the scent of lilacs. In World War II, this was mixed with the smell of gunsmoke and the stench of death in the jungle.

The geography is confusing. The Solomon Islands were so named by explorers who thought they had reached India. Individual island groups thereafter were given native, French, and British names. Kolombangara is upward from Guadalcanal, where a number of heroic sea battles began in August 1942. It was nine months later before American forces could move up to New Georgia, Vella Lavella, and a storied channel called Blackett Strait. The actions here were suitable only to small ships, and that meant that they were fought by young men. Some of the young men did glorious things. Many died. And a few wrote almost incredible epics of survival after their ships had been shot from under them.

I came that way later, island-hopping after reporting to Halsey's staff in Noumea. Noumea is a lovely place, with a climate San Diego or Honolulu might wish to have; Noumea also has lovely New Zealand ale. My job was taking care of press correspondents, who were mainly sitting out a lull in the fighting, living in Quonset Hut Number Nine, drinking beer and composing limericks and bawdy songs. When any of them finished a bottle, he shouted "Timber!", and everybody ducked. The bottle sailed over their heads and shattered on the forward bulkhead, where there was a pile of broken brown-bottle glass three feet high. One song we sang, to the tune of *Stars and Stripes Forever*, went:

> *Three cheers for old hut Number Nine,*
> *It's the best goddammed hut in Noumea;*
> *The boys and the girls are so fine,*
> *They are really a wonderful group . . .*

This had been brought to the South Pacific by a former teacher, who enchanted everybody by singing the original corn:

> *Three cheers for the Jones Junior High,*
> *It's the best Junior High in Toledo . . .*

(Shortly after the war, I checked on this fantastic bit of folklore while in Toledo. Believe it or not, there was a Jones Junior High.) Such songs were reminiscent of an incident in World War I, when a field-artillery piece was stuck in the mud, and a group of muddy soldiers trying to move it were heard singing sweetly, "Jesus wants me for a sunbeam." This proves something. A singable song can take the place of profanity, and always helps relieve the chore at hand, just as the lusty old sea chanteys helped with the heave and haul.

When I went on up the chain of islands to Espiritu Santo, Guadalcanal, and Bougainville, we were envious of a song that was being sung in the Mediterranean theater about "Dirty Gertie from Bizerte," and we composed a counterpart called "Ella from Vella Lavella." It did not catch on, perhaps because the action

113

had been stepped up and everybody was on the move. But Blackett Strait had already become famous, mostly due to an operations order that must have been occasioned by the enthusiastic way in which Arleigh "Thirty-one Knot" Burke's destroyers put to sea. The dispatch said:

EFFECTIVE THIS DATE DESTROYERS OF THIS COMMAND WILL NOT REPEAT NOT MAKE SPEED IN EXCESS OF TWENTY KNOTS WHEN PROCEEDING THROUGH BLACKETT STRAIT X RAY IT HAS BEEN DETERMINED THAT THIS SPEED GIVES ARMY PRIVIES ALONG THE SHORE A GOOD FLUSHING OUT WITHOUT DESTROYING THEM X RAY THE PRACTICE OF PAINTING THE SILHOUETTES OF ARMY PRIVIES ON THE BRIDGE WITH A HASHMARK FOR EACH ONE SUBSEQUENTLY DESTROYED WILL BE DISCONTINUED.

This fell under the general classification of a "beno order," like "there will be no scrub and wash clothes on the foc'sle," or "Now there will be no smoking topside during refueling." Somebody was always taking the fun out of life. The Army privies were built out over the water, and used the whole wide sea for a sewer. It was great sport to whip down the channel at thirty-one knots, and throw a tremendous bow wave that knocked down the pilings and dumped the Army privies into the sea—along with their occupants. A newspaper correspondent who observed this astutely noted that the Army men were interred, but not dead.

But then things began happening fast, and the Navy had to forget about having fun.

Destroyers were known as Small Boys, although there were some even smaller boys around, and all with the itch to fight. The Japanese still had warships in the area, and other ships assigned to supply their numerous shore installations. IFF (Identification Friend or Foe) was especially difficult during night actions. Occasionally, U.S. Commanders had to send plaintive signals over TBS (Talk Between Ships) to their own side, saying: "Tell your boys to stop shooting at us." In at least one case, the Commodore of a destroyer squadron replied, "Sorry, but the next salvo is already on the way."

I would not say that destroyers are trigger happy, but I am

sure they are the shootingest ships in the Navy. I know of only one case in which they were urged to use restraint. During the pre-invasion bombardment of Saipan, Captain Donald C. Varian was the commodore of a destroyer squadron. He thoughtfully provided each of his ships with charts so detailed that they marked each building ashore. (Naval Intelligence is a wonderful thing.) Then he sent a signal that said: DO NOT REPEAT NOT FIRE ON THE WHOREHOUSES.

Here again was a matter of logistics, and the careful conservation of supplies. Naturally, Varian became a Rear Admiral, and had a very distinguished career.

U.S.S. *Strong* was one of four destroyers covering the landing of American troops on New Georgia Island, on the night of 5 July, 1943. She was torpedoed. The torpedo blast alone would have sunk the ship, but now the Japanese on the island illuminated her, and began pouring a withering fire into her from their shore batteries.

Despite this bombardment from about two miles away, destroyers *Chevalier* and *O'Bannon* promptly came to *Strong's* aid. *O'Bannon* fired back at the shore batteries; *Chevalier* rammed her bow into the gash in *Strong's* side, and threw across lines and rescue nets. She took off 240 survivors in seven minutes, and then had to pull away.

Strong had been hit again and again. She sank in the darkness at 0122 time. Seven officers and thirty-nine men had been killed by the torpedo—and seven officers, in a destroyer, is a lot.

Twenty-three men went over the side as the ship went out from under them. One of these was Lieutenant Hugh Barr Miller, Naval Reserve. He had been an All-American quarterback at the University of Alabama, but there was little he could do now to call the signals.

As the *Strong* went down in the alien sea, the depth charges racked on her fantail began exploding—as they were designed to do—from the pressure. Every man in the water felt the terrible, jolting, rupturing force of the concussions. They clung desperately to a life net and to pieces of wreckage, and tried to stay together. But some of them had been mortally injured.

It was a totally black night. No rescuers found them, and they drifted with the current. One by one, the injured men lost their hold on the net or the flotsam, and were drowned. This ordeal went on for four days. Then six men—all that were left of the twenty-three—drifted onto the beach at Arundel Island.

They were so weak from immersion and the lack of food or water that they had to crawl on the sand like land crabs. Two of the six died there in the pitiless sun before they could reach the jungle.

That left four. Hugh Barr Miller was one of them.

He suffered from hemorrhages, and thought he was dying. By now it was nine days after the loss of the *Strong*. There were a few emergency rations, running out. Lieutenant Miller ordered the other three men to leave him and try to find help. He divided his clothing among them, and kept only a pocket knife for himself. He made it plain that an order was an order, and that they would obey. They did.

Hugh Barr Miller lay down to die. But two days later, a rain came up. He roused himself out of a coma, drank some rain water, and decided not to die, after all. He had given one of the men his shoes, and now he set out barefoot. He found a coconut, and drank its milk and ate its meat—the first real food he had taken in nearly two weeks.

Then he found a dead Japanese soldier, and stripped the corpse of field rations and hand grenades, and he was in business. Two days later, he ambushed a Japanese patrol of five men, killed them all with the grenades, and took what he needed from them.

Hugh Barr Miller put Robinson Crusoe in the shade for all time, because he not only survived on the island, but carried on a one-man war. He lived on Arundel Island for forty-three days before he was picked up by a Marine Corps Reserve seaplane piloted—appropriately enough—by Major Goodwin R. Luck.

He had killed more than thirty Japanese soldiers in his personal island war.

[*iv*]   Blackett Strait is off Vanga
Vanga, on the Kolombangara coast. If you have not been there,
the names suggest coral beaches and fronded palms, and even
romance under a tropical moon. But if you were there during the
war, you will remember Spam, and bugs, and an atabrine tan,
along with infinite boredom.

Blackett Strait became famous months before the Army
erected its privies along the shore. It was known for a loud, swift,
and shattering night action on 1 August, 1943, when Japanese
planes bombed the PT boat base at Rendova.

PT boats are the Motor Torpedo Patrol Boats, which are
much smaller boys than the destroyers. They are the Navy's hot-
rodders, dashing and swerving and attacking at high speed, and
of course they are commanded by very junior officers. Nobody
else could handle them.

In the 1 August action, seventeen PT boats were present. Two
were sunk, and the other fifteen made a night attack on five Japanese destroyers. The Japanese ships were retiring when the
destroyer *Amagiri* rammed PT-109, perhaps more accidentally
than purposefully. At any rate, PT-109 was cut in half.

Quite a bit has been written about this incident, but I prefer
the simple and factual Navy Intelligence report made by Lieutenant (j.g.) Byron R. White, USNR, and Lieutenant (j.g.) J. C.
McClure, both attached to Motor Torpedo Boat Flotilla One. I
think this document has not been published except in an official
Navy publication. I present it here unchanged, except that I call
the commanding officer "the Skipper." The text follows:

> The time was about 0230. Ensign Ross was on the bow as look-
> out; Ensign Thom was standing by the cockpit; the Skipper was at
> the wheel, and with him in the cockpit was Maguire, his radioman;
> Marney was in the forward turret; Mauer, the quartermaster, was
> was standing beside Ensign Thom; Albert was in the after turret; and
> McMahon was in the engine room. The location of other members
> of the crew upon the boat is unknown.
>
> Suddenly a dark shape loomed up on PT 109's starboard bow
> 200–300 yards distance. At first this shape was believed to be other
> PT's. However, it was soon seen to be a destroyer identified as the

Ribiki group of the Fubiki class bearing down on PT 109 at high speed. The 109 had started to turn to starboard, preparatory to firing torpedoes. However, when PT 109 had scarcely turned 30 degrees, the destroyer rammed the PT, striking it forward of the forward starboard tube and shearing off the starboard side of the boat aft, including the starboard engine. The destroyer, traveling at an estimated speed of 40 knots, neither slowed nor fired as she split the PT, leaving part of the PT on one side and part on the other. Scarcely 10 seconds elapsed between time of sighting and the crash.

A fire was immediately ignited, but fortunately, it was gasoline burning on the water's surface at least 20 yards away from the remains of the PT which were still afloat. This fire burned brightly for 15–20 minutes and then died out. It is believed that the wake of the destroyer carried off the floating gasoline, thereby saving PT 109 from fire.

The Skipper, Ensigns Thom and Ross, Mauer, Maguire and Albert still clung to the PT 109's hull. The Skipper ordered all hands to abandon ship when it appeared the fire would spread to it. All soon crawled back aboard when this danger passed. It was ascertained by shouting that Harris, McMahon and Starkey were in the water about 100 yards to the Southwest while Zinser and Johnson were an equal distance to the Southeast. The Skipper swam toward the group of three, and Thom and Ross struck out for the other two. The Skipper had to tow McMahon, who was helpless because of serious burns, back to the boat. A strong current impeded their progress, and it took about an hour to get McMahon aboard PT 109. The Skipper then returned for the other two men, one of whom was suffering from minor burns. He traded his life belt to Harris, who was uninjured, in return for Harris's waterlogged kapok life jacket, which was impeding the latter's swimming. Together they towed Sharkey to the PT.

Meanwhile, Ensigns Thom and Ross had reached Zinser and Johnson who were both helpless because of gas fumes. Thom towed Johnson, and Ross took Zinser. Both regained full consciousness by the time the boat was reached.

Within 3 hours after the crash all survivors who could be located were brought aboard PT 109. Marney and Kirksey were never seen after the crash. During the 3 hours it took to gather the survivors together, nothing was seen or heard that indicated other boats or ships in the area. PT 109 did not fire its Very pistols for fear of giving away its position to the enemy.

Meanwhile, the IFF (Identification Friend or Foe) and all codes aboard had been completely destroyed or sunk in the deep waters of

Vella Gulf. Despite the fact that all water-tight doors were dogged down at the time of the crash, PT 109 was slowly taking on water. When daylight of August 2 arrived, the 11 survivors were still aboard PT 109. It was estimated that the boat lay about 4 miles north and slightly east of Gizo Anchorage, and about 3 miles away from the reef along northeast Gizo.

It was obvious that the PT 109 would sink on the 2d, and decision was made to abandon it in time to arrive before dark on one of the tiny islands east of Gizo. A small island 3½–4 miles to the southeast of Gizo was chosen on which to land, rather than one but 2½ miles away which was close to Gizo, and which, it was feared, might be occupied by Japs.

At 1400 the Skipper took the badly burned McMahon in tow and set out for land, intending to lead the way and scout the island in advance of the other survivors. Ensigns Ross and Thom followed with the other men. Johnson and Mauer, who could not swim, were tied to a float rigged from a 2 x 8 which was part of the 37 mm. gun mount. Harris and Maguire were fair swimmers, but Zinser, Starkey and Albert were not so good. The strong swimmers pushed or towed the float to which the non-swimmers were tied.

The Skipper was dressed only in skivvies. Ensign Thom, coveralls and shoes, Ensign Ross, trousers, and most of the men were dressed only in trousers and shirts. There were six 45's in the group (two of which were later lost before rescue), one 38, one flashlight, one large knife, one light knife, and a pocket knife. The boat's first-aid kit had been lost in the collision. All the group with the exception of McMahon, who suffered considerably from burns, were in fairly good condition, although weak and tired from their swim ashore.

That evening the Skipper decided to swim into Ferguson Passage in an attempt to intercept PT boats proceeding to their patrol areas. He left about 1830, swam to a small island ½ mile to the southeast, proceeded along a reef which stretched out into Ferguson Passage, arriving there about 2000. No PT's were seen, but aircraft flares were observed which indicated that the PT's that night were operating in Gizo not Blackett Strait and were being harassed as usual by enemy float planes. The Skipper began his return over the same route he had previously used.

While swimming the final lap to the island on which the other survivors were, he was caught in a current which swept him in a circle about 2 miles into Blackett Strait and back to the middle of Ferguson Passage, where he had to start his homeward trip all over again. On this trip he stopped on the small island just southeast of "home" where he slept until dawn before covering the last ½ mile to join the rest of his group. He was completely exhausted, slightly feverish, and slept most of the day.

Nothing was observed on August 2 or 3 which gave any hope of rescue. On the night of the 3d, Ensign Ross decided to proceed into Ferguson Passage in another attempt to intercept PT patrols from Rendova. Using the same route as the Skipper had used and leaving about 1800, Ross "patrolled" off the reefs on the west side of the Passage with negative results. In returning he wisely stopped on the islet southeast of "home," slept and thereby avoided the experience with the current which had swept the Skipper out to sea. He made the final lap next morning.

The complete diet of the group on what came to be called Bird Island (because of the great abundance of droppings from the fine feathered friends) consisted of cocoanut milk and meat. As the cocoanut supply was running low, and in order to get closer to Ferguson Passage, the group left Bird Island at noon, August, 4th, and, using the same arrangements as before, headed for a small islet west of Cross Island. The Skipper, with McMahon in tow, arrived first. The rest of the group again experienced difficulty with a strong easterly current, but finally managed to make the eastern tip of the island.

The new home was slightly larger than their former, offered brush for protection and a few cocoanuts to eat, and had no Japanese tenants. The night of August 4th was wet and cold, and no one ventured into Ferguson Passage that night. The next morning the Skipper and Ross decided to swim to Cross Island in search of food, boats, or anything else which might be useful to their party. Prior to their leaving for Cross Island, one of three New Zealand P-40's made a strafing run on Cross Island. Although this indicated the possibility of Japanese, because of the acute food shortage the two set out, swam the channel, and arrived on Cross Island about 1530. Immediately they ducked into the brush. Neither seeing nor hearing anything, the two officers sneaked through the brush to the east side of the island and peered from the brush onto the beach. A small rectangular box with Japanese writing on the side was seen which was quickly and furtively pulled into the brush. Its contents proved to be 30–40 small bags of crackers and candy. A little farther up the beach, alongside a native lean-to, a one-man canoe and a barrel of water were found. About this time a canoe containing two persons was sighted. Light showing between their legs revealed that they did not wear trousers and, therefore, must be natives. Despite all efforts of the Skipper and Ross to attract their attention, they paddled off swiftly to the northwest. Nevertheless, the Skipper and Ross, having obtained a canoe, food and water, considered their visit a success.

That night the Skipper took the canoe and again proceeded into Ferguson Passage, waited there until 2100, but again no PT's appeared. He returned to his "home" island via Cross Island where he picked up the food but left Ross who had decided to swim back the following morning. When the Skipper arrived at base about 2330, he found that the two natives which he and Ross had sighted near Cross Island had circled around and landed on the island where the rest of the group were. Ensign Thom, after telling the natives in as many ways as possible that he was an American and not a Japanese finally convinced them whereupon they landed and performed every service possible for the survivors.

The next day, August 6, the Skipper and the natives paddled to Cross Island, intercepting Ross, who was swimming back to the rest of the group. After Ross and the Skipper had thoroughly searched Cross Island for Japanese and had found none, despite the natives' belief to the contrary, they (the natives) showed the two PT survivors where a two-man native canoe was hidden.

The natives were then sent with messages to the Coastwatcher. One was a penciled note written the day before by Ensign Thom; the other was a message written on a green cocoanut husk by the Skipper informing the coastwatcher that he and Ross were on Cross Island.

After the natives left, Ross and the Skipper remained on the island until evening, when they set out in the two-man canoe to again try their luck at intercepting PT's in Ferguson Passage. They paddled far out into Ferguson Passage, saw nothing, and were caught in a sudden rainsquall which eventually capsized the canoe. Swimming to land was difficult and treacherous as the sea swept the two officers against the reef on the south side of Cross Island. Ross received numerous cuts and bruises, but both managed to make land were they remained the rest of the night.

On Saturday, August 7, eight natives arrived, bringing a message from the coastwatcher instructing the senior officer to go with the natives to Wana Wana. The Skipper and Ross had the natives paddle them to [the] island where the rest of the survivors were. The natives had brought food and other articles, including a cook stove, to make the survivors comfortable. They were extremely kind at all times.

That afternoon, the Skipper, hidden under ferns in the native boat, was taken to the coastwatcher, arriving about 1600. There it was arranged that PT boats would rendezvous with him in Ferguson Passage that evening at 2230. Accordingly he was taken to the rendezvous point, and finally managed to make contact with the PT's at 2315. He climbed aboard the PT and directed it to the rest of the survivors. The rescue was effected without mishap, and the Rendova base was reached at 0530, August 8, 7 days after the ramming of the PT 109 in Blackett Strait.

So ends a routine Intelligence report made on 22 August, 1943, after the survivors of PT-109 had been interviewed. It is an official document from the Navy's archives, and if at any point it lacks literary grace it at least contains stark and elemental drama.

One wonders what happened to that message the Skipper wrote on a green cocoanut husk? One report had it that it was found years later, and was presented to the Skipper. At any rate it would have been quite a collector's item, because the Skipper was Lieutenant John F. Kennedy.

9. NOW HEAR THIS!

Ensign to Chief Petty Officer: "Chief, have you got change for a dollar, for the cigarette machine?"
Chief: "Yeah, I think so."
Ensign: "Now, wait a minute! Is that any way to speak to a commissioned officer? Let's run through that again. Have you got change for a dollar for the cigarette machine?"
Chief: "No, sir."

IN HIS MEMOIRS, the famous and colorful Marine Corps General, Lewis B. (Chesty) Puller, said that "paper work will ruin any fighting force." He added: "We make generals today on the basis of their ability to write a damned letter. Those kind of men can't get us ready for war."

Perhaps not. But when General Puller's marines were surrounded in Korea, and he observed, "Now we can fire in all directions," somebody should have put it into a dispatch. It may be unfortunate, but it is true that combat leaders are often longer remembered for what they *said* than for what they *did*. General Puller was expressing what Major Gilbert D. Hatfield had told Sandino, in Nicaragua, years before: "Water, or no water, marines *never* surrender!"

A classical military bon mot was Douglas MacArthur's "I shall return!" even if it did earn him the Navy's nickname of "Dugout Doug." (This was because it was said that he "dug out" from the Philippines.) The earliest examples go back to the ancient Greeks, and to Julius Caesar's *"Veni, vidi, vici."* Compare this alliterative brevity with the message Navy Lieutenant Donald F.

Mason sent on 8 January, 1942:

SIGHTED SUB, SANK SAME.

No, the man who can make a clever signal, or a clever retort, does his career no harm. Posterity will remember him.

The almost legendary Commodore Joe Fyffe, U.S. Navy, was a past master of the clever retort. Not long after he had made flag rank, his flagship broke down, and he had to order a tow from one of the ships in his own squadron, which was approaching Gibraltar. The Captain of the towing ship, knowing Joe Fyffe, decided he would have a little fun. He made a signal:

UNLESS THE WIND AND TIDE ABATE

I CANNOT TOW YOU THROUGH THE STRAIT.

Joe Fyffe was quite equal to the challenge. His answer, hoisted only a minute later, said:

AS LONG AS YOU HAVE WOOD AND COAL,

THEN TOW AHEAD, GOD DAMN YOUR SOUL.

On the China Station in the 1880's, Joe Fyffe ordered a twenty one–gun salute on Queen Victoria's birthday. Twenty-one guns, of course, is the ultimate in salutes. And salutes are always in odd numbers: in the old days, an even-numbered gun salute meant that the ship's Captain or Master was dead.

The gunner's mate was drunk, an occupational disease of many gunner's mates in the Old Navy. He stood on the flying bridge where the saluting battery was mounted, one gun to starboard and the other to port. Seamen fired the guns, but in those days before stopwatches, the gunner's mate stood between the guns and timed the intervals by reciting the Gunner's Chant:

> *If I wasn't a gunner, I wouldn't be here,*
> *Ready, starboard, fire!*
>
> *Away from my wife and my home so dear . . .*
> *Ready, port, fire!*

He ran through a whole list of relatives he was away from, but he also lost count, and ran through twenty-two guns.

There was a British flagship present, with a senior British Admiral embarked. The Admiral was either stuffy, or he knew Joe Fyffe. He made a signal:

WHAT WAS THE MEANING OF THAT SALUTE?

Joe Fyffe's reply promptly broke out on the flag hoist:

TWENTY ONE GUNS FOR QUEEN VICTORIA AND ONE GUN FOR MRS. COMMODORE JOE FYFFE BY GOD.

It can still happen, despite stopwatches. In 1957, Vice Admiral Roscoe F. Good, Commander Naval Forces Far East, inspected the Marine Corps First Division on Okinawa, and felt highly honored to have his three-star flag saluted by a field battery of four guns. The salute for a Vice Admiral or a Lieutenant General is fifteen guns. This means fifteen shots, fired by a battery of four guns.

The Number-2 gun misfired the second time around. The boys picked it up smartly, so as not to break the intervals, and guns 1, 3, and 4 finished the salute. About fifteen seconds later, Number-2 gun cooked off.

But the marines saved face. At lunch for all the officers of the First Division, Admiral Good was introduced as the only Vice Admiral in the Navy ever to be correctly saluted by the Marine Corps—fifteen guns for his flag, and one gun for the court martial he should have had many times over.

[ii] Honors between warships are not always rendered by gun salutes, which are reserved for special occasions. But when one ship passes another, the rail is manned by all hands, at attention. This is an ancient courtesy, and the British Navy is especially particular about observing it.

The old *Arizona* was standing up to Istanbul. She passed a British battleship, and the rail of the British ship was promptly manned. The *Arizona* anchored a little farther up the channel, and at once dragged her anchor and drifted downstream. As she went by, the British sailors once more were piped to the side . . .

The *Arizona* got up steam, and went up the channel again. When she came abreast of the British battleship, the same honors were rendered. I am indebted to Warwick Tompkins for this story. He was a signalman aboard the *Arizona* at the time, and he later became a famous salt-water sailor, sailing around Cape

Horn in a small schooner. He wrote a good book about that experience, *Fifty South to Fifty South.*

I had been transferred from Halsey's staff just before he took command of the Third Fleet, and was in San Francisco when he sent his famous dispatch to the Fleet on 15 August, 1945, after the Japanese surrender:

CEASE FIRING BUT IF ANY ENEMY PLANES APPEAR SHOOT THEM DOWN IN A FRIENDLY FASHION.

Halsey was not merely being clever here. There were Japanese slow to get the word, and some who did not believe it, and others who wanted to die for the emperor. (We have an unfortunate but very natural tendency to call this attitude "fanaticism" if it belongs to the enemy, and "patriotism" when it is practiced by our own people.) But thirteen days after the Halsey signal, the destroyer *Callaghan* was sunk off Okinawa by a Kamikaze pilot.

Halsey *was* the Third Fleet. Nimitz *was* the Pacific Fleet when he observed, "The Lord gave us two ends, one to sit on and one to think with. Heads we win, and tails we lose."

Both were capable of salty and humorous remarks, but both were too busy, in most cases, for such levity. One cannot be too sure that Commander (later Captain) James Bassett did not suggest some of the famous Halsey dispatches. When he congratulated General Alexander M. Patch on his victory at Gaudalcanal, Halsey punned:

HAVING SENT GENERAL PATCH TO DO A TAILORING JOB ON GUADALCANAL I AM SURPRISED AND PLEASED AT THE SPEED WITH WHICH HE REMOVED THE ENEMY'S PANTS TO ACCOMPLISH IT.

When the Third Fleet made a series of devastating air attacks over Luzon to protect the Palau operations, Halsey got off a message of congratulations to the commander of his fast carrier task forces. This said:

THE GATE RECEIPTS FROM THE RECENT EXCEPTIONAL PERFORMANCE AT LUZON WERE GRATIFYING AND ALTHOUGH THE CAPACITY AUDIENCE [the Japanese] HISSED VERY LITTLE WAS THROWN AT THE PLAYERS. AS LONG AS THE AUDIENCE HAS A SPOT TO HISS IN THE PERFORMERS WILL STAY ON THE ROAD.

It is well known that the war was fought by young studs, old fuds, and lieutenant commanders. I became a lieutenant commander not long after the war started, by virtue of my name appearing on an ALNAV (or *to all the Navy*) dispatch.

Even commanders were notified of their selection in this informal way, perhaps a hundred at a time. The skipper of a submarine approaching the Golden Gate in a heavy fog went on voice radio to request a navigational fix from the radar station. Fixes were not given out until it was certain the ship was American.

"Sing for your fix!" the enlisted radarman said.

The sub skipper complied:

"Super-suds, Super-suds, lots more suds with Super-suds-s-s!"

At that juncture, the radar station Commander entered. He had just made three stripes, and felt his rank. He got on the horn.

"It is not necessary to sing for your fix," he said.

The ebullient submarine skipper, filled with happy thoughts of liberty in San Francisco, came back joyously with:

"Super-suds, Super-suds, lots more suds with Super-suds-s-s!"

"I repeat," the shoreside Commander said tartly, "that it is not necessary for you to sing for your fix. This is Commander Whosit speaking."

The reply came back at once. "Roger, dodger, you old codger —I'm a Commander, too!"

A number of years before World War II, a Japanese ship groping through dense fog off North Carolina sent a hesitant radio message to the Cape Lookout station, asking for a navigational fix. The station promptly replied. The ship's radioman was obviously working with a Japanese English dictionary in his left hand. After a few minutes, he slowly spelled out:

DEAR MR CAPE LOOKOUT PLEASE DO NOT SEND SO FURIOUSLY VIRGIN OPERATOR AT THIS END.

George Hickman, expert in communications and linguistics, remembers when he, too, was a virgin operator. It was in a destroyer, the old four-stacker *Borie*. He was a fireman third, striking for radioman.

The *Borie*'s only two radiomen went ashore in Guantanamo, leaving Hickman to handle the twelve-to-four afternoon watch. They said, "Remember this: you'll be the only man aboard who knows the code. If anybody questions an incoming message, just tell them 'That's what he said!' "

Hickman was both proud and nervous as he sat in the communications shack and fiddled with the dials. Things were quiet, but finally a message came to all ships present from Naval Station Guantanamo. It said:

CAPTAIN YARNELL WILL ARRIVE GUANTANAMO BY PLANE.

Hickman went to the yeoman's office to get this typewritten for delivery to the *Borie*'s captain, Lieutenant Commander George E. Brandt. But the yeoman, like the two radiomen, was over on the Gitmo Base, lapping up some 3.2 beer. Hickman typed it himself, but he was excited, and not too familiar with the typewriter. He summoned a Filipino mess steward, and told him to take the copy to the skipper.

In a little while, Commander Brandt appeared at the door of the radio shack with the message in his hand. Hickman beat him to the punch by blurting out, "That's what he said!" He repeated this twice before Brandt could tell him to pipe down. Then Brandt said, "It says here that Captain Yarnell will arrive Guantanamo by *phone,* and . . ."

"That's what he said!" Hickman croaked again.

Brandt looked at him for a space, and then said, "Okay—you sit in this radio room and listen for the phone call. But *I'm* going out on the foc'sle and watch for a plane!"

Guglielmo Marconi died in 1937, and let us hope that before his death he had been both amazed and amused at the uses to which his invention had been put. When the Navy is at sea, Marconi's wireless telegraphy brings everything from war alerts and operational orders to personal messages that are very important to morale: notices, for instance, of births, deaths, and other vital statistics; pleas for a larger allotment to keep up the payments on the car, and such things as

GRANDFATHER DIED AND SPOILED MY LEAVE REQUEST FIVE DAY EXTENSION.

(He got it.) Or the case of a newlywed ensign who had gone to Atlantic City for his honeymoon, and dispatched his ship:

IT IS WONDERFUL HERE REQUEST FIVE DAY EXTENSION OF LEAVE.

When the latter message was received, the temptation was too great, and the commanding officer sent back:

IT IS WONDERFUL ANYWHERE REPORT TO YOUR SHIP.

Another man, asking extension of leave because his wife was about to have a baby, was told

I CAN UNDERSTAND THAT YOU HAD TO BE ON HAND WHEN THE KEEL WAS LAID BUT I DO NOT CONSIDER YOUR PRESENCE NECESSARY AT THE LAUNCHING.

An ensign aboard the cruiser *Concord* in 1928 had been married some six months, and knew that his wife was expecting when he sailed on an extended cruise. He did not want to be kidded in the wardroom, and told his bride to work out a code message that would announce the baby's arrival. As the date neared, he haunted the radio shack to keep the message from falling into other hands.

But of course it did. It said:

CURTAINS ARRIVED TODAY, ONE WITH TASSELS AND ONE WITHOUT.

Commodore Joe Fyffe's wife was living aboard ship with him, on the China Station. In some moment of crisis, the Navy Department ordered all dependents sent home. Joe Fyffe answered:

WIFE NO GO. WHAT DO?

Mrs. Fyffe had a French maid. The toilet facilities aboard the flagship were somewhat crude: for the dependents, they consisted of a sort of Chic Sale rig which hung over the taffrail. One day when the maid sat down there, a sailor was suspended just below her in a bosun's chair, painting the ship's stern . . .

Caught up by the allure of an unpainted surface, he lifted his brush and made a wide swipe. The girl fled shrieking, and soon the sailor was had up by Joe Fyffe.

"God dammit!" said the Commodore. "How many times do I have to tell you people that you never—*never*—paint a seam until it has been caulked?"

Admiral Albert Gleaves, who was retired in 1922, told the story of an American ship on a west coast South American cruise in the days when the wardroom could still serve wine. At Callao, she fell in with a British ship, and had to entertain.

The group of young passed midshipmen (midshipmen who had made the grade) aboard the American ship asked their British counterparts over for dinner, although they had been under hack (restricted to the ship) for some time, for various escapades.

They had no glassware. The Captain of their ship had just bought an elaborate set of stemware for his wife, and they asked him to lend them this. The Captain agreed, on condition that if one glass was broken, they would all go under hack for the remainder of the cruise. They agreed.

They knew the British custom of toasting the Queen, or the President, and then tossing the wine glass over the shoulder, so they decided that there would be no such toasts. But not all of the midshipmen got the word. During the party, after various toasts had been made, one youngster said, "Isn't it about time that we toasted the Queen and the President?"

The worried mess president, guarding the glassware, forgot himself and said, "Oh, the hell with the Queen!" And in the general melee that followed, *all* the glassware was broken.

Admiral Gleaves told the story to some English Admirals in World War I. One of them chuckled, and said he had been one of the visiting midshipmen. "You know," he said, "I have wondered for forty years just what you birds had against the dear old Queen!"

The old *Monongahela* had in her crew a lookout who had grown up on the San Francisco Embarcadero. His name was Cahoon, and he prided himself upon having very sharp vision.

But maybe Cahoon dozed while on watch. On a cruise from San Francisco to Hawaii, he failed to report a ship that was hardly a mile off the beam. The officer of the deck threatened to throw him in the brig. Cahoon argued that he had the sharpest eyes in the Navy, and said that if he failed to report the next ship in sight, he would take double brig time.

The officer of the deck agreed to this, and gave Cahoon permission to go below for a drink of water before going on watch in the crow's nest.

When it was getting light, at four bells in the morning watch, Cahoon sang out:

"Sail ho! One point off the port bow—a large steamer, two masts, three stacks, and a yellow band around the middle one!"

The officer of the deck peered from the port wing of the bridge, but saw nothing. After an hour, when it was lighter, he could still see nothing. But, then, Cahoon had a much loftier vantage point.

"Do you still see her?" the O.O.D. yelled up at Cahoon.

"Yes, sir!" Cahoon answered. "I can still see her, as plainly as I can see that cockroach on the capstan head!"

Well, the capstan head was a long way forward, and this was too much for the O.O.D. He sent for Cahoon, and told him, "If there is no cockroach, you go into the brig. If there *is a* cockroach, you'll get a medal for the sharpest eyes in the Navy . . . that is, of course, if your ship shows up! "

Then he sent a messenger forward—and this man brought back a dead cockroach from the capstan head. The steamer did not appear, and Cahoon was consigned to durance vile for making a false report.

But two days later, at almost exactly the same hour, a large steamer showed on point off the *Monongahela's* port bow, with two masts, three stacks, and a yellow band around the middle stack.

So, they let Cahoon out of the brig, and he received some sort of prankish decoration as a man with such sharp eyesight that he could see into two tomorrows. At the time, no one knew the true story. Having been reared on the San Francisco waterfront, Cahoon could identify all the ships sailing from the Golden Gate on the Hawaiian run. He also knew their sailing schedules, and their approximate positions at almost any hour of the voyage.

This steamer had fouled him up by having engine trouble that delayed it for exactly two days.

The cockroach on the capstan? Cahoon had killed it when he went below for his drink of water, and had planted it there when he came back topside.

[*iii*] A chaplain was giving some advice to men who were being paid off, or were going home on leave after a long cruise. This took the line of acknowledging Kipling's assertion that "single men in barricks don't grow into plaster saints," but deplored the use of certain adjectives men learned in the Service. "When you ask your mother to pass the butter," the chaplain said, "don't describe it."

From the earliest days, the Navy has had what is probably a natural and a healthy tendency. If it can't do it, it can talk about it—to such an extent that flag officers have frequently felt the need to launder the sailors' language. One Admiral sent a dispatch:

A RESOUNDING OATH UTTERED IN RIGHTEOUS ANGER HAS ITS PLACE BUT I CAN SEE NO NEED FOR THE CONTINUOUS USE OF THE BIOLOGICAL PARTICIPLE.

That was a Clever Dispatch which caused chuckles in wardrooms, but went over the heads of a great many enlisted men who didn't know what a biological participle was. Vice Admiral Robert B. ("Mick") Carney, then Chief of Staff to Admiral Halsey, made these remarks to the staff officers on 27 March, 1943, the nation then being in a state of war:

> Prolonged absence from normal restraining and refining influences is resulting in an increase of senseless obscenity that does no credit to the ship, the offending individual, nor the home and stock from which he hails. The nature and character of our enemies are such that considered use of such terms as "son-of-a-bitch" and "bastard" are not without considerable merit at appropriate times; but continuous loud and pointless reference to the malodorous residue of digestive assimilation certainly shows a dreary lack of imagination, and as a means of emphasis is not convincing. By the same token, repetitious and wholly inapplicable mention of the procreative function adds nothing to conversational clarity.

That sort of language is not useful, forceful, expressive, nor amusing. I hope I will in future hear less about bodily excrescences, such manifest absurdities as rain squalls or swabs indulging in the sexual act, and illegitimate and depraved shipmates of canine descent on the distaff side.

Admiral Carney later became Chief of Naval Operations. His discourse cleaned up the conversation in the wardroom after eliciting some hearty chuckles. It was aimed only at the staff officers, and its scholarly language would have gone over the heads of many of the people in the foc'sle. Admiral Carney probably wisely concluded that the situation there could best be handled by a salty CPO, who would roar: "Knock off that kind of — talk, you bastards! "

[iv]

Oh, the officers ride in a motorboat,
The Captain, he rides in his gig;
It don't go a doggoned bit faster,
But it makes the old bastard feel big . . .

    Sing tooral-a-tooral-a-tooral-aye,
    Sing tooral-a-tooral-a-A,
    Sing tooral-a-tooral-a-tooral,
    A-tooral-a-tooral-a-A!

The enlisted men ride in a motor launch,
The Admiral rides in his barge;
It don't go a doggoned bit faster,
But it gives the old bastard a charge . . .
    (Repeat chorus.)

Yes, the "people" always have their stories about the commissioned officers. I am not so sure but what the Navy should collect these stories, and consider them along with officers' fitness reports when selection boards convene. They would reveal a great deal not available from any other source.

Somewhere around the middle 1930's, cribbage became a very popular pastime in the peacetime Pacific Fleet, and even threatened to outrank the Navy's traditional and ancient game of Acey-Deucie. Championship cribbage tournaments between battleships were even being played off by radio.

Commander Blank, the executive officer of one battleship, was one of the most avid cribbage players, and had largely been responsible for starting the craze. He went below decks one day, and saw the watertight door of a storeroom open, and a light on. He put one foot over the storm sill, and then observed two bluejackets sitting on a blanket and playing cribbage. They were so intent upon the game that they did not see the Commander.

One sailor suddenly slapped down and scattered his cards, with the exclamation, "I win!" He advanced the cribbage peg. The other man protested, "Now, wait just a goddam minute! I didn't see your hand!"

"Well, you can take my word for it, can't you?"

"I'm not so sure about that!"

"Now, look!" said the winner. "You've been back around the wardroom, and you've seen the Exec and them other officers playing cribbage. Did you ever hear one of them ask to see the other's hand?"

His opponent reflected for a minute. "Well, no," he admitted. "But, then, hell—them bastards are supposed to be gentlemen!"

The Exec quietly withdrew his foot from the storeroom, and softly stole away, thinking of the fitness of things. As the famous historian, Thomas B. Macaulay, said of another time: "There were gentlemen and there were seamen in the Navy of Charles II. But the seamen were not gentlemen, and the gentlemen were not seamen."

The difficulties of docking or mooring a ship under adverse wind and sea conditions have contributed much to Navy language, most of it profane. I am indebted to that walking Navy encyclopedia, Captain Roy C. Smith III, for straightening me out on one well known Navy story: it did not happen in the U.S. Navy, but is a Royal Navy classic. Admiral Viscount Cunningham, commanding in the Mediterranean in World War II, was well known for demanding excellence in shiphandling. A new Captain, reporting, made a botched landing at Alexandria, and was scared stiff.

Then the signal messenger came with "a message from the flag ship, sir," and the skipper was much relieved when he saw that it read GOOD. A moment later came the crusher:

TO MY PREVIOUS MESSAGE ADD WORD GOD.

Admiral Cunningham certainly was a master of such things. When Admiral Sir James Somerville—already knighted—was made a Knight of the Bath after sinking the *Bismarck*, Cunningham sent:

CONGRATULATIONS. TWICE A KNIGHT, AND AT YOUR AGE.

Mooring a destroyer alongside a nest of other destroyers swinging around a buoy can be difficult, indeed, but may be nothing compared to docking an aircraft carrier. In World War II a big carrier was trying to make Pier Five at the Naval Operating Base at Norfolk. Wind and tide were both off the pier, and there were not enough tugs. In desperation, the skipper turned up the engines of aircraft parked outboard on the flight deck—perhaps the first case of "Operation Pinwheel." Still no go.

Finally another tug came churning up from the Navy Yard to lend a hand. But the carrier could not get a line to her because both heaving lines and shot lines blew away in the wind. Then the Captain ordered a three-pounder line-throwing gun broken out, and fired it off.

The projectile went squarely through the tug's stack. Whereupon the boatswain's mate who was the skipper of the tug promptly ripped off his white skivvy shirt, and ran it up the halyard as a signal of surrender.

When Admiral Don Varian was Commodore of a destroyer squadron, one of his tin cans—the *William R. Rush*—somehow became the subject of an unfavorable report by higher authority. Varian blew his stack. He knew the ships in his squadron were Four-Oh, which in the Navy means perfect, and he especially liked the skipper of the *Rush*—Commander Theodore Robert Vogeley, a tall, dedicated Pennsylvanian who neither smoked nor drank, and who lived, loved, and breathed Navy.

What followed is called "administrative jocularity." Varian put a forwarding endorsement on the report, and sent it along the chain of command, both to the *William R. Rush* and to the higher authority:

First Endorsement
1. Forwarded.

2. If toilet tissue is in short supply aboard *William R. Rush,* it is suggested that this report be used in lieu thereof.

Administrative jocularity adds much fun to Navy life. Any officer needs a sense of humor, and the higher his rank, the greater his sense of humor must be. An Admiral should be a man the enlisted men can respect and also poke a little fun at—and it is a wise flag officer who understands this. It makes him more human.

Take, for instance, the case of Rear Admiral D.F. "Dog" Smith, Jr., recently Commander of the Naval Air Test Center at Patuxent River, Maryland, and formerly the very popular skipper of the carrier *Randolph.* Admiral Smith has a tic that affects the right side of his cheek, but in no way affects his ability. To some, this would be a handicap; to Admiral Smith it is an asset, identifying him. On at least two occasions, when he found juniors mimicking him, he said: "I got mine from syphilis. Where did you get yours?"

This, naturally, left the juniors with nothing to say.

It does not always pay to MODIFY MY PREVIOUS any more than it pays to correct a typographical error. The classic example which comes to mind is the editor who referred to a citizen as a "battle-scarred veteran," only to have it come out as "battle-scared veteran." When he apologized in print for this, it came up as "bottle-scarred veteran." You can't win.

On the China Station, an Admiral who wanted his white uniforms laundered had a semaphore signal sent to the headlands of Luzon. It said:

HAVE ADMIRAL'S WOMAN REPORT FOR DUTY AT 0800 HOURS.

This occasioned a little mirth in the fleet, but not nearly so much as when someone sent another signal that said:

REFERENCE MY PREVIOUS MESSAGE INSERT WASHER BETWEEN ADMIRAL AND WOMAN . . .

10. UNDER THE ONE STAR

Most of the early settlers came by way of
the sea, embarking at Mobile and New Orleans.
Because of their innocence, or because of a certain love of independence, they entered through
whatever ports on the Gulf seemed most expedi-
ent. The ports of entry which Mexico attempted
to establish for the collection of customs duties
were an early cause of friction which contributed
to the Texas Revolution. And during the Revolution, the tiny Texas Navy, built around three
sloops of war under Commodore (Charles E.)
Hawkins, was able to establish control of the
Gulf of Mexico. These ships were the *Independence,* the *Invincible,* and the *Brutus.* With
them, Hawkins controlled the sea approaches to
Texas, blocked reinforcements to Santa Anna,
and contributed in large part to the many difficulties which beset the Mexican Army in its long
overland march to the Alamo, Goliad, and San
Jacinto battles of 1836. So it was that Texas established a naval tradition to stand alongside the
brilliant military record achieved on land.
—*Fleet Admiral Chester W. Nimitz, 16 January,
1944*

JUST ABOUT EVERYTHING that had happened to the young
and victorious Navy of the United States also happened to the
Texas Navy during the years of the Lone Star Republic. It had its
triumphs over superior Mexican forces; it had a bloody mutiny at
sea; it suffered shipwreck. And, finally, the entire Navy was put

137

up for sale to the highest bidder—just as the infant United States had sold the last ship of her Navy in 1785.

It also had an incident in June of 1836 that has been unmatched by any other Navy in the world's history. This was an amphibious operation on horseback, pulled off in reverse, and of course it involved the vaunted Texas Rangers, who had no intention of being left out of any kind of fighting. Some thirty Rangers under Major I. W. Burton sighted a suspicious ship off the coast at Copano. Burton concealed most of his men in the chaparral thickets, but had a few run out on the beach and make distress signals.

The ship did what most ships of that time did in the way of identification. She first hoisted the Texas flag, which the men ignored. She raised the Stars and Stripes, and still got no response. The she hoisted the Mexican flag, and the men on the beach jumped and cheered.

That did it. In came a boat from the schooner, which proved to be named the *Watchman*. The Texans fell upon this boat, and captured it.

Sixteen Rangers, booted and spurred, then rowed the boat back to the ship, and opened fire with their rifles. This may have been the only ship taken by rifle fire, but taken it was. Meanwhile, the other Rangers rode horseback into the surf, and kept up a supporting fire.

Burton and his men parked their horses somewhere, and enjoyed sailing the *Watchman* for a few days. They captured two Mexican ships, the *Fanny Butler* and the *Comanche*, and then came into Galveston harbor.

Their exploits were shortly being celebrated by a ballad:

> *I'm Captain Jenks, of the Horse Marines;*
> *I feed my horse on corn and beans . . .*

[ii] Famed historian Hubert Howe Bancroft attributed the colonization of Texas, her rebellion against Mexico, and even her part in the U.S.–Mexican War, to slave-holding interests. I believe Bancroft was wrong in this regard, especially as it pertains to the era of Mexican rule, and until

after Texas won her independence. The people who crossed the Sabine or came to Texas by ship were mostly young adventurers and hunters who wanted room, and were hungry for land; they were not the type wealthy enough to own slaves.

They found land in plenty, and abided by Mexican rule until it became plain that there could be no justice for the Mexican provinces of Coahuila and Texas so long as the Mexican legislature sat in far-off Monclova. Of course it is significant, too, that Texas settlers did not renounce their American citizenship when they removed to an alien country. Looking back, one might believe that the Texas Revolution was planned from the beginning of the first settlements.

On 6 April, 1830, Mexico issued a decree which banned further immigration from the United States, and set up a military rule intolerable to the Texans. This, and certain already existing trade, tariff, and maritime regulations brought on the Revolution. The complaints of the Texas settlers were very similar to those of the New England Colonies against Britain in 1776.

And the solutions to the problems were much the same. Sea power again was the answer. The Texans early manned three small schooners—*Austin, Red Rover,* and *Waterwitch.* Later, Stephen F. Austin bought four schooners to found the real Texas Navy. They were the *Liberty,* 60 tons, and the *Invincible, Brutus,* and *Independence,* each 125 tons. Then in 1839 the Texas Navy acquired a proud flagship, the sloop-of-war *Austin,* which was 600 tons and mounted 38 guns.

When General Sam Houston touched off the "Runaway Scrape" by retreating toward the Gulf after the fall of the Alamo, was he being scared, cautious, or crafty? The settlers abandoned everything they owned, and fled after him in a disorganized mob. Santa Anna pursued him with a not very big army, but Santa Anna's real reason for heading to the coast was that he had arranged to get supplies, and reinforcements of two thousand men, *by sea.* He also fondly hoped to return to Mexico by ship after he had conquered the upstart rebels; he was a man who indulged in opium, and liked his comforts.

He got reinforcements, all right, from General Cos, but they

139

came by land and were not enough to give Santa Anna the over-whelming strength he had hoped for—because the insignificant Texas Navy had bottled up the Mexican ships at Matamoros. Then Santa Anna was bottled up on the Plain of St. Hyacinth (San Jacinto) and was whipped in one of the most significant battles in history. He had some 650 men killed, and 750 captured. Amazingly, the Texans had only nine killed.

They had won the battle with guts and straight shooting—but in the final analysis, they had won it because of sea power.

It had begun nearly a year earlier. In August 1835, the schooner *San Felipe* was bringing impresario Stephen F. Austin back from Mexico after some eighteen months' imprisonment. When the *San Felipe* approached the mouth of the Brazos, she saw the Mexican revenue cutter *Correo* firing on a small Texas ship. As *San Felipe* came near, the cutter fired on her, and *San Felipe* fired back. Gunnery on both sides was poor: the two ships blasted away at each other all afternoon, and then *Correo* finally surrendered.

Austin had the *Correo* escorted to New Orleans for a piracy trial. This turned out to be quite a dramatic hearing. The two opposing attorneys threw law books and ink wells at each other; the judge dismissed the Mexican crewmen—and sent both lawyers to jail.

That was when Austin decided to buy his four ships and put Texas on a sound maritime basis.

In the beginning, the Texas Navy was under command of Captain Charles Hawkins, who should have rated the title of Commodore, but apparently was never called such. He sent the tiny *Liberty* to patrol the North Mexican coast, under Captain William S. Brown. All sixty tons of the *Liberty* took on the Mexican schooner *Pelicano*, killed seven of her crew, and captured the rest. The *Pelicano*'s cargo of flour was found to contain a large quantity of rifles and ammunition.

This was just before the Texas war for independence. When that war came, the Texas Navy was in full control of the Gulf, and Santa Anna was caught—as the Texas saying goes—between a rock and a hard place.

During the ten years of the Texas Republic, Santa Anna had no intention of abiding by the terms of his surrender or the peace treaty. He planned successive invasions of Texas to avenge his defeat at San Jacinto. But he had learned, the hard way, that marching his troops across the desert was not so good, and now he planned his principal attack by sea.

He built up a rather formidable Navy, commanded for the most part by raffish adventurers, including naval officers on leave from the British Navy, and a Yankee renegade or two. His ships included something new: the 775-ton iron vessel *Guadaloupe*, built in Scotland, and armed with two long 68-pound guns, and four 12-pounders.

This was the first iron ship ever to be engaged in battle. Oddly enough, she did not do very well. A warship is no better than the crew that mans her, and for some reason the Mexicans of that era —although excellent cavalrymen—did not take kindly to the sea.

Texas Minister Ashbel Smith, in London, invoked every principle of international law in an effort to prevent the *Guadalupe* and other ships from sailing. He was unsuccessful. Some twenty years later, shipyards along the Firth and the Clyde were making millions by building ships for the Confederacy—and Charles Francis Adams could not stop them, either. Business will find a way.

Meanwhile, the Texas Navy had also found itself involved in diplomacy, a role it played well. It encouraged the revolt of Yucatan, and its secession from Mexico; it played up the dispute between France and Mexico, and more or less egged the two countries to war. The French fleet for awhile was supreme in the Gulf of Mexico, and thus history repeated itself. Just as the French fleet had made possible the victory at Yorktown in the American Revolution, so did it forestall Mexican invasions of Texas when Texas was weak.

[*iii*] The Texas Navy had to be called in for "bottomry," or repairs. *Invincible* and *Brutus* went to

New York yards; the *Liberty* and *Independence* to New Orleans. Texas lost the *Liberty*, being too bankrupt to pay the repair bill. Captain Hawkins died of the smallpox, and the *Independence* was left in New Orleans.

In August 1837, the weather did what the Mexicans had not been able to do. A fierce Texas norther destroyed both *Brutus* and *Invincible*, just after they had captured six Mexican ships.

Texas was now without a Navy. The terrible financial panic of 1837 struck all three nations—the United States, Mexico, and the Republic of Texas. Then the French–Mexican war came along, and gave Texas a chance to rebuild her fleet. Mirabeau Bonaparte Lamar became president of Texas—and the French loved that name. Lamar chose a U.S. Navy lieutenant—twenty-nine–year-old, black-bearded Edwin W. Moore, as Commodore of the Texas Navy.

But the Texas Congress did not appropriate sufficient monies to rebuild and maintain sea power. Moore must have been an extremely able man, skilled in diplomacy: he promoted ships through his personal credit.

Lamar's administration ended in December, 1841, and Sam Houston was inaugurated for his second term. He came near to sinking the Texas Navy for all time.

Houston was an anomaly. His personal courage and his sagacity could not be questioned. But there had been no sea power in the Bayou of San Jacinto when he defeated Santa Anna; sea power, in his opinion, did not help him defeat Santa Anna. He was irascible, opinionated, and vainglorious.

Upon his second inauguration, he at once began his drive to recall, decommission, and sell the Texas Navy's ships. Moore saved the day by arranging a deal under which the Navy would protect the Yucatan Peninsula while the former state of Yucatan negotiated for re-entry into the Mexican nation. Yucatan paid $8000 per month for this protection against Mexican warships, and that sum came near supporting the Texas fleet. Unfortunately, the arrangement only lasted four months. Yucatan stopped paying, and Sam Houston ordered the operation ended.

It was shortly afterward that the Texas Navy had a mutiny aboard the small ship *San Antonio*, which had been a member of the Yucatan squadron. She had been sent to New Orleans for supplies. At night, on 11 February, 1842, a few of her sailors and marines got drunk, tomahawked the duty officer, and finished him off with bayonets. They wounded three other officers and threw them down a hatch, then they lowered a boat and rowed ashore.

The crew of a United States revenue cutter, the *Jackson*, heard the noise, captured thirteen men, and restored good order and discipline. The prisoners were turned over to civil authorities. Some months later, the ringleader of the mutiny, Sergeant Seymour Oswald, escaped. Another marine died. Some of the remainder were tried by general court martial. One was acquitted, and another pardoned. But three men got 100 lashes apiece, and four were hanged from the yardarms of the *Austin* on 26 April, 1843. The whole affair was more violent and bloody than any such incident had ever been in the United States Navy.

Meanwhile, Sam Houston was pushing his program to sink the Texas Navy. Some historians think that Houston was being as sly as a fox, and wanted to present Texas as completely unarmed and defenseless—thereby hoping to enlist United States aid, and promote annexation to the Union. Others believe there was a bitter personal feud between Houston and the Navy's commander, Commodore Moore, who had not been a Houston appointee.

The latter theory may have been strengthened later in 1843 by Moore himself. He met the Mexican ships in a pitched battle, and whipped them soundly. Moore lost only five men; his enemy had eighty-seven killed and many more wounded. The Mexican fleet was so terribly damaged that it could not longer support any attempted invasion of Texas.

Moore wrote, then, "I expect 'Old Sam' will hang me, for I have traveled out of the course his instructions dictated."

This was the last battle, on land or sea. A couple of years later, Texas was annexed by the United States, and her Navy became a part of the U.S. Navy. Houston had given Commodore Moore a dishonorable discharge—but Moore appealed to Congress, and was not only acquitted, but came out with resolutions honoring him.

It gives me pleasure to report that there is a Texas Navy today. It was reactivated on 21 April 1958—a fitting date, since it was an anniversary of the battle of San Jacinto. It has its own insignia of Lone Star and fouled anchor, and is an active arm of the civil defense of Texas. It is an honorary outfit made up of privately owned yachts and power cruisers, but one which could do very valuable patrol work in wartime.

II. NEVER SEEN AGAIN...

Eternal Father! strong to save,
Whose arm hath bound the restless wave,
Who bidd'st the mighty ocean deep
Its own appointed limits keep:
  O, hear us when we cry to Thee
  For those in peril on the sea!
—William Whiting (The Navy Hymn)

THE MOODS OF the sea are as unfathomable as its deeps. It can be beautiful and benign, sullen and sorrowful, capricious and cruel by turns. Peace treaties and disarmament or declarations of war mean nothing to it. The United States Navy has lost literally hundreds of ships to enemy action; it has also lost hundreds of ships to the sea in both peace and war.

For example, we lost fifty-two submarines in patrols and combat action during World War II, with 374 officers and 3,131 enlisted men. Those fifty-two subs were 18 per cent of our combat undersea vessels. A man was much safer, say, aboard a battleship or aircraft carrier, and perhaps a little safer—but not much—in a destroyer. Yet, practically no one in submarines ever requested transfer to less hazardous duty. The men who wear the dolphin insignia have a tremendous *esprit de corps*.

Germany learned the hard way, in World War I, that U-boat duty offered better than a 50 per cent chance of fatality. She had 272 subs in commission for that war, and lost 178 of them—mostly to Allied warships. In World War II, she apparently had

145

no trouble recruiting young Nazis for her *unterseebootes*—and she lost more than 700 subs. Some of these simply vanished, but the majority fell victims to the greatly improved methods of anti-submarine warfare. The Japanese lost 128 submarines in World War II, and had only fifty-eight remaining at the time of the surrender—quite a few of them not in operating condition.

Disappearance of our own nuclear submarine *Scorpion*, which was officially declared "presumed lost" on June 5, 1968, remains a mystery. Ninety-nine men went down in her. The Navy concentrated its search in a vast area some four hundred miles southwest of the Azores, mainly using the oceanographic research ship *Mizar*, which reportedly is equipped with underwater listening devices that are secret. The Navy will not talk about these, except to say that the 266-foot *Mizar* carries a "fish"—a 1400-pound, tubular-shaped assembly of electronic and optical gear which is sent to the bottom. This device finds metal objects by measuring the intensity of a magnetic field; it also has lights, underwater cameras with wide-angle lenses—and even a TV camera that transmits pictures to a laboratory in the ship, by means of a co-axial cable.

Shortly after the *Scorpion*'s radio fell silent, the Navy had sixty ships and thirty airplanes looking for her. *Mizar*, originally built as an ice-breaking re-supply ship and assigned to the Navy's Military Sea Transportation Service, was headed for a refit period in Norfolk when she was diverted. She knew her job—she had located wreckage of the sunken submarine *Thresher* in 1964, and had helped find an H-bomb lost off Palomares, Spain, in 1966.

Her search took eighteen weeks. Aboard *Mizar* was her crew of eleven officers and thirty-one men, along with nineteen scientists. She took some 150,000 photos on the bottom of the Atlantic, and about 12,000 of them showed wreckage of the *Scorpion*, fearfully smashed and broken by the tremendous pressure of 10,000 feet—about 8,800 feet below maximum depth for the sub. Foul weather finally ended the search in November, and a Navy court of inquiry began the task of studying the photographs. At this writing, no report has been made on the court's findings.

What happened to drive *Scorpion* to her doom probably will never be known. A streak of superstition persists in many seafaring men, and they—not the scientists—may say the submarine was jinxed by her name. The Navy has had other *Scorpions.*

This one was the fourth. Away back in 1812 we had a two-gun schooner by that name, and whether she was lost or simply decommissioned does not seem to be of record. A little later we had a "block sloop" called *Scorpion:* she was in Joshua Barney's flotilla on the Chesapeake, and afterwards burned. The third *Scorpion* was a submarine (SS-278) in World War II. Commanded by Commander M. G. Schmidt, she left Pearl Harbor for her fourth war patrol on 29 December, 1943, with a crew of seventy-six men. She refueled at Midway and sailed from there on 3 January, 1944, for the northern East China and Yellow Sea area. She was never heard from after 6 January, and on 6 March, 1944, was listed as "presumed lost."

Before she vanished, the World War II *Scorpion* had made quite a record. On her first three patrols, she sank ten Japanese ships totaling 24,000 tons, and damaged two more vessels to account for an additional 16,000 tons. She is believed to have been destroyed by a Japanese mine.

[ii] The writing of the sad official report, "and was never seen again," began early. On 8 August, 1800, the U.S.S. *Insurgent,* 36 guns, sailed from Norfolk for the West Indies. She was never seen again, and 340 lives were lost.

The *Insurgent* had had an impressive history. In the Quasi War with France, we captured French ships and changed their names; the French captured our ships and changed their names —and then we captured some of them back. We lost the schooner *Retaliation,* for instance. It had been *La Croyable* before we took it from the French fleet. When the French recaptured it, it became *La Magicienne*—probably because it was changing nationality so often that a sleight-of-hand seemed to be involved.

The *Insurgent* had been *L'Insurgente* of the French Navy. She was taken in February 1799 in a classic action by Captain

Thomas Truxtun of the *Constellation:* the action was classic in more ways than one, because Truxtun had aboard Midshipman David Porter and First Lieutenant John Rodgers, both of whom were to become naval heroes. (Porter was also the foster father of David Glasgow Farragut.)

It was *L'Insurgente* that had recently recaptured the schooner *Retaliation,* and so things were confusing. But not to Truxtun. When his signals were not properly answered, he began to shoot. He gained the weather gauge on the enemy—meaning he took advantage of the wind—and raked her thoroughly. Captain Barreault of *L'Insurgente* apparently later dreamed up having seen two big British ships bearing down upon his vessel, and decided to surrender to Truxtun. Truxtun's report made no mention at all of any British vessels.

Barreault came on board *Constellation* to surrender, and asked, "Why have you fired upon the French flag? Our two countries are not at war."

They were not at war officially, but it was one of the hottest unofficial wars, or police actions, that America has ever seen. And Truxtun, reporting to the Secretary of the Navy, said, "The French Captain tells me I have caused a War with France; if so I am glad of it, for I detest Things being done by Halves."

Thus, *L'Insurgente* became U.S.S. *Insurgent.* She was refitted as a 36-gun frigate at Norfolk, and went on, the next year, to her mysterious end.

On 20 August, 1800 U.S.S. *Pickering*, a 14-gun brig in Commodore John Barry's squadron, sailed from New Castle, Delaware, for the island of Guadalupe. Never seen again. Ninety lives lost.

On 20 June, 1805, U.S. Gunboat *Seven* sailed from New York for the Mediterranean. Never seen again.

On 22 November, 1812, the U.S. Schooner *Etna*, 11 guns, vanished near New Orleans. Thirty lives lost.

On 9 October, 1814, the U.S.S. *Wasp* informed the Swedish brig *Adonis* that she was standing for the Spanish Main. Never seen again. A hundred and forty lives lost.

14 July, 1815, U.S. Brig *Epervier* passed Gibraltar enroute to the United States. Never seen again. No record exists of the lives lost.

11 January, 1820, U.S.S. *Lynx* sailed for the Gulf of Mexico. Never seen again. Fifty lives lost.

28 October, 1824, U.S.S. *Wild Cat* sailed from Cuba for Thompson's Island, West Indies. Never seen again. Fourteen lives lost.

10 September, 1829, U.S.S. *Hornet*, 18 guns, driven from her anchorage at Tampico by a gale. Never seen again. A hundred and forty lives lost.

1831 . . . *Sylph*, one gun. Sailed for West Indies. Never seen again. A small crew, but no figures are available for many of these early losses.

25 February, 1839, U.S.S. *Seagull*, converted pilot boat, sailed from Orange Harbor, Tierra del Fuego. Never seen again. Sixteen lives lost.

14 March, 1843, Schooner *Grampus* sighted off Charleston, S.C., and then never seen again. Believed lost in a heavy gale.

1850—Coast Survey ship *Jefferson*, operating in Straits of Magellan. Vanished and never seen again.

21 September, 1854, U.S.S. *Porpoise*, 224-ton brig, parted company with the U.S.S. *Vincennes* in the Straits of Formosa, and was never seen again.

29 September, 1854, the U.S.S. *Albany* sailed from Aspinwall for New York. Never seen again. A hundred and ninety-three lives lost.

18 September, 1860, U.S. Sloop *Levant* sailed from Hawaii for Aspinwall, Nicaragua. Never seen again.

4 March, 1918, U.S.S. *Cyclops*, a collier, 19,360 tons, sailed from Barbados, West Indies. Never seen again. Two hundred and eighty lives lost.

23 March, 1921, U.S.S. *Conestoga*, tug, sailed from San Francisco for Samoa. Never seen again. Forty-three lives lost.

17 December, 1942, *Natsek,* Coast Guard converted trawler, vanished in Belle Isle Strait, Newfoundland. Twenty-four lives lost.

These are the most famous of the mysteries, their secrets so jealously guarded by the sea. The ships lost to enemy action are of record in most cases, and their sinkings hurt somewhat less because we know they went down fighting. On 7 March, 1778, the U.S.S. *Randolph* was engaged with the British ship *Yarmouth.* Fire reached the *Randolph*'s magazine, and it exploded. Of her entire crew of 315 men, only four survived the blast—the worst wartime disaster of the Navy until the attack on Pearl Harbor a hundred and sixty-three years later.

[*iii*] Strangest of all the mysterious ship disappearances was that of the collier (coal ship) *Cyclops.* Her route from Barbados was through calm seas. It was wartime, but after the Armistice the German High Command stated that not a single German submarine had been anywhere near the area.

She was a big ship, only eight years old; she was well over five hundred feet from stem to stern, and displaced 10,000 tons when empty. At the time of her sailing, she carried nearly 11,000 tons of manganese which had been loaded in Rio de Janeiro. Manganese, it has been said, is a very tricky cargo, given to sudden shiftings.

She had radio equipment. Surely, even if she rolled due to a shifting of her dangerous cargo, there would have been time for an SOS before she foundered. But no radio transmission was ever heard.

In what must have been part of a hysteria in World War I, much was made of the fact that the captain of the *Cyclops,* George Worley, was of German birth.

Apparently he was a tough and exacting skipper. He was had up once before a court of inquiry, on charges that he drank too much and was too hard on his men. Worse than that, he was

accused of having fraternized with the skippers of German ships
that had been interned in Norfolk. He pointed out, however, that
such fraternization ceased the minute the U.S. declared war.

The *Cyclops* had engine trouble on its way to Rio de Janeiro
to load the cargo of manganese. It was so bad that it could not be
corrected in that port; she would have to limp back to Norfolk for
repairs. When she left Rio, she carried a number of civilians, and
one seaman accused of murder.

Six weeks after the *Cyclops* sailed from Barbados, the Navy
began asking about her. A search was ordered. Nothing was
found. The declaration that she was lost and all aboard her le-
gally dead was signed by Acting Secretary of the Navy Franklin
D. Roosevelt.

Then the speculation began, in its hysterical way. Maybe
Captain Worley had taken her back to the Germans. Perhaps her
passengers had mutinied, and then scuttled the ship. Maybe U.S.
Consul Alfred Gottschalk, from Rio, who was aboard as a pas-
senger, had been a German sympathizer. Maybe this and that.
Many German names appeared in her list of passengers.

And then, in New York, Naval Intelligence turned up a report
on a German named Hohenblatt, employed by the shipping firm
that arranged for the *Cyclops'* cargo of manganese. This report
was not released for many years. It said that Hohenblatt burned
hundreds of letters from Germany at the time of the *Cyclops'* disappearance, told fellow workers "they'll never get anything on
me!" and then vanished.

However, one must allow for the dramatics and braggadocio
that always turn up in such a case. Two Germans in Rio de Janeiro boasted in saloons that they had secreted a time bomb in
the manganese ore.

This was likely enough. But there is another school of thought.

Mahlon S. Tisdall, now Vice Admiral, U.S. Navy, retired,
served in U.S.S. *Neptune,* a sister ship of the *Cyclops,* in 1916. In
1918, he made a ten-day cruise in the *Cyclops* under George
Worley, and went through an Atlantic storm.

Tisdall says he personally saw the clinometer register rolls of 56 degrees to starboard, and 48 degrees to port. He said Worley's topside tanks were open at all times, whereas those in *Neptune* were always closed because they were above the center of gravity, and if filled with water could start a dangerous roll.

Admiral Tisdall wrote an article which was published in the *Naval Institute Proceedings* for January, 1920, entitled, "Did the Cyclops Turn Turtle?". It was, and still is, his contention that the ship capsized. He may very well be right . . . but whatever happened will never be known.

[*iv*] A look at a chart of the Atlantic will show that the *Cyclops,* the nuclear submarine *Scorpion,* and most of the other ships listed on the preceding pages vanished in an area known as the Bermuda Triangle. It is bounded on the west by Florida and the Middle Atlantic coast, on the south by Cuba and the islands of the Spanish Main, and its northeast corner touches Bermuda.

Something is very strange about the Bermuda Triangle. A number of ships belonging to other nations have disappeared there, as well as those flying the American flag. The story always has been the same: no storm or adverse sea conditions, no distress calls, no recovery of bodies, no sighting of the debris that ordinarily bobs to the surface when the ship goes down. It is such an eerie story that one could almost believe in the existence of gigantic sea monsters, able to drag vessels to the bottom. Except for one thing: the disappearances have not been confined to surface craft, and even the most superstitious would find it hard to imagine that a sea monster could bring down planes.

Some score of planes have flown into the Bermuda Triangle, made no report of trouble, and never returned to base. Nor were these all single flights, by any means. For example, in December 1945, five Avenger torpedo bombers took off from the Naval Air Station at Fort Lauderdale for a two-hour routine patrol flight. They flew in formation, and certainly if one ship had had difficulty, others could have reported it. Instead, there was some confused communication between the Naval Air Station and the flight commander, and then with another officer who had inexplicably taken over from the flight commander. They could not see land, they said. They didn't know where they were.

This was odd, since Avengers had the best of navigating instruments. The Fort Lauderdale station immediately launched a Martin Mariner with a crew of thirteen, and all rescue equipment. The Mariner is a flying boat that can handle rough seas.

In a very few minutes, the station lost contact with the Mariner, and it never returned. Now there were six aircraft missing, instead of five. A Coast Guard search was instigated at once, and scores of Navy planes took off. They found nothing—no storm, no oil slicks, no flares, and not a bit of flotsam. Next morning at daybreak, the carrier *Solomons* stood out with some twenty other smaller ships, for the search. More than 250 planes flew above, and a number of shore parties prowled the Florida beaches.

Nobody found anything.

We are always finding out new things about electronics. Considering the absence of distress signals from any of the ships and aircraft that have been lost in the Bermuda Triangle—is it possible that here is an area where for some reason electronics do not work?

There is another such sea area in the world, between Iwo Jima and Marcus Island. The Japanese call it the "Devil's Sea," and point to a large number of mysterious losses there. They sent out a survey ship carrying scientists, and that ship vanished, too.

The Japanese have lived intimately with earthquakes and volcanoes, and their scientists and vocanologists are among the best in the world. They think that underwater volcanoes and earthquakes on the bottom of the sea can cause sudden and very high waves—high enough to swamp a ship. They could be right.

The Navy and the Coast Guard are trying to find out things about the Bermuda Triangle. The work under way, known as Project Magnet, will investigate electro-magnetic gravitational and atmospheric disturbances. At this writing, no report has been made.

153

It sounds terribly scientific. Meanwhile, if there are other ship losses in the Bermuda Triangle, or in Japan's Devil's Sea, old-timers will hoist another beer and say, "I told you so!"

[*v*] Everybody has heard the legend of the *Flying Dutchman,* a ghost ship most often "sighted" off the Cape of Good Hope. Richard Wagner heard the legend and wrote an opera about it in 1841. But back in the mid-Thirties there were U.S. Naval officers still extant who swore that they saw the *Flying Dutchman,* and they were men of veracity.

It wasn't off the Cape of Good Hope, but near the tip of Scotland. The old U.S.S. *South Carolina* was fighting a heavy gale when a coal passer, about to go below on watch, sang out to the bridge that a sailing vessel was on the port hand.

The people on the bridge saw her, too. She was surrounded by a ghostly aura, and was doing the impossible by sailing dead into the eye of the wind with her yards cock-billed. All hands on the *South Carolina*'s weather decks said they saw the apparition sail across the head of the column, and then vanish in a squall. The coal passer who first sighted her was killed a few hours later by an explosion of gas in a coal bunker. It is part of the legend that the first man in any ship to sight the *Flying Duchman* dies before the day is out . . .

Some of the Navy's disasters are well recorded. The side-wheeler *Saginaw* ran aground on the reef at Ocean Island, Pacific, on 29 October, 1870, and this mishap had a most heroic and tragic aftermath.

In the actual grounding, all hands managed to scramble ashore, and apparently were able to salvage provisions and drinking water from the wreck, because Ocean Island certainly could not long support life.

Then five volunteers took the *Saginaw*'s gig—a sailboat—and headed for Hawaii, 1800 miles away. They left on 18 November, and made a small boat voyage rivaling that of Captain Bligh, victim of the mutinty in H.M.S. *Bounty.* The cruise took exactly thirty days. The gig reached the island of Kauai, only to be capsized in the heavy surf as it attempted to land. Coxswain William

Halford was the only survivor. He gasped out his story to Hawaiian officials, and the Royal Hawaiian Government sent a ship to take the other members of the *Saginaw's* crew off Ocean Island.

Submarines and surface vessels are not the only Navy craft to vanish mysteriously. On 22 March, 1920, a Navy free balloon took off from Pensacola, and was never seen again.

Free balloons were once used for observation, and to spot artillery fire, but with the development of anti-aircraft guns they became too much of an easy mark. In 1920, the Navy was using them to train dirigible crews: if the engines quit in a dirigible, it could still be operated as a free balloon.

These wicker basket jobs with sandbags hanging over the side for ballast had not come far from Jules Verne, or the lone hot-air aeronauts who used to thrill people at county fairs. They carried five or six men. They navigated, not by star and compass, but by —of all things—sand and a roll of toilet paper.

I made a couple of training flights in one with Chief Warrant Officer George Steelman, who had competed in national balloon cup races, and knew his business. Once we were up and had attained a state of suspension where we sat in the sky and went neither up nor down, Steelman began his navigation.

He shredded toilet tissue into confetti, and threw it over the side, then watched it. A hundred feet down, it might bend briefly westward with an air current; two hundred feet down, it could turn in any other direction.

Steelman ordered, "Valve one second!" or "Valve two seconds!" and the equilibrium of the balloon was so sensitive that the release of a little gas made it drop. If he was about to overshoot the desired level Steelman ordered, "Out one handful!" or "Out two handfuls!" and ballast sand was dropped over the side.

The maneuverability of a free balloon, selecting its wind currents, is amazing. Free ballooning could be a wonderful sport— but rather expensive.

Something very strange must have happened to the Navy balloon from Pensacola. Ordinarily, it should have been able to find a wind that would bring it back to base. It should have been able to climb quickly above any sudden storm.

155

12. IN HARM'S WAY
—THE DESTROYERS

Of all the tools the Navy will employ to
control the seas in any future war, the most useful of the small types of combatant ships—the destroyer—will be sure to be there. Its appearance
may be altered and it may even be called by another name, but no type, not even the carrier or
the submarine, has such an assured place in future
Navies.
—*Admiral Chester W. Nimitz*

Scratch one pig boat. Am searching for more.
—*U.S.S.* Borie *to U.S.S.* Card, *1 Nov., 1943*

THE *Borie*, DD-215, was a product of World War I, which is to
say that she had a thin skin, a flush deck, and four pipes, or
stacks. She was known as a "tin can." In World War II, she and
all other destroyers became known as "small boys," but oddly
enough were still referred to as "she." Regardless of gender, they
wrote an epic of sea warfare.

Before the war was over, the United States had lost 57 destroyer types in the Pacific, and 25 in the Atlantic. But the tin
cans gave much better than they took, and a tremendous amount
of enemy submarines and other shipping went to the bottom because of them.

The *Borie* is only a case in point. She was much over age as a
small boy, in 1943. Nobody expected much of her, not even her
own people, or her Captain, Lieutenant Commander Charles H.

Hutchins, U.S. Naval Reserve. But Hutchins and all the men serving under him were determined to do their best.

The beginning of the war found the *Borie* attached to the 15th Naval District, which is the Panama Canal Zone. There were some sinkings by U-boats off the Canal, but it was not a place where classic naval battles were likely to be fought, since we had a pretty good air patrol of the area. And nothing in *Borie*'s previous history indicated that this particular small boy would become a hero or a heroine—take your choice. In fact, some of the remarkable things that have happened to her in peacetime can only be explained by the feeble statement, "Well, that's a destroyer for you!"

Back in the 1920's, the *Borie* had in her crew a wonderful character in Chief Water Tender Joseph C. Pulusky. He was a champion swimmer—in fact, he was the champion swimmer of the Scouting Force, which meant the Atlantic Fleet. Known as "Ski," he was a big guy, well over six feet and displacing 250 pounds, but he was a fish in water. In the words of a contemporary, Ski could do a back flip into a bottle of ink, and never spill a drop.

Very well. A new ensign, fresh caught from the Naval Academy, reported aboard *Borie*, and was given the dual assignment of commissary officer and athletic officer. It is not of note that the chow was improved, but as athletic officer, the ensign was out to qualify all hands as swimmers. The ability to swim, he pointed out, was a good thing to have if you were drowning.

He had been on the Academy swimming team, and knew his stuff. Word got around the *Borie* that he had competed with swimmers from Yale, Harvard, Smith College, and Bryn Mawr. He lost no time getting out of his uniform and into Navy swimming trunks—which in that era fit like a blacksmith's apron. All hands were called to the foc'sle and told to fall in ranks. They had to dive off the foc'sle, swim back to the fantail, and then back to the gangway in order to qualify.

A few days after this routine started, Joe Pulusky came up from the fire room, covered with sweat. The ensign said, "Chief—

you, too! Get your swimming suit on!"

Ski went down to the CPO quarters, and came back wearing a black silk bathing suit with SCOUTING FORCE across his chest in gold letters. But this meant nothing to the ensign.

The ensign said, "Go up there to the eyes of the ship, dive off, swim back to the fantail, and you will be qualified."

Half the *Borie*'s crew were standing around burning their bare feet on the deck, but they said nothing. They did not tell the ensign that Ski habitually dived from the crow's nest every morning, unless he had the watch below.

Ski said, "Sir, I am a big man. If I hit the water from this height, it will bust me wide open!"

The ensign said, "Don't be a big baby! I'll hold your hand and go off with you, and I will absolutely bring you up and back!"

Ski stuck out his hand. It was about the size of a banjo, and his fingers were like bananas. It swallowed the fist of the ensign.

They went over the side. The whole crew of the *Borie* was manning the lifelines to see what happened.

All they saw was the bottoms of the two men's feet, with Ski hanging on to the ensign with one hand and swimming powerfully for the bottom with the other.

This was in the Gulf of Guayacanabo, where the water was clear. But the Navy could never either spell or pronounce the name of the place, so they called it Scrub and Wash Clothes Bay . . .

A long way down toward the bottom, Ski turned loose of the ensign's hand. Then he swam under water a hundred feet or so to make the gangway. The ensign surfaced and yelled, "Where is he?" and the helpful audience yelled, "Over there!' and the ensign dived again. This happened several times. Ski was at the rail, himself, when the ensign asked "Where is he?" and Ski answered, "He's over there."

But finally the gag was over. The ensign went below to get into uniform, and never again held a swimming class on the *Borie*.

The *Borie* went to Marseilles, and then to Mentone—and Ski, with nine dollars, wanted to break the bank at Monte Carlo. He did not succeed, but as he left the casino, he managed to steal a young and beautiful fox terrier, which he named Monte Carlo.

The dog quickly became the pet of the ship. The U.S.S. *Tracy,* (DD-214) in the same division, had a female brindle bull terrier. Soon there was quite an exchange of messages: was Dorothy, the brindle bull, in heat? Was she at this stage, or past it?

Finally the two ships were alongside each other. Monte Carlo and Dorothy got together. But Monte Carlo, due to his low stature, was not up to what the Navy calls the Plimsoll line of Dorothy. Ski put both dogs on a slack awning, and both fell over the side. Ski had to dive and save Monte Carlo, and a man from the *Tracy* saved Dorothy. It is not of record that there were puppies . . .

[*ii*] Destroyers date back to coal-burning days, to 1902, when DD-1, the U.S.S. *Bainbridge,* was commissioned. It is not too much to say that they revolutionized sea warfare, since their development kept pace with that of the submarine as an offensive weapon, and they have produced as many naval heroes as the submarines themselves. Submarines are sneaky; destroyers are cheeky—and dashing. They roll a lot in heavy seas, being narrow of beam, and time was when one could nearly always pick out a destroyer man ashore, because he had the same sort of seagoing roll to his walk.

Bainbridge is an historic name, which fortunately has been preserved on the Navy's roster. The first *Bainbridge,* launched in 1842, was a brig of 259 tons, a hundred feet long and carrying a crew of 100. She served the Union with a glorious record in the Civil War, until August 1863, when she capsized in a storm off Cape Hatteras. All but one man of her crew were drowned.

The second *Bainbridge* was the first destroyer. She was only 420 tons, and although more than twice as long as the *Bainbridge* brig, carried only seventy-five men. But she could do nearly thirty knots, which was very fast, indeed, for warships in 1902. She served long with the Asiatic Fleet, went on convoy duty in

World War I, and was put out of commission in Philadelphia Navy Yard in 1919.

Just a year later, the third *Bainbridge* was launched at Camden, New Jersey, and became DD-246. She was a four-piper, flush-decked, and the design of destroyers had grown so much over her predecessor that she displaced 1,200 tons.

The *Bainbridge* became a hero in one of the most dangerous and spectacular rescue operations the Navy has ever known. In December 1922, in the Sea of Marmora, she went alongside the burning French Army transport *Vinh-Long* and saved 482 of the 495 men and women aboard. Exploding ammunition twice blew the *Bainbridge* away from the transport, but she came back, and finally rammed her bow into the flaming vessel to carry out the rescue with munitions exploding all over her foredeck. She was decommissioned in 1930, put back into service in 1933, placed in the reserve fleet in 1937—and still called up again in 1939 to work with the Neutrality Patrol. Her final decommissioning was in 1945, after she had won battle stars.

The fourth destroyer *Bainbridge* is nuclear powered, and very modern, indeed. There is no doubt that in the event of war, she will uphold the glory of her name. As Admiral Arleigh A. Burke, the most famous of all destroyer men, has put it: "Throughout the years, destroyer men have been a proud breed . . . No task has been too difficult for them to tackle. . . ."

None ever will be.

In April 1917, German submarines had been sinking neutral ships at such a great rate that we declared war. Our first act was to send the destroyers, six of them—*Wadsworth, Wainwright, Conyngham, Davis, McDougal,* and *Porter*—to Queenstown, Ireland. These ships were under command of Commander J. K. Taussig.

"How soon will you be ready to go out on patrol?" asked British Vice Admiral, Sir Lewis Bayly.

"We are ready now, sir," Taussig said, "that is, as soon as we finish refueling . . ."

Soon there were 34 American destroyers working with the

British, and before World War I was over, there were 80 such ships in the fighting. Destroyers *Fanning* and *Nicholson*, in a joint attack, sank U-Boat 58, but mostly the destroyers' part in that war was one of defense that thoroughly discouraged U-Boat attacks.

We lost Destroyer *Jacob Jones* to a German submarine, and we had Destroyer *Cassin* badly damaged by a torpedo. Gunner's Mate Osmond Kelly Ingram, of Alabama, saw the torpedo coming; it was headed for the fantail of the *Cassin*, with its rack of deadly depth charges. Without hesitation, Ingram ran to release these ash cans. He was blown over the side, and his body was never recovered, but he had saved the ship. In World War II, he was honored by having a destroyer (255) named U.S.S. *Osmond Ingram*.

Jacob Jones was torpedoed in the English Channel, and sank in eight minutes. The U-Boat had the grace to help some of the survivors get aboard life rafts, and to send a radio message giving the position of the sinking, for rescue purposes.

The destroyer *Ward* was built in one war, and became famous in the next one. She slid down the ways at Mare Island in May, 1918, a little late for World War I. But she was launched with a great deal of proud and prophetic fanfare, to the tune of "She's Some Baby," and it happened that she lived up to the boast.

On the morning of 7 December, 1941, the *Ward* was returning to Pearl Harbor from a routine patrol. She was commanded by William W. Outerbridge. I have served with Outerbridge, and can personally testify to his decisiveness and his aggressive bull-dog attitude. That morning he was suddenly faced with a terrible decision: he found a submarine operating in restricted waters, where no submarine had a right to be. Without the slightest hesitation, he followed his orders: he attacked with depth charges, and gave her the deep six.

She was a midget Japanese sub. Almost before Outerbridge could report the sinking, Pearl Harbor was attacked. The destroyer *Ward* had made the first kill in the Pacific.

The peacetime Navy had its share of tragedy for destroyers.

My Love Affair with the Navy

On the foggy night of 8 September, 1923, a destroyer squadron in follow-the-leader formation made a "9 turn" (a 90-degree change of course) too soon off the California coast, and seven destroyers—*Delphy, Fuller, S. P. Lee, Chauncey, Nicholas, Woodbury,* and *Young*—piled up on the cruel rocks of Point Honda, and were lost. The disaster was blamed on faulty navigational signals from a shore radio-compass station at Point Arguello, although its exact cause was never fully determined. The remarkable thing was that only twenty-two lives were lost when the leading ships struck and were turned over. It could have been much worse.

A shipmate of mine, Chief Radioman Frederick W. Fish, was aboard one of these destroyers. Next morning, he was in a small boat, helping in the search for survivors or bodies. He had escaped wearing only dungarees. He spotted a gold-braided Commander's cap floating in the water, sullied only by a little fuel oil, and he put this on with no other thought than that of keeping his head warm. A little later, he saw something that looked like a body near one of the other boats, and shouted over to alert its crew. The cox'n of the boat saluted, and said, "Aye, aye, sir!"

Fred thought nothing of this until it happened the second time. Then he realized that he was Commander-for-a-day—and he relaxed against the thwarts and had a great deal of fun ordering the boats of the flotilla here and there. He never found out who owned the brass hat. No Commander was lost in the Honda disaster. But there may have been more than one lieutenant commander who was hopeful of making that extra half stripe, and had a brass hat ready.

America began the Battle of the Atlantic on 3 September, 1939, after a German submarine torpedoed the British liner *Athenia,* off Ireland.

The U.S. was not prepared. She had a total of 140 old destroyers, all but thirty of them decommissioned and in mothballs. Forty of the old-time four-stackers were recommissioned, and a few new subs joined them on the Neutrality Patrol, protecting and escorting merchant ships in the waters west of Iceland.

It has been said that a mistake was made in naming Iceland and Greenland: Iceland, which has thermal hot springs around its shores, is wonderfully green, while Greenland is terribly icy. Iceland is bathed by the Gulf Stream, and is only 530 miles from Norway. In World War II, Norway had been occupied by the Nazis, and in the spring of 1941 American destroyers were assigned the job of patrolling the Icelandic sea approaches, to protect American merchant ships. Whether the rest of the country knew it or not, the Navy foresaw that sooner or later these tactics would be a factor in bringing on U.S. involvement in the war.

An American destroyer, U.S.S. *Niblack*, fired the first shot some eight months before Pearl Harbor. Her captain was Lieutenant Commander E. R. Durgin, and she flew the pennant of Commander D. L. Ryan, who was commodore of Destroyer Division 13. On April 10, 1941, she had just picked up survivors from a torpedoed Dutch freighter when she made a sonar contact on a Nazi submarine. Ryan ordered the *Niblack* to drop a pattern of "ash-cans"—depth charges—and the U–Boat, perhaps severely shaken up by the attack, speedily departed on other business.

A few months later, in the fall, I had the good fortune to be ordered aboard *Niblack* for her second cruise to Reykjavik. We were one of numerous destroyers escorting the first American convoy that carried troops to Iceland. Durgin was still the skipper, and to all intents and purposes, war had been declared. We dropped a numer of depth charges after making sonar contacts, and there was no doubt that German submarines were in the area.

Destroyers are beautifully fast and maneuverable, and can turn on a dime. After one depth-charge attack, we turned about and cruised through the area. There was oil on the surface. Somebody said that it looked like whale oil, and this was reported in the ship's log. But you get whale oil only after a process of boiling and rendering the blubber, and there is a good chance that the oil was Diesel.

The voyage was without other incident, except that the landing of thousands of troops in Iceland was not appreciated by the Icelanders, who wanted only to be left alone. In Reykjavik's Hotel Borg, the statuesque Icelandic girls, all Nordic beauties and many of them six feet tall, wanted little to do with the Americans. According to a Continental custom, they retired to their own side of the dance hall after each dance. My stay was too short for me to form an opinion, and I have often wondered how the occupation troups finally made out.

[*iii*] We come back, now, to U.S.S. *Borie,* a typical four-stack, flushed-deck, over-age destroyer. She was patrolling off Panama and Yucatan in 1942, and it was a busy area, because U–Boats were out in force to sink Panama Canal traffic.

War is hell, indeed, but it also is people, and they vary. One Nazi submarine skipper machine-gunned the swimming survivors of the torpedoed *Atwater,* but another U–Boat commander trumpeted in a German accent, "Sorry I had to do it . . . hope you make it in!" to the survivors of the *Alcoa Puritan.* One German submarine made a lee for a raft in a heavy wind and sea, and held up one man by a boathook until the raft could take him aboard. This sub also informed the survivors that land was 270 miles away, and that they should take it easy—they were in a shipping lane, and would likely be picked up.

The *Borie,* in 1942, had neither radar nor modern detection gear for submarine hunting. Early in June, she was called in to hunt for U-Boat 159, which had downed six ships off Panama in a few days. *Borie* did not find the submarine, but she did rescue eight tattered and starving survivors of the cargo ship *Merrimack* from their raft. It was the destroyer *Landsdowne,* which had been in commission only two months, that finally sank U-159 in 1500 fathoms of ocean. *Landsdowne* was commanded by Lieutenant Commander W. R. Smedberg, III, who climaxed his naval career as a Vice Admiral, and was Chief of Naval Personnel. Smedberg has been quoted earlier.

In the fall of 1943 old flush-deck, four-pipe *Borie* was part of a task group under the escort carrier U.S.S. *Card*. And here she covered herself with glory.

Seven hundred miles north of the Azores, the *Card's* radar picked up two submarines. She sent *Borie* in search, under Lieutenant Commander Hutchins. Huchins was shortly reporting to *Card:*

"Scratch one pig boat am searching for more."

The second kill was tougher. The U–Boat fled into a blinding rain squall, but this time *Borie* had radar equipment and could see in the darkness. She plunged through 15-foot seas, and caught up with the submarine on the surface, where they shot it out. The U–Boat had deck guns equal to those on the *Borie,* and almost immediately she hit the destroyer both amidships and on the bridge.

The gunfight lasted nearly an hour, both ships blasting each other with everything they had. *Borie* let loose machine-gun fire that drove the German gunners from their mounts, and then Hutchins saw a chance to ram. He hit the submarine's afterdeck at a speed of 25 knots, and sliced neatly through her hull, virtually cutting her in two. His own bow was crumpled by the collision, and for awhile the two ships were interlocked.

At such close range, *Borie* could not bring her deck guns to bear. The German sailors swarmed up out of the conning tower, and a hot fight raged, hand to hand, with rifles, Lugers, Very pistols, and sheath knives. The *Borie's* machine guns set the sub's conning tower on fire with incendiary bullets.

Then the heavy seas broke the two vessels apart. Damaged as she was, the submarine dared not dive, but tried to escape on surface. *Borie,* taking water in her forward engine room, pursued. After a dramatic chase, with both ships badly hurt, *Borie* missed with a spread of torpedoes, but caught the submarine in the hairs, or the sight, of the main battery. The sub surrendered, and went down just after her crew took to their rubber boats.

Borie was too badly damaged to stay afloat very long. She went down next afternoon, despite salvage efforts by destroyers

Barry and *Goff*. Twenty-seven of her crew were lost to the stormy seas. The *Borie* sank, but she had put U-405 on the bottom ahead of her.

[*iv*] Destroyers are wonderful, and spectacular. Books have been written about their operations in World War II, and there is no space here to repeat their accomplishments. But we might tell about Destroyer Escort *Buckley*, whose crew heard a command not used in the Navy for more than a hundred years—the command to "Repel boarders!"

Buckley, in May 1943, was one of the hunter-killers in the screen of the carrier *Block Island*. She was commanded by Lieutenant Commander B. M. Abel, U.S.N.R., and was about 500 miles west of the Cape Verdes islands, hot on the tail of a German submarine, U-66.

It turned out to be another surface battle. Abel's lookouts sighted the sub in the moonlight at 2500 yards. She opened fire at 2200 yards, and the submarine fired back. The two ships raced each other for a time, barely 20 yards apart, shooting with everything they had. Then *Buckley* swung over sharply, and rammed the submarine, her bow riding high over the U–Boat's deck.

The Germans swarmed out of the U–Boat, shooting with rifles and small arms, and for some moments drove the *Buckley*'s gunners from their posts. Guns could not be brought to bear, anyway, so the fight became hand-to-hand, and that was when the old, classic order was issued to "Stand by to repel boarders!"

The crew of the *Buckley* stood by, gallantly enough, and fought with pistols, hand grenades, fists, coffee mugs, and anything else they could throw at the enemy. The DE finally broke clear of the U–Boat's hull, and the ships moved alongside each other, the crews still fighting with everything they had. The submarine rammed the *Buckley* with a glancing blow—and somebody aboard the DE threw a hand grenade into the U–Boat's conning tower.

That did it. There was an explosion, and a fire, and the submarine went down. The *Buckley,* her bow twisted out of line, proceeded to Bermuda and then New York. She was the first Navy ship to repel boarders since the days of Stephen Decatur.

[*v*] The last time anybody saw Commander James E. Kyes, skipper of the destroyer *Leary,* he was on the bridge, handing his kapok life jacket to a mess attendant who did not have one.

This was on Christmas Eve, 24 December, 1942, at two o'clock in the morning, and an icy wind blowing. The *Leary* had just been hit by two torpedoes from the submarine she was stalking. She was struck aft and starboard, and the greedy sea rushed into her wounds, with no way of stopping it.

At 0025, Commander Kyes ordered his men to the boats. A few minutes later, there were two more explosions. The *Leary* had been hit by at least a third torpedo.

She sank almost at once. Commander Kyes, who was holding to the tradition that says the Captain is the last to leave his ship, went down with her.

Leary had had a busy career. She was the first U.S. destroyer to contact enemy submarines on radar, and had done a lot of convoy escort duty on the Icelandic run—later the Murmansk run—in the fall of 1941, before the war began. She had dropped many depth charges into these same submarine-infested seas.

The escort carrier U.S.S. *Card* was on the job. Despite high seas, the flat-top circled in the dark—a perfect target for the German submarine—until she had picked up many of the *Leary's* survivors. Even so, nearly one hundred of the *Leary's* crewmen were lost.

Captain A. J. "Buster" Isbell, of the *Card,* did his best, and but for his efforts the entire crew of the *Leary* probably would have died in the icy water.

By the summer of 1943, our destroyers had the German wolf packs on the run. On 11 April, Admiral Doenitz reported to Hitler: "I fear that the submarine war will be a failure if we do not

167

sink more ships than the enemy is able to build." And in the following June, German submarines accounted for only nineteen merchant ships.

The decline was on. Germany was coming up with a revolutionary submarine device, the "schnorkel," which permitted a sub to breathe beneath the surface, but she was also losing an average of twelve undersea boats a month to U.S. anti-submarine warfare, and with them her trained submarine crews.

The time came when Commander Tenth Fleet could say:

For each U–Boat destroyed in 1941, about 16 Allied vessels went down. For each U–Boat destroyed in 1942, the Allies lost about 13 vessels. In 1943, the Allied figure was reduced to 2. And by the spring of 1944, a U–Boat was going down for almost every Allied vessel sunk.

And Fleet Admiral Ernest J. King told the Secretary of the Navy: "Submarines have not been driven from the seas, but they have changed status from menace to problem."

He might have added that this was largely due to the effectiveness of the destroyers . . .

There is no space aboard destroyers and submarines where athletes can work out, but both the tin cans and the subs have long been famed for the smokers they hold ashore, and for the baseball and football teams they field. For many years, the annual football game between Des Pac and Sub Pac (Destroyers and Submarines, Pacific) was nearly as big an attraction as games in the Rose Bowl.

Sometimes the contests take on an international flavor. When Rear Admiral Mark Lambert Bristol commanded a number of destroyers in Turkish waters in the early 1920's, each ship had a baseball team hopeful of winning the Mediterranean Fleet championship. They were happy to teach the Turks to play the game, and thus further Admiral Bristol's people-to-people program. Eventually, the Turks developed a few fairly good players, including an outstanding pitcher. Then they challenged the destroyer champions.

The game was played with much fanfare, and many dignitaries of both nations were on hand. The game developed into a real cliff-hanger. The score was still tied at 2–2 in the top half of the ninth, when the Turks came to bat.

The first Turk batter prayed aloud, "Oh, Allah, give me a home run!" and struck out. The second beseeched Allah for a base hit, and grounded out. The third batter only asked Allah to get him on base, and then struck out.

Then the first bluejacket stepped up to bat, rapped the bat on the plate in time-honored fashion, looked up at the heavens, and cried, "You know me, Al!" He hit the first pitch for a home run, to win the game.

13. WARFARE IN
THE DARK—
THE SUBMARINES

The ships destroy us above
And ensnare us beneath.
We arise, we lie down, and we move
In the belly of Death.

The ships have a thousand eyes
To mark where we come . . .
But the mirth of a seaport dies
When our blow gets home.
—Rudyard Kipling, "Tin Fish," from *Rudyard*
Kipling's Verse: Definitive Edition

THE SUBMARINES are dangerous in many ways. And for that reason, submarine duty is very attractive to Navy recruits, who are hell-bent for adventure. Submarine men are very carefully chosen: not every man can pass the rigid physical tests, and each must prove he does not suffer from claustrophobia. Those who do qualify really become a band of brothers.

Submarine losses began very early. On 20 June, 1904, the Russian submarine *Dolphin* vanished with her crew of twenty-three. In 1923, a Japanese submarine sank at the dock in Kobe, with the loss of eighty-five lives; in 1924, a Japanese submarine, No. 43, sank after a collision off Sasebo—forty-nine lives lost. In 1925, the American submarine S-51 went down off Block Island after collision with the *City of Rome,* and thirty-four men died. That same year, the British submarine M-1 had a collision in the English Channel, and sixty-nine men perished. In 1927, the S-4 went down off Provincetown, Mass., after a collision. Forty dead.

The list is very long. U.S.S. *Squalus*, sunk off Portsmouth, N.H., twenty-six dead. British sub *Thetis*, lost in the Irish Sea, ninety-nine dead. French sub *Phenix*, Indo-China, sixty-three lost.

Add to this what has happened in the last couple of years—the losses of the nuclear submarines *Thresher* and *Scorpion*, which we have already covered—and you can readily see that submarining is a very dangerous business. We will later take into account the American submarines lost in World War II, along with their splendid record of sinking enemy ships.

Today's submarines are equipped with both radar and sonar, and carry Momsen escape lungs. We also have a number of submarine rescue ships (ASR, or Auxiliary Submarine Rescue) carrying the diving bells that can bring up eight men at a time. These work efficiently at any depth where a diver can operate, a diver being necessary to secure the downhaul cable to the submarine's hatch. But they cannot work in depths of thousands of feet, where the *Scorpion* sank. The pressure there would already have crushed the *Scorpion*'s hull like so much cardboard; it would kill any man in a diving rig before he came anywhere near reaching the bottom.

So, it is hard to say why submarine duty is popular.

On the day after Pearl Harbor, all thinking Americans knew that we were irrevocably in a two-ocean war. We had 175 warships in the Atlantic—one new battleship and seven old ones, four aircraft carriers, thirteen cruisers, ninety destroyers, and sixty submarines. All of these would be desperately needed to escort convoys and keep the Atlantic sea lanes open.

In the Pacific, far flung along a supply line that was much more extended and imperiled, we had left after the Japanese blitz some hundred warships, mostly small, and could count on the assistance of about fifty Allied ships, also small. At the moment,

Japan had at least 170 combat vessels.

In the Pacific, half our strength was in submarines. We had fifty-one of them—but, again, the Japanese outnumbered us by more than a dozen subs already in commission, and were turning out new undersea craft at a formidable rate. Aside from ocean-going subs, Tokyo was especially concentrating on the building of small subs, useful in harbor defense.

The Japanese Sixth Fleet Submarine Force was off Pearl Harbor on the fateful morning of 7 December. With it were at least five of the midget subs, including the one the destroyer *Ward* sank before the attack. Another midget made it into the inner channel, and was near Ford Island when the attack began. She carried two torpedoes, and fired them, but both hit the mud —and then our seaplane tender *Curtiss* sank her. Another midget was captured near Bellows Field the following day. Although classified as a "midget," she was seventy-nine feet long, carried two torpedoes, and could make top speed of twenty-four knots. That was pretty good, compared to some of our earlier subs.

The Japanese overlooked a great bet when they attacked Pearl Harbor. Their fliers either had expended all their bombs and torpedoes on Battleship Row, or were so elated at their success they did not want to stretch their luck too far. At any rate, the Japanese torpedo planes flew almost directly over the Submarine Base on their approach, and then returned over it. Five good submarines were tied up there—*Cuttlefish, Cachalot, Narwhal, Dolphin,* and *Tautog*—along with the tender *Pelias.* These would have made a fat and profitable kill.

Tautog and *Narwhal* fired on the planes that swept over Merry Point that December morning. So did a destroyer that was tied up near the Submarine Base. One plane was shot down, and all three ships got credit for downing it.

Then *Tautog* shot down a Japanese plane single-handed, the first ship to do so in World War II. But meanwhile, the damage had been done and the horror written—nineteen warships sunk or blasted, and more than three thousand men killed.

The Submarine Base and the submarines there were not hit,

despite the fact that the Japanese planes flew over the base twice. In the next two years, Japanese militarists would have many reasons to regret this tactical oversight.

Meanwhile, the baby Japanese submarine sunk by *Curtiss* was given a most unusual and significant burial. Its two-man crew was dead. Some people may think that what happened was atrocious; others will agree that it was fitting and honorable. A new concrete pier was being built at the Submarine Base, and fill-in material and steel support was needed. The midget submarine was slammed into the concrete—following a very proper Christian burial service for the dead. And so the little Japanese sub, and the bones of its two-man crew, became a part of the solid foundations of the pier at the Submarine Base.

[*ii*] In July, 1944, an outfit known as the "Headhunters" was operating in Formosa Straits. It was so called because it consisted of the submarines *Hammerhead, Steelhead,* and *Parche.* The *Parche* was commanded by Lawson P. Ramage, who had red hair and was known as "Redhead"— which rounded out the Headhunters' name.

And Ramage carried it off very successfully with this wolf pack of submarines. He was assigned to an area called "Convoy College," between Luzon and Formosa. It was a business of chasing ghosts, but Red Ramage was just about to change that.

He took on an entire Japanese convoy just after three o'clock in the morning, and in a time of rain squalls that diminished his visibility. Ramage had been a destroyer man, and he used his submarine like a destroyer—charging at twenty knots into the ring of Japanese ships, firing his torpedoes.

The range closed fast. Ramage got off his bow torpedoes and sank one tanker, then swung around and fired his stern tubes and sank another tanker.

Ordinarily it would have been over, then, but for a long time the redheaded Ramage had been training his crew in reloading torpedo tubes under any conditions at sea—and this can be extremely difficult. Standard practice, after surface firing, was to dive the submarine and then level off and reload the torpedo tubes from a much steadier platform. A submarine on the surface rolls heavily—more than sixty degrees—if there is any kind of sea, and one torpedo going adrift in the boat could sink her and kill all hands.

But Red Ramage's crew had been trained to reload tubes on the surface, and Ramage had no intention of diving so long as he had torpedoes and targets. Now, in the very middle of the Japanese convoy and under blistering gunfire, *Parche* reloaded. She went hard right and hard left, and escaped getting rammed by a Japanese ship by only fifty feet—and then she slammed three torpedoes into a big enemy troop transport and sent her down.

The fight had lasted more than an hour and a half, and there was so much shooting at close range the Japanese vessels could not depress their guns enough to hit the *Parche*—but they must have hit each other. Ramage had expended nineteen torpedoes; he had only five left. He might need them on the rest of *Parche*'s patrol. It was getting daylight.

"Set course 330 degrees true!" Ramage ordered. "Take her down!"

A number of *Parche*'s people were awarded Silver Star Medals, and the whole crew got a Presidential Unit Citation. Red Ramage himself became the first living submarine officer to get the Congressional Medal of Honor.

Many books have been written about the heroism of American submariners in World War II. Their deeds conform to a pattern and in the telling may become repetitive and monotonous—a singular thing, because one does not usually associate monotony with continual danger. Of course on some submarine patrols it was true that war became a period of long boredom, interspersed with moments of intense action, and intense fear.

But none of the submariners admitted that fear, or expressed it.

In this account, I can only report some submarine actions which were atypical of the whole gallant record. Submarines made up only 2 per cent of the Navy: they sank 1,314 Japanese ships, both warships and merchant vessels. Small craft such as sampans and junks were destroyed, but were not counted.

The submarines cut off Japanese supplies from Southeast Asia, and denied the Empire oil, rice, and rubber. They saved many downed fliers, landed coast-watchers, evacuated American Army and Navy nurses from Corregidor, and performed many other missions. U.S.S. *Trout* used as ballast twenty tons of gold bullion and silver *pesos* from Manila banks. A rumor had it that the *Trout*'s crew divided this wealth. Unfortunately, it was not true.

Besides Red Ramage, six other submarine skippers won Medals of Honor in the Pacific. Captain John Cromwell, Commander Howard Gilmore, and Commander Sam Dealey were honored posthumously. Eugene Fluckey, Richard O'Kane, and George Street lived to receive the highest military honors this nation can bestow.

Fluckey earlier had the remarkable record of having won three Navy Crosses for "extraordinary heroism." What kind of man was this? Let's take a look at him, and let him stand for all the other pigboat people who fought so valiantly in the war.

[*iii*] After having been graduated from the Naval Academy in 1935, Eugene Bennett Fluckey saw his first service in the old battleship *Nevada*. But he was soon in the submarine *Bonita*, where he qualified for submarine command, and then he took over submarine *Barb*.

Like Lawson P. Ramage, he was red-haired and freckled—and it may be that such coloring goes with pugnacity. It was in *Barb* that he won those astounding three Navy Crosses.

Another submarine wolf pack—*Growler, Sealion,* and *Pampanito*—had hit a Japanese convoy in the South China Sea, sinking two warships and several transports and freighters. The transports were jammed with British and Australian prisoners of war—some 2,100 of them—who had been captured after the surrender of Singapore. They were in very bad shape physically, and many died. But more than two hundred made it to the life rafts, covered with oil. They saw Japanese destroyers rescue the

Japanese, but they were left behind.

Then, after a long time, they were sighted by the U.S. submarines. *Barb* was called in from more than four hundred miles away, to help in this rescue.

Fluckey was eager to get at the enemy with his torpedoes, but he wrote in his log, "The measure of saving one Allied life against sinking a Japanese ship is one which leaves no question, once experienced. I would forego the pleasure of an attack on a Japanese Task Force to rescue any one of them."

The castaways were in bad shape, and Fluckey saved most of them in weather so rough that his own men had to wear lifebelts. The winds were from twenty to fifty knots; the *Barb* rolled thirty degrees. Fluckey stayed in the area until the typhoon passed, but found no other survivors. Those picked up were given clothing donated by the *Barb*'s crew—along with some $300 in cash.

Gene Fluckey was only getting under weigh. He sank 28,000 tons of enemy shipping on his third patrol. Then, after dark on the night of 23 January, 1945, he chased a Japanese merchant ship into Namkwan Harbor, on the China coast—and went in after her. He had already sunk a transport and a freighter on this cruise, and climaxed this attack by blowing up an ammunition ship. It was recorded that the explosion as so severe that it created a vacuum that almost pulled men in the *Barb* up the hatch from the control room, and actually did suck their skivvie shirts up over their heads.

The chase into Namkwan Harbor was a story-book action, and it was based upon reports from coastwatchers working for then Commodore Milton E. Miles, who became famous and beloved as "Mary" Miles.

Fluckey went in with the *Barb*—past minefields, shore batteries, dangerous rocks and shoals—and he was soon in waters where a submarine could not dive at all. The approach was slow and agonizing. It was a couple of hours later before he was on target. He made the attack just after 1 A.M.

And then he saw he was in the midst of dozens of Japanese ships, all within a little more than 4000 yards. He couldn't miss . . .

"Fire one! Fire two!"

In half a minute, *Barb* had launched four torpedoes. She swung around, launched her stern torpedoes,—and then started speeding out of Namkwan Harbor.

The whole area exploded. Fluckey's second and third torpedoes blew up a large freighter. His first missed this ship, but hit another vessel in the second column. The fourth torpedo did away with a big freighter in the third column. An ammunition ship blew up with a tremendous bang, and shells exploding from her sank other ships alongside.

Barb got out fast, then. Escorts were after her, firing blind.

Fluckey always had a sense of humor. He was yearning for deep water—forty fathoms or more, so he could dive. He wrote in his log: "The Galloping Ghost of the China Coast crossed the 20-fathom curve with a sigh. Never realized how much water that was before. However, life begins at forty—fathoms. Kept going."

Fluckey got the Congressional Medal of Honor for this particular bit of business on the China Coast, and he richly deserved it.

But Gene Fluckey wasn't through, by any means. He sold Admiral Lockwood, boss of the submarines in the Pacific, on the idea of raiding the Japanese fleet north of Hokkaido. He also demanded that *Barb* be equipped with a rocket launcher.

Rockets were new. No submarine had a rocket launcher. But Fluckey carried his point. A few minutes before he sailed, a rocket launcher and some one hundred rockets were delivered aboard *Barb*. Nobody in the crew really knew how to fire them.

The target was a Japanese cable station on Sakhalin Island. Just when Fluckey took off, the Navy decided that this target wasn't worth four million dollars' worth of rocket equipment—they wanted the equipment back. They were too late: Fluckey had already latched it onto his hull. In doing this, he might well be considered the grandfather of nuclear missiles aboard our modern submarines. More important at that time, he proved that rockets were important armament, and before long they were being issued to all our submarines.

The bold and imaginative Gene Fluckey was busy on still another project. He was training some of his men as a boarding party, as a special weapons group designed for commando and espionage work. Their training was thorough: it even included a course in how to crack a safe with TNT, thus qualifying the submariners for a career in burglary on the Outside. But it was important, because it enabled them to take ship's documents from any vessel the *Barb* sank. And it supplied part of the wonderful finesse Fluckey was using to build up a Task Force of his own—a group of real gangsters.

This, of course, was extra duty, because no submariner is supposed to function on land. Fluckey called this group an Assault Team.

In July 1945, members of the Assault Team were chafing for action, and Fluckey decided it was time to unleash them. He thought about all the things submarines had never done, and came up with the novel idea of blowing up a train.

The Japanese railroads have long held a reputation for great efficiency, and pride themselves on operating schedules to the second. But, of course, none had ever remotely considered such a thing as a submarine attack.

Fluckey had great fun planning this. Observing from offshore, he chose a system of railroad tracks on the Japanese east coast system, a complex where three rail lines merged. He had watched the trains from offshore, and had written down a fairly accurate timetable of their runs. Then he ordered the *Barb*'s Assault Team ashore with a 55-pound demolition charge.

The *Barb* could go in without running aground some thousand yards offshore at Karafuto. Fluckey planned to send his gangsters in on a lonely beach, some seven hundred yards from the village.

At 10 P.M. on the 22nd, the submarine surfaced off Karafuto. Two rubber boats were inflated. The Assault Team was in charge of Lieutenant William Walker. It included Signalman Second Class Francis Sever, Motor Machinist's Mate First Class John

Markuson, Motor Machinist's Mate Second Class James Richard, Chief Gunner's Mate Paul Saunders, Ship's Cook First Class Lawrence Newland—a good man with a cleaver—and Torpedoman Third Class Edward Klinglesmith. It probably would have meant nothing to the Japanese, but the team also included Electrician's Mate Third Class Billy Hatfield—whose ancestors had fought the notorious Hatfield-McCoy feud in Kentucky. Billy Hatfield was no man to have mad at you.

Signals were worked out. That for an alert was two bobwhite whistles. For assembly, whippoorwill whistles. (Nobody learned until later that there are no whippoorwills in Japan.) There were others, for blinker guns and Very stars. The *Barb* could well be driven to sea, leaving her party stranded, and one Very star from her signified that she was having trouble, but would return every night.

Thus the adventure began, and the rubber boats were put over the side. Fluckey told the men that if they had trouble, they should head north for Siberia, 130 miles away.

Nothing came off according to plan. There was fog, and the rubber boats landed in the wrong place—in the rear of a Japanese house. They were in the middle of the small town. Fortunately, no Japanese *inu* barked, and they made a highway and did their best to get their bearings. Walker said, "Follow me!" and immediately fell into a deep ditch. A little farther, though, they found the railroad tracks.

A tense and trying time followed. The tools they had made aboard the *Barb* were inadequate for digging in the roadbed, and they ended up planting the demolition charge by hand.

A train came by, and they all had to hit the ground. Hatfield began to swell visibly. His lifebelt had been inflated by the carbon dioxide cartridges.

"You're not shot!" the others told him. "You're just pregnant."

Finally, the demolition charge was in place, and the raiders made their way back to the beach and the rubber boats.

At 1:45 A.M., the people aboard *Barb* heard a northbound train coming around the bend, and the men in the rubber boats stopped paddling. Two minutes later, the charge went off.

The locomotive blew up. Cars went off the rails. Japanese newspapers, blaming an aerial bomb, said 150 people were killed. The rail complex was out of order for several days.

No other submarine has ever destroyed a train.

[iv] Time was when the Navy was smaller, and so were the submarines. In that day, a man serving in the subs could come to know almost all the other people in that branch. Crews were small, too, but the boats remained terribly crowded.

But let my friend "Rojo" Hickman tell the story to illustrate just how crowded they were . . .

"I want to tell you about an old shipmate I introduced to [Captain] Roy C. Smith," Rojo says. "This friend, Monk Irvin, was a radioman nearly all of his career—he shipped in 1914, and did more than thirty years. Monk runs a paint and varnish shop in Alexandria, Virginia.

"Roy wanted to buy some varnish one day while we were visiting with him. I said, 'Let's go get it from Monk.' Roy said OK, because he is always interested in anyone and everything re the U.S. Navy. We went into the store, and after the introduction, Roy told Monk that the late Rear Admiral Montgomery Meigs Taylor was his uncle, and asked if Monk knew him.

" 'Do I know that old buzzard?' Monk said. 'You should have seen him the night he caught his nose in my skivvies!'

"Roy nearly did a backflip, but, man, was he interested. Monk said, 'I was on a pigboat with him in Coco Solo, when he was a lieutenant. He used to go ashore every Friday night, and was never known to return to the boat until Monday morning.

" 'On a pigboat, it's hard to find a place to hang your clothes after you have scrubbed them. So I used to run a line across his cabin after he went ashore, and then did my washing and hung it up in his room. This worked fine until one night when he returned to the boat after all hands had turned in.

" 'He stumbled around in the darkness of his cabin, trying to find the light switch; he got all fouled up in my clothesline, and stuck his schnozzle right into a pair of regulation, nansook skivvies. When he finally got the light on, he read "A. S. Irvin" stenciled on the waistband of those skivvies.

" 'I was transferred the next day.' "

Well, the submariners were and are a hearty and lusty crew, and so much the better, according to the Navy, because there is a strong tendency in the Navy to believe in Bayard Taylor's:

> *The bravest are the tenderest—*
> *The loving are the daring.*

and the Navy has long theorized that a man who won't make love won't fight. A test, perhaps, of masculinity?

As this is being written, a new chapter on Navy submarines is being recorded. The Joint Committee on Atomic Energy has called upon the Navy Department to stop holding up construction of a super-silent electric-drive submarine that could track Soviet warships.

Work on this submarine was started months ago, and then was halted pending a decision as to whether the ship should not be scrapped in order to save money.

It is all a very technical problem. The super-silent electric-drive submarine would be slower than the super-fast—and considerably noisier—boats driven by steam turbines.

The answer, of course, is that the Navy needs both types, and should have them. Both are atomic powered.

The submarines with the speed advantage can either join the engagement, or withdraw from it, Admiral Thomas B. Moorer, Chief of Naval Operations, testified. The other ship could do nothing about it.

This is an example of the sad case in which the Navy needs two types of warships, but because of limited appropriations must choose one type over the other. Come war, and the restriction to a single choice might prove regrettable, indeed.

No material on submarines would be complete without some reference to that colorful old submariner, Fleet Admiral Ernest J. King, Commander in Chief during World War II. The Navy insisted the "J" stood for "Jesus."

My Love Affair with the Navy

In the early 1920's Commander E. J. King took command of a submarine division at New London—small, ancient boats of World War I vintage. Because they were so small, it was the custom for their crews to live aboard the submarine tender when in port. King ordered them back aboard the boats, so they could get under weigh at a minute's notice.

Morale declined rapidly. Rear Admiral Montgomery Meigs Taylor sent for King and suggested that reconsideration might be in order. King said that his boats would always be ready for sea, and that the order would stand.

Admiral Taylor looked at him, and said quietly, "Tell me, Commander, will you rescind your order, or shall I?" It was the only time in his life that Ernest J. King ever rescinded an order.

When King was graduated from the Naval Academy, he bet with a classmate on who would have the first son, in spite of a two-year period before marriage was allowed. In due time, both married and had children—both girls. The bet was doubled, but the next children also were girls. Doubled again, and still girls.

Finally, the classmate's fifth child was a son, while King's was a daughter, and he paid off. The King family continued on to a sixth child, and a first son. Admiral King told this story at a Washington dinner many years later, and his dinner partner asked what he had named the boy. "Why, Ernest Joseph Junior, of course," he said. She replied, "Oh, no, Admiral—you should have named him Ernest Endeavor!"

During World War II, King spent most of his nights working aboard his flagship U.S.S. *Dauntless* in the Washington Navy Yard, rather than going home to Admiral's House, where there was too much social distraction. One evening he had to go aboard the President's yacht for a dinner conference. On boarding, he handed his briefcase to the messenger of the watch with the injunction, "Hold this in your own hand until I come back for it."

The messenger, a fresh-caught young lad with stars in his eyes, said: "Yes, sir, Admiral—your slightest wish is my command!" Whereupon Ernest J. glared at him with his frosty blue eyes and said, "You're goddamned right it is, son!"

14. THEY
WANTED WINGS

. . . they shall mount up with wings as eagles . . .
—Isaiah XL 31

I wanted wings till I got the blank-blank things—
Now I don't want them any more!
—South Pacific Navy song

THE WRIGHT BROTHERS, Wilbur and Orville, had started it all in 1903 when Orville flew 120 feet in twelve seconds. Six years later the Navy was interested enough to request that it be supplied with two "aeroplanes." The Acting Secretary of the Navy turned thumbs down on this, saying, "The Department does not consider that the development of an aeroplane has progressed sufficiently at this time for use in the Navy."

The Acting Secretary may have been right. But on 18 January, 1911, Eugene Ely, a private pilot, landed a Curtiss pusher-type plane on a platform 30 feet wide and 132 feet long that had been built on the deck of the armored cruiser *Pennsylvania*. This historic first took place in San Francisco Bay.

It was a stunt, but it proved something. Ely's "aeroplane" was turned around, and he took off from the ship to land at Selfridge Field.

If he could land and take off from a man-o'-war, he could not only serve as eyes for the fleet, with a range of vision greatly exceeding the twelve miles from the crow's nest—he just might be able to carry and drop a bomb.

A couple of months later, Wilbur and Orville Wright offered the Navy a deal. They would train an aviator if the Navy would buy just one plane, for $5000. The deal was not made.

Considering the fantastic strides it has made, naval aviation got off to a very slow start, but in January 1913, a small aviation detachment was used for the first time in fleet maneuvers—it had to be land-based, of course. But the idea caught on, and a year later the first school for naval air training was commissioned at Pensacola.

This was the beginning of what became known as the "brown shoe" Navy, as against the traditional "black shoe" and blue uniform of line officers. It was the beginning of an entirely new Navy language—with hand gestures showing the relative positions of two planes, not understandable to the line officers in officers' clubs. These upstarts could not hand, reef, or steer; they were not qualified to stand a watch in the engine room. They were visionaries, but dedicated ones, believing in their dangerous trade—and a few lived to see their prophecies fulfilled. On 21 April, 1920, the Navy commissioned U.S.S. *Langley*.

The *Langley* was a most ungainly and unlovely craft—a makeshift job. They had taken the old collier U.S.S. *Jupiter,* and roofed her over with a flight deck to become our first carrier. She was named gloriously enough for Samuel Pierpont Langley, a scientist and aviation research pioneer who headed up the small Naval Academy observatory away back in 1866. He died in 1906, but by then he had attempted—without success—to build a plane that would carry a man.

The *Langley* quickly became known as the "Covered Wagon" —after a very popular motion picture of the era. She had her mishaps—planes of that day had no brakes, and in landing on deck were stopped by a series of wires that ran athwartships and engaged hooks on the tails of the aircraft—but not always. Many a *Langley* flier went right on off the bow, and had to gun his engine to keep from splashing. Many splashed, and has to be rescued by boats.

But the Navy pilots were pioneering, and learning.

And teaching. They passed their lore along. A classic example was the legendary pilot, dying of burns, whose last words were, "Tell them to cut off the ignition before they crash . . ."

Much was owed, of course to the light-hearted adventurers of the Lafayette Escadrille in World War I. But aviation ashore and aviation afloat are entirely different. The pitching and rolling flight deck of a carrier looks like a postage stamp from a few thousand feet of altitude, and allows for no errors. A plane being shot from a catapult on a battleship could break a man's neck unless he had it properly braced against the sudden momentum.

The Navy's first aviator, Commander T. G. Ellyson, survived in a remarkable fashion, considering his perils. He kept flying, and was killed in a crash on 27 February, 1928, after a spectacular career.

Another famous pioneer in naval aviation was P. N. L. Bellinger, a junior grade lieutenant, who had begun flying in 1912. In April 1915, he established a seaplane record by climbing to 10,000 feet in one hour and nineteen minutes.

(Progress: on 23 February, 1955, forty years later, a Douglas F4D Skyray reached the same altitude of 10,000 feet *in less than a minute!*) And in April 1958, Lieutenant Commander G. C. Watkins, in an F11–1F at Edwards Air Force Base, set a world altitude record of 76,938 feet.

Professor Langley's problem of a heavier-than-air machine that would carry one man had been solved. In March 1949, the Navy's *Caroline Mars* set a world record by carrying 269 men from San Diego to Alameda. The record was short-lived. Two months later, another Mars flying boat ferried 308 men from Alameda to San Diego. (It is easier, the fly-boys say, when you are going downhill.)

[*ii*] Navy fliers are young, ebullient, full of hell, in the peak of physical condition—and therefore much given to horseplay. A single anecdote, having to do with

two of the most famous naval aviators, will serve as an example.

In 1939, before the war, Commander Austin K. "Artie" Doyle was commander of the Air Group in U.S.S. *Saratoga.* The famed Dixie Ketcham was the *Saratoga's* Air Officer, and Commander Charles R. "Cat" Brown became Ketcham's assistant.

Cat Brown was a notorious practical joker. Artie Doyle was out of the class of 1920 at the Naval Academy, and a year the senior of Brown—but this made no difference. Doyle went to the Commerical Club in Honolulu, as an honorary member. Of course he introduced himself and told what his job was. Then Cat Brown came in, and was duly introduced to the civilian members . . .

Cat looked at these, and said, "Did this gentleman [Doyle] tell you he is a naval aviator? And did he tell you he is in command of the Air Group aboard the *Saratoga?*"

The civilians nodded. Cat Brown waggled a finger at Doyle, and said, reprovingly, "At it again, Artie!"

There seemed to be no way to get back at Cat, although Artie Doyle laid for him for years. Finally, in May of 1952, the chance came. Doyle by then was a Rear Admiral, Carrier Division Commander in the Sixth Fleet, with his flag in U.S.S. *Midway,* in the Mediterranean. Cat Brown had just made his broad stripe as Rear Admiral, and was ordered to relieve Doyle at Gibraltar. Brown's new flag was in the Coral Sea.

Artie Doyle chuckled to himself all day, knowing what would happen. Cat Brown would have to ask what the uniform would be for the change-of-command ceremony.

Finally the dispatch came. It said:

REQUEST UNIFORM OF THE DAY FOR ENTERING PORT.

With great glee, Artie Doyle told his flag lieutenant to answer:

UNIFORM OF THE DAY FOR CORAL SEA FOR ENTERING PORT IS SERVICE DRESS BLUE BAKER, WITH SHOES.

And he laughed all night. The Sixth Fleet, in the Mediterranean, was a tremendously smart, spit and polish outfit. The Coral Sea could hardle hope to cope with such elegance.

They Wanted Wings

A Consul General and other Foreign Service officers were aboard *Saratoga* next morning, for the ceremony. The barge bearing Cat Brown came alongside, and he grinned up under the visor of his brand new brass hat.

Then he boarded *Saratoga* in his bare feet—carrying his shoes in his hand. "You did not say whether or not to wear them!" he trumpeted at Artie Doyle.

You just can't get back at some guys . . .

[*iii*] "Coordination" is defined in the Random House Dictionary as "harmonious combination of interaction, as of functions or parts." A shorter definition could be, simply, "teamwork."

When the Battle of Midway was fought on 4 and 5 June, 1942 —and it was the decisive battle of the Pacific war—America was very fortunate in having Admiral Chester W. Nimitz in command of the Navy in the Pacific. Nimitz not only understood the principles of teamwork, but was personally the most coordinated man I have ever known, both physically and mentally.

He was fifty-nine when I served on his staff in 1944. He still played a championship brand of tennis, when he had time for a game. He was completely ambidextrous, and never used a backhand shot. If the ball came toward his left, he simply shifted the racquet to his left hand, and slammed out another forehand.

He also had a horseshoe-pitching rig outside his quarters on Makalapa Heights, and delighted in taking guests to the cleaners at two bits a throw. One of his cruiser captains was his victim one day, and after losing three in a row to the Old Man, the Captain said, "Admiral, you're too good for me!"

Nimitz said, "Oh, come on—one more game, and I'll pitch left-handed!" Then, in *sotto voce* to Roscoe Good, who was then a captain, he said: "That'll make it an even buck!" And it did . . .

The point may seem far-fetched, but it need not be. The U.S. Forces at Midway were commanded by Rear Admiral Raymond A. Spruance and Rear Admiral Frank Jack Fletcher. But behind both, and in overall command—behind all the intelligence work

187

that broke the Japanese code and all the combat and logistical planning for the Midway operation—was the superbly coordinated man who was CINCPAC.

He had some wonderful assistance from his staff. Commander Joe Rochefort broke the Japanese code; Commander Edwin T. Layton handled Intelligence. Both knew the Japanese people, their language, and their ambitions. Nimitz trusted them, and he was not the kind of leader who has to look back to make sure he is being followed. It was teamwork all the way.

It was Nimitz's decision, at Midway, to call in the entire force of Pacific Fleet submarines to back up Fleet operations, rather than let them continue their very profitable but independent raids on Japanese shipping. There were twenty-nine such undersea boats, some of them quite new. Not one submarine had been lost to the Japanese since the war began.

Nimitz divided the surface warships into two groups. Rear Admiral Raymond A. Spruance had the carriers *Hornet* and *Enterprise,* six cruisers, and ten destroyers—along with two tankers—to make up Task Force 16. Rear Admiral Frank Jack Fletcher, with his flag in the carrier *Yorktown,* had two cruisers and six destroyers to make up Task Force 17.

The combined strength sounds formidable. But wait. Approaching Midway, Admiral Isoroku Yamamoto (a year older than Nimitz) had a main force of six battleships, three cruisers, and a number of destroyers at his disposal. His striking force was made up of four aircraft carriers. He had two more battleships, eight cruisers, and a number of destroyers to escort the transports he expected to land troops on Midway.

Neither side had any monopoly on brains, ability, or courage. Admiral Yamamoto was a very wise man—and a prophetic one. He had studied at Harvard, and had served as a naval attaché in this country. He knew our industrial capacity. But he obeyed orders. In 1941, he said, "If I am told to fight, I shall run wild for the first six months or a year, but I have utterly no confidence in the second and third years of the fighting."

It turned out, indeed, that he was a prophet without honor in his own country.

Admiral Spruance was a "black shoe" Navy man who had never dealt with carriers before, and this caused some muttering among the "brown shoe" fly boys. He came to command of Task Force 16 because of an odd and trivial thing—such as often affects the course of history. Admiral "Bull" Halsey, who otherwise would have been in command, was hospitalized at Pearl Harbor with an itch so raging that he had to bathe in oatmeal.

There really was nothing funny about Halsey's dermatitis, nor was there anything funny about the way Spruance handled his job. The two task forces rendezvoused on 2 June, and Nimitz, still calling the play, ordered them to proceed north of Midway. The submarine force was sent out to be advance scouts.

And the battle was about to begin. A supposed Japanese attack on the Aleutians had not fooled Nimitz, any more than an Army belief that the attack would be on San Francisco.

[iv] The Battle of Midway began in the air, and it began bravely and tragically, as a portent. This was how war was going to be, from here on out. The physical strength, courage, and daring of an individual could no longer be counted upon to vanquish a lesser man—not if the lesser man happened to be operating a superior machine. It was the story of the Gatling gun and the machine gun all over again, cutting people down to size: in a sense, the Age of Automation had arrived, only now it came in an airplane.

Early in May, Admiral Nimitz had flown to Midway for a personal look at the defense installations: he was sure, that far ahead, that Midway was going to be the target. When he went back to Pearl Harbor, he began beefing-up Midway's strength. He sent a battery of eight 37-millimeter antiaircraft guns; he sent the Marine Corps' famous Carlson's Raiders; he sent Army B-26 planes converted to carry torpedoes, B-17's, and twelve Navy

PBY's. Altogether, Midway had about a hundred planes.

Admiral Frank Jack Fletcher, being the senior, took command of the joint task forces at the rendezvous on 31 May. He had three aircraft carriers, eight cruisers, and fourteen destroyers. As it turned out, this wasn't very much.

Seven hundred miles from Midway on the morning of 3 June, Ensign Jack Reid, in a Navy PBY, saw some spots on the sea. He broke out his binoculars, and quickly got off a cryptic signal that said "Main Body."

Midway went on the alert. Back in CINCPAC at Pearl Harbor, with all the intelligence information at hand, they could be more calm. They asked for more details.

Reid reported that there were eleven ships, steaming at 19 knots, on a course of 090 degrees. Then he was ordered back to Midway before he ran out of fuel.

In CINCPAC again, the team of Nimitz and Rochefort and Layton received Reid's report in their coordinated way. Nimitz had the whole Pacific at his fingertips, and this just didn't tie in. The Japanese feint at Alaska's Dutch Harbor had just come off as predicted. The "Main Body" sighted by Reid was coming from the wrong direction—it would be the transports of the Japanese Invasion Force. Japanese carriers could still be expected to hit Midway next day from the northwest.

THAT IS NOT REPEAT NOT THE ENEMY STRIKING FORCE.

Nimitz warned Midway immediately. It was like a chess game being played by radio. Nimitz sat back in CINCPAC headquarters, and called all the moves.

On the night of 3 June, planes from Midway attacked the Japanese ships Ensign Reid had sighted. A couple of hits—or probable hits—were observed, but there was nothing conclusive. Next morning the island's PBY's found the Striking Force coming from the northwest, only 200 miles away.

All of Midway's planes took off. But the Japanese planes, approximately one hundred, carrying torpedoes and bomb, were already on their way. They had a fighter escort of Zeroes. A few miles offshore, Marine planes from Midway challenged them.

We learned a sad and startling lesson then. Fifteen of the Marine Corps planes, under command of Major Lofton R. Henderson, were very quickly splashed. Henderson was killed. Some of the planes made it back to Midway, but never flew again. One, piloted by First Lieutenant Daniel Iverson, had 259 holes in it from machine-gun bullets and flak; Iverson's microphone had been shot off his throat—it was that close—and he had only one wheel, and no flaps. But he landed, and made a written report that said, "My plane was hit several times . . ."

In a way, this was all incredible. America had a vaunted and acknowledged superiority in the field of engineering and aeronautics. Yet the Japanese Zero of that year could outclimb, outmaneuver, and outdistance any plane we had. Part of this was due to the fact that the Zero was of very low weight, and was being flown by a smaller man. A single well-placed shot could destroy it, since it was extremely flimsy. But the Zeroes usually dived from above, with their machine guns blazing—and that one well-placed shot was very difficult to manage.

Midway badly needed the Task Force ships under Fletcher and Spruance, but although these were steaming at flank speed they did not arrive until daylight of 4 June. Japanese flying scouts spotted the carriers, *Yorktown*, *Enterprise*, and *Hornet*. The Japanese carriers *Akagi*, *Hiryu*, *Kaga*, and *Soryu* stopped loading their planes with bombs to blast the island, and began loading them with torpedoes, instead.

This was a break for our side. The Japanese Striking Force had changed course abruptly, and our carrier planes had trouble finding it—some of them ran out of gas, and had to ditch or land at Midway. *Yorktown*'s fighters finally sighted the Japanese force, and guided the pilots from *Enterprise* and *Hornet* to the target. They struck while the enemy planes were being rearmed—and there could have been no better timing.

The *Kaga* took four bomb hits that left her a splintered shambles, dead in the water, her deck wrecked and her flight island destroyed. *Akagi* was set aflame. *Soryu* met the same blazing end. *Hiryu* got away.

The story of Midway lacks continuity and cohesion: too much was happening simultaneously. The destroyers and the submarines were just as busy as the fly-boys, and all did their jobs. Historians do not agree on who sank which, and how many: it was a confused picture.

But the gallant lads of *Hornet*'s Torpedo Squadron Eight deserve special mention. Torpedo Eight was commanded by Lieutenant Commander John C. Waldron, who vowed he was going to sink a Japanese carrier. Each of his fifteen planes carried a "pickle"—a torpedo—which they had never done before. There is an old saying: "You pay to learn."

Torpedo Eight paid dearly. Its planes took off from the *Hornet* on a flight of nearly two hours, with Waldron leading them low over the water. For some reason, the fighter cover they were supposed to have did not make the rendezvous—but they ran into some thirty Zeroes circling over the Japanese force.

Commander Waldron's plane was one of the first to go down. His boys did not change their course by one degree. They kept flying—and they all went down.

Ensign George "Tex" Gay, the squadron navigator, was flying the tail-end Charlie position, under fire. He pinched a bullet out of his arm, and was flash-burned on his leg. He looked back to see that his radioman, Bob Huntington, had been killed. Then the TBD, terribly shot up, hit the sea about a quarter of a mile from a Japanese carrier. As it struck, Gay heard his torpedo explode against the carrier's hull.

One wing shattered, and the plane began filling with water. Gay fought desperately to get out of the cockpit, and finally made it. But now there was a new peril: the Zeroes were circling overhead, strafing the helpless men in the water.

A black seat cushion from the plane bobbed up to the surface, along with the deflated yellow rubber boat. The straps holding both in the plane had been literally shot away. Gay latched onto these providential items, and pulled the seat cushion over his head for concealment that enabled him to escape the machine-gun fire, although he came very close to being run down by a destroyer.

A few minutes later dive bombers from the American carriers swept overhead and began dropping their lethal loads on the enemy ships. Torpedo Eight had not died in vain: Waldron had managed to radio the carriers. This brought a quick response, and the Japanese flat-tops were caught rearming and refueling their war birds. The dive bombers gave them a two-hour blitz, and Tex Gay had a ringside seat from which he watched them burn.

The cost was high. *Yorktown, Enterprise,* and *Hornet* had launched forty-one torpedo planes, and only six returned.

After a long time, Gay inflated the yellow life boat, and climbed into it. He was rescued next day by a PBY seaplane being flown by Lieutenant "Pappy" Cole. Considering the circumstances, the rescues were fantastic: they went on for ten days, and the PBY's picked up twenty-seven airmen who were adrift, salt-caked and sunburned.

When Ensign Gay was in clean pajamas and a clean bunk, doctors asked him what he had done to treat his wounds. The sole survivor of Torpedo Eight said, "Well, I soaked them for several hours in salt water."

It helped, later, to know that Torpedo Eight had been avenged. A flight of sixteen torpedo planes from the Japanese carrier *Hiryu* attacked U.S.S. *Yorktown* in much the same manner —and all of them were shot down by the sky guns of *Yorktown* and her destroyers, *Anderson, Hammann, Hughes, Morris,* and *Russell.* There was some good shooting that day.

[*v*] But *Yorktown* had been very badly damaged by the Japanese bomb attack. She was hit by eighteen bombers and eighteen Zero fighters. Torpedo Eight's suicide mission was repeated here by the enemy. The attackers ran into a vicious fire, but ten of the Japanese planes managed to break through the fire curtain long enough to drop their bombs before they were shot down. The others came on—and they also were splashed.

About this time, the Japanese carrier *Soryu,* some distance away, was torpedoed by the American submarine *Nautilus*. *Kaga* followed her to the bottom a little later, and that night *Akagi* went to what the Navy calls the "deep six."

That left *Hiryu*. That night she was given a terrible beating by American planes, and the next morning a Japanese torpedo sent her to her last resting place.

Amazingly U.S.S. *Yorktown* stayed afloat, despite her injuries, and became a legend. She was still functioning and fighting two days later. But on 6 June, when destroyer *Hammann* was alongside, pumping out *Yorktown*'s water and fighting her internal fires, Japanese torpedoes hit them both.

It was a spread of four torpedoes, fired by Japanese submarine I-168 in a very daring attack. The first fish hit *Yorktown*. Then *Hammann* was struck.

The destroyer began sinking. Berlyn Kimbrel, Torpedoman First Class, raced to the fantail and set the depth charges on "Safe" to insure that they would not explode as the ship went down. He lingered too long in doing this, and was killed by one of the explosions he tried to avert. A gunner's mate, Osmond Kelly Ingram, had died in exactly the same way, back in World War I, and had had a destroyer named for him.

The destroyer *Hammann* sank, and so did the carrier *Yorktown*. These were our ship losses at Midway, which was principally an air battle.

The Japanese lost four aircraft carriers and a heavy cruiser.

Theodore Roscoe, distinguished historian for the United States Naval Institute, has summed up the Battle of Midway like this:

> Midway was where the war tide stood still. The point where the Japanese onrush was halted. The beginning of its ebb. And the place where the Imperial Japanese Navy suffered its first defeat since 1592. The victory was costly enough for the United States. Total American losses included 150 American aircraft, and 307 officers and men, as well as carrier *Yorktown* and destroyer *Hammann*. But these losses were light compared to those suffered by the enemy.

[*vi*] It seems curious, now, that at the time of the Battle of Midway, General Douglas MacArthur

and Fleet Admiral Chester W. Nimitz had never met. They fought a common enemy in the South and Southwest Pacific before they finally got together late in April 1944.

Why was this? MacArthur had been in Australia and New Ginea since March 1942. He was Supreme Commander in the Pacific. Surely, by the time of Midway, he should have been ready to acknowledge that it was largely an ocean war. He could have directed Nimitz to fly down and confer with him, but he did not, and Nimitz could not very well ask for such a talk. Finally, during the Solomons campaign, MacArthur sent not for Nimitz, but for Admiral Bull Halsey. It may be presumed that they talked about amphibious warfare and island-hopping. Amphibious warfare was neither strictly naval, nor the sole business of the troops; it required close Army and Navy collaboration.

In those days, Halsey was not authorized to issue communiques—these came from MacArthur. They minimized the efforts and the importance of the Navy at every turn. Pride of outfit is a wonderful thing, and no one will deny MacArthur his greatness as a General. But he must have had his blind side.

The Navy told stories about MacArthur's famous crushed hats, which he designed himself. The Navy referred to him as "Dugout Doug," that "seasick General," and "God's cousin." Bull Halsey, however, never lent himself to any such disrespect, and it is quite apparent that Halsey greatly respected MacArthur.

It was then left to the Navy's old fuds, young studs, and lieutenant commanders to vent their spite on MacArthur. At the time, I was a lieutenant commander. On Guadalcanal, a number of press correspondents lent their talents to compose a song called "Doug's Communique . . ."

For two long years, since blood and tears have been so very rife,
Confusion in our war news burdens more a soldier's life;
But from this chaos daily, like a hospice on the way,
Like a shining light to guide us, rises Doug's Communique.

For should we fail to get the mail, if prisoners won't talk,
If radios are indisposed and carrier pigeons walk,

My Love Affair with the Navy

We have no fear because we'll hear tomorrow's news today
And see our operations plan in Doug's Communique.

Here, too, is told the saga bold, of virile deathless youth
In stories seldom tarnished with the plain unvarnished truth;
It's quite a rag, it waves the Flag, its motif is the fray,
And modesty is plain to see in Doug's Communique.

"My battleships bombard the Nips from Maine to Singapore,
My subs have sunk a million tons, they'll sink a billion more;
My aircraft bombed Berlin last night." In Italy, they'll say
"Our turn's tonight, because it's right in Doug's Communique!"

"My armored tanks have moved his ranks, so Rommel's gone to hide,
And the frozen steppes of Russia see my wild Don Cossacks ride;
My brave beleaguered Chetniks make the Axis sweat and pray"—
It's got to be, it's what we see in Doug's Communique.

His area is quite cosmic, and capricious as a breeze,
Ninety times as big as Texas—bigger than Los Angeles;
It springs from lost Atlantis up to where the angels play . . .
And no sparrow falls unheeded, it's in Doug's Communique.

He used to say, "And with God's help," but lately it would seem
That his patience is exhausted, and God's on his second team.
And the Cabots and the Lodges, too, have long time ceased to pray
That they'll ever squeeze a by-line into Doug's Communique.

And while possibly a rumor now, some day it will be fact
That the Lord will hear a deep voice say, "Move over, God, it's Mac."
So bet your shoes that all the news, that last great Judgment Day,
Will go to press with nothing less than Doug's Communique . . .

15. WHAT SO PROUDLY WE HAILED...

ASK AN AVERAGE American citizen about the War of 1812, and unless he happens to be a real history buff, he is likely to reply vaguely that this was the conflict in which Francis Scott Key wrote the words of The Star Spangled Banner, and Captain James Lawrence uttered his immortal order of "Don't give up the ship!" And—oh, yes—the British invaded Washington, and burned the U.S. Capitol . . .

All this is true. But it was a very strange war that need never have been fought, and probably wouldn't have been fought if there had been something like radio, or a transatlantic cable.

England lifted her embargo on American merchant ships on 16 June, 1812, but communications were slow. Two days later, the United States declared war. It had not got the word.

By the same token, the single decisive land battle of the war— the battle of New Orleans—was fought four days after a treaty of peace had been signed in Ghent!

Neither side won this war. It had been fought because of the British practice of boarding U.S. merchantmen, seizing both American-born and naturalized U.S. citizens, and impressing them into the British Navy. A "press gang" today means nothing more menacing than the newspaper press-room crews who come out for lunch wearing the traditional box caps made of newsprint.

197

But in 1812, a press gang was something else. I say nobody won the War of 1812, because a half-century later, British warships were still impressing seamen.

The War of 1812 deserves some space here, because this is a book about the Navy, and because—again—only the Navy came out shining. The blunders on land were often absurd, and were atoned for only in the final battle at New Orleans. There, the Tennessee or Kentucky long rifle wrought terrible damage against the British.

The gallant English officers took the most forward positions, and most of them were killed. With typical English bulldog courage and tenacity, they kept charging. When the fight was over, they had 700 of their men killed, 1,400 wounded, and 500 were made prisoner. Incredibly, the Americans had accomplished this victory with only eight men dead, and thirteen wounded.

The war had its lighter moments, and some of them, unfortunately, could never happen again today; if they could, Navy recruiting stations would be swamped. U.S.S. *Essex*, a frigate, commanded by Commodore David Porter, sailed from Delaware Bay on 28 October, 1812. *Essex* was to join up with *Constitution* and *Hornet*, in southern waters. She carried 319 men and a good stock of provisions.

She did not contact the other two ships, but went on across the Equator, and took the British ship *Nocton*, which was carrying gold worth $50,000. Porter took the gold, gleefully, and sent the *Nocton* on her way with a prize crew. She was shortly recaptured—ships changed hands frequently in that war—but Porter had the money. He sailed on, and rounded the Horn on St. Valentine's Day of 1813.

Now the high living began. On the coast of Chile, the *Essex* dropped the hook long enough to put boats ashore and shoot wild pigs, a welcome change from salt horse; actually, salt beef. She went into Valparaiso, and was royally wined and dined. After a few days, however, Porter again weighed the anchor.

He captured a Peruvian corsair, freed some American whalermen who were prisoners, and went on to the British whaling grounds off the Galapagos Islands—where he raised hell by capturing a dozen British whaleships, along with whale oil worth more than $2,000,000 and sent them home with prize crews. Then he sailed across the Pacific to the Marquesas Islands, reaching them in October.

Here began the idyll that could have been a Navy recruiting officer's dream. The Marquesans were a beautiful people, tawny and tall, with proud-breasted women who did not conceal their endowments. There was a little internecine war going on between the people who lived on the shore and those residing in the hills. Porter lent his strength to the coastal group, which was soon victorious.

The fruits of victory were surprising to the Yankees as in the *Essex*. The Marquesans were so grateful that they turned all their wives and daughters temporarily over to the officers and crew of the *Essex*.

Still, Porter had a job to do. When he announced that it was time to sail, the Marquesan women lined the beach and beat their breasts and wailed. The crew of the *Essex* couldn't take this, and began grumbling. Commodore Porter mustered all hands topside, read the *Article of War*, and demanded that the men willing to obey his orders fall in on the starboard side. Those against him would take the port.

There is a great story here—if only the names, the facts, and especially the sequel had been recorded. Only one seaman of the entire crew stood against Porter; obviously he was a man who knew what he wanted, and he stood firmly.

This man was put on the beach, and the ship made sail. The last seen of the lone American, he stood on the shore, smiling happily and surrounded by a large group of the lovely, full-breasted island women and girls. There is no further record of him, but he must have enjoyed his exile.

[*ii*] Not all of the war, however, had tender moments. When it broke out, the U.S. Navy had some twenty ships of 500 guns. There was not one ship of the line, or

first class fighting ship. We had nine frigates, of which several were laid up for overhaul, three sloops, and five brigs, along with some two hundred gunboats. The British had more than a thousand warships, including 150 ships of the line, 164 frigates, and 134 sloops. A sizeable portion of this force was on the American station, distributed between Halifax and Jamaica: 5 ships of the line, 19 frigates, 41 brigs, and 16 schooners.

The situation at sea was accepted as hopeless. If the war could be won at all, it would have to be won ashore.

It didn't work out that way. The British took Detroit, which of course was only a small town in those days, but nevertheless its capture was significant. We lost several skirmishes and battles along the Canadian border, and what was proposed as an invasion to take Canada failed dismally.

It was up to the Navy. Congress had said that this would be a land war, and nothing was expected upon the sea beyond some commerce raiding by our privateers—and that went off very well around the home islands of Britain.

The Army generals were old men, covered with glory. The Navy captains, on the other hand, were young. The Administration of Thomas Jefferson had reduced the roster of Navy officers from some five hundred by more than half. Commodore John Rodgers, Captain Stephen Decatur, and most of the others were no more than in their forties.

Captain Isaac Hull of the *Constitution* fought a unique battle with several British warships, in which none of the ships could move because of a dead calm, but had to be kedged—towed by oarsmen in small boats. This severe exercise went on for two days, with no ship getting an advantage. Finally a breeze came up, and Hull made all sail and managed to escape from the superior force. But it was not long after this that *Constitution* engaged the British frigate *Guerriere*, of 38 guns, and whipped her. Legend says that Isaac Hull wore very tight breeches, and split them from waistband to knee in this engagement. Whether this is true or not, he really did take the pants off the enemy: *Constitution* had 14 men killed and wounded out of a crew of 456; *Guerriere* lost 79 out of her crew of 272. She sank.

The American Navy's gunfire was greatly superior to that of the British. There was a reason for this. The American Navy had been trained in Preble's tough school of the sea and had kept in practice during the Quasi War with France and the war with the Barbary Pirates. The British had plenty of practice in the Napoleonic Wars—but they had become overconfident. At any rate the Americans did the better shooting.

This was again demonstrated when the U.S. sloop *Wasp*, 18 guns, encountered the British *Frolic*, also 18 guns, and they fired at each other from a distance of fifty yards. *Wasp* shot away the *Frolic*'s masts and rigging, and then boarded her with pikes and cutlasses. What was left of the *Frolic*'s crew laid below; there was no hand-to-hand fighting and the colors were struck without opposition. The British had lost an incredible proportion of their men—90 dead and wounded out of a crew of only 105. The *Wasp*, on the other hand, had sustained losses of only 5 killed and 5 wounded.

But the *Wasp*'s victory was short-lived. A little bit later, the British ship of the line *Poictiers*, mounting 74 guns, bore down on the *Wasp* and took her prisoner, along with her prize. Such were the fortunes of war.

And such was the story of the War of 1812. It was an age when personal gallantry still counted in conflict, and chivalry still flowered. Stephen Decatur, in the frigate *United States*, of 44 guns, vanquished the British frigate *Macedonian* in short order— there was hardly that much disparity in their armaments. When the *Macedonian* surrendered and her skipper offered his sword, Decatur said, "Sir, I cannot receive the sword of a man who so bravely defended his ship. But I will receive your hand . . ."

By the time the war ended, it found that the small United States Navy had sunk or captured more than eight thousand tons of British men-of-war, with a loss of only 820 tons. In addition, nearly fifty prizes had been taken by the Navy, and these did not include the ships captured by the privateers.

Joshua Barney, the boy captain now grown up, fought quite a

war on sea and land. He had a strong force of gunboats in the Patuxent River, to defend Washington and Baltimore, but it was not strong enough. When the British warships invaded, Barney abandoned his thirty gunboats and went ashore with 400 armed men. The skeleton crews he left aboard the gunboats were under orders to blow them up rather than let them fall into British hands.

[*iii*] It was such a strange war that President Madison and his Cabinet set out to have a personal look at it. (They may well have felt that if they stayed in their offices in Washington, they would be captured.) Here you had the President, the Secretary of State, the Attorney General, the Secretary of the Treasury, the Secretary of the Navy, and the Secretary of War (who was a little late reporting) all on hand for the battle of Bladensburg, Maryland. Before the battle began, Commodore Barney, with apparently no respect whatsoever, for rank, gave the Secretary of the Navy a terrific chewing-out in blistering seagoing language. It seems that the Secretary had ordered Barney to stay behind and guard the Washington Navy Yard, but when Barney had finished speaking his piece, the orders were changed.

What happened at Bladensburg was confusion. The Americans outnumbered the British by nearly two to one, but somehow imagined that they were pitted against a force of 10,000 British regulars. They broke and ran.

The British—and this may surprise you—used rockets for the first time in warfare, and they terrified American troops. Commodore Barney's men held fast, and continued a telling fire against the enemy, but 500 sailors could not long withstand 3000 British. Barney was wounded, and his defense collapsed.

Not long after the Battle of Bladensburg, the British invaders swarmed into Washington. They set fire to one end of the Potomac Bridge, and we set fire to the other.

Dolly Madison was finally prevailed upon to leave the White House, where she had been firmly entrenched while President Madison and most of his Cabinet were away at the wars. She wrote to her sister that she could hear the noise of the cannon at Bladensburg.

After Commodore Barney was wounded and had been captured, the British Admiral, Sir George Cockburn, and the British General, Robert Ross, who knew him either personally or by reputation as a gallant seaman, had his wounds treated and gave him every courteous and humane attention. And then, when the British were advancing on Washington, a sniper—supposedly one of Barney's men—fired a shot from a house and killed General Ross's horse.

This was a mistake. A horse may perhaps be unfairly classified today along with a piece of mechanized equipment, but the fact remains that a horse always has been and always will be a noncombatant. Everybody loves a horse.

General Ross and the rest of the British were so enraged by this act that they may have become more determined to put Washington to the torch. It might have been easier for the city if the bullet had hit General Ross. A soldier asks to take his chances; a horse does not.

Madison crossed the Potomac by boat, mounted a horse, and made a rough ride of some eighteen hours. He was more than sixty, and this was quite an ordeal. He found Dolly waiting for him at an inn in Virginia. The Attorney General, the Secretary of the Navy, and others were also in their saddles alongside him.

Meanwhile, Washington was burning. In the Washington Navy Yard, the invaders had great good fun mutilating the Tripoli monument, but the fun and the vandalism ended tragically enough when a British soldier dropped a firebrand into a dry well. The well was a powder storehouse, and the explosion was immediate and loud. It killed twelve soldiers, and wounded thirty more.

[*iv*] Young Captain James Lawrence was in command of the U.S.S. *Chesapeake*, a 38-gun frigate. This was the ship that had had bad luck in her engagement with the British *Leopard*, and sailors said she was jinxed. She

was in Boston harbor, which was being blockaded by H.M.S. *Shannon,* also a frigate of 38 guns. And now a most unusual thing happened.

The *Shannon*'s commander, Captain Philip Bowes Vere Broke, wrote to Lawrence suggesting that the two ships meet, "to try the fortunes of our respective flags."

Lawrence accepted this courteous challenge to a duel. He took the *Chesapeake* down to Massachusetts Bay on 1 June, 1813, although his crew was still complaining about being jinxed.

At four in the afternoon, *Chesapeake* fired one shot to begin the action. Both ships sought the weather gauge, and more than an hour and a half later, they were yardarm to yardarm, exchanging broadsides. *Shannon* had a superior weight of metal, and after twelve minutes of fighting, *Chesapeake*'s upper works had been mostly shot away, and she would not obey her helm.

Lawrence had already been slightly wounded; now he fell to the deck mortally hit. Before he died, he gave the Navy his immortal maxim of "Don't give up the ship!"

Sadly enough, the admonition was not heeded here. The British boarded and hauled down the American flag. *Chesapeake* had lost 48 men killed and 98 wounded; Shannon had 26 killed and 58 wounded.

Once again the British observed all military courtesies and honors toward the slain Americans, paid them tribute, and then sent their bodies from Halifax to the United States for a state funeral. It had been a duel in all the old sense of knighthood.

Now, for the first time in our history, we had a fresh-water Navy. This was an anomaly: the Navy was nothing if not salty. But after they took Detroit, the British had a flotilla on Lake Erie, and could command what was then known as our northwest. Something had to be done about it.

We came up with a naval genius in the person of young Oliver Hazard Perry. As a lieutenant at twenty-seven, he had commanded a flotilla of gunboats, like Joshua Barney. He was promoted to the Lake Erie command, where we were building some ships at what is now Erie, Pennsylvania. Two brigs and three gunboats were already under construction.

It was winter time, and Perry went up by sleigh with 150 of his best men, and, incidentally, recruited his fifteen-year-old brother on his way. His adversary on Lake Erie was first a Captain Finnis of the Royal Navy, and then Captain Robert H. Barclay, who had served under Nelson—and, like Nelson, had lost an arm.

The story of the epic battle is too well known to be detailed here. It began badly for the American forces, and Perry was forced to transfer from one ship to the other, carrying the banner that bore Lawrence's words, "Don't Give Up the Ship." But the tide of battle turned, and after more than two and a half hours of fighting, the British squadron was hammered to pieces.

Perry went back to the *Lawrence* for the surrender ceremony, in which he graciously refused the British officers' swords. His main concern at the moment was for his young brother, Alexander. It was thought that the boy had been washed overboard. But, after a search, Alexander was found in his bunk, soundly asleep.

It was then that Perry took an old envelope, and wrote his famous signal to General Harrison:

"We have met the enemy and they are ours; two ships, two brigs, one schooner and one sloop. Yours with great esteem and respect. O. H. Perry."

Lake Erie was secure.

16. SOME VOYAGES
OF DISCOVERY

Behind him lay the gray Azores,
Behind the Gates of Hercules;
Before him not the ghost of shores,
Before him only shoreless seas.
He gained a world; he gave that world
Its grandest lesson: "On! Sail on!"
—Joaquin Miller, *"Columbus"*

IT IS hard to remember, now, when jet planes cross the Atlantic in a few hours, that Christopher Columbus sailed into a mystery far less known than what we know today of outer space.

The important thing to remember now is that the challenge and the motivation were the same then as they are today, and will be the same always.

The challenge was a frontier. The motivation was a burning desire to learn what lay beyond that frontier. Put the two together, and you have what it takes to make an explorer.

America became great because of the fact that she has always had a frontier. At first, it was physical: it was Kentucky and Tennessee, then Texas, the western plains, and California. Fortunately, there are still frontiers today, infinitely more vast than any we have conquered before. The new frontiers are in space and the stars. You may be sure that the United States Navy is doing its part toward interstellar exploration and navigation.

Whaleships began it all for this country. In 1791, seven whalers rounded Cape Horn and entered Pacific waters that were about as unknown as the sea into which Columbus sailed. This was private enterprise, and fitting for a democracy: whaling was becoming a big and profitable business. Where business goes upon the sea, the Navy must go too, for protection for commerce. But it took a little time for the Pacific whaling trade to become that important.

The U.S.S. *Essex,* under Preble, rounded the Horn in 1800, to protect American shipping in the East Indies. *Essex* and U.S.S. *Ontario* went around the Horn in the War of 1812. It was not until 1819 that U.S.S. *Macedonian* was sent into the Pacific with the assignment of protecting American commerce. But U.S.S. *Ontario,* in 1818, established our claim to land on both sides of the Columbia River, in what is now Oregon. This was important: it was our first move to extend the country from coast to coast.

Macedonian's cruise was hard on the wives and families of its crew; it lasted for two years and nine months. Nearly sixty thousand miles were logged by the ship. She came back to Boston minus twenty-six men of her original ship's company: nineteen had died of illness, four were lost overboard, a midshipman had been killed in a duel, and two men had been slain by the Spanish in Callao. The Navy in those days was a hard and dangerous calling. This may explain why another warship of that era—U.S.S. *Monocacy*—had a crew made up of men from nineteen different nations. These men were truly sailors of fortune, or, in a very real sense, mercenaries. They remained loyal to the American Flag in time of battle, because that appears to have been a trait of mercenaries. Officers in the *Monocacy* had to give commands in several different languages, if they expected them to be obeyed.

But things were about to change. A naval officer named Matthew Calbraith Perry—younger brother of Oliver Hazard Perry, the hero of 1812—had some ideas. He thought that the selection of midshipmen for the Navy was too haphazard, and that seamen should be given some sort of training before they began performing their duties at sea. In the long run, and despite many difficulties, Perry's theories were largely responsible for training cruises for boys and cadets—and even for the establishment of the U.S. Naval Academy, itself.

The Navy was getting only foreign seamen, and the riffraff of this country's waterfronts. But it appears that things changed when the Navy really began to sail to far places—it had much less difficulty, then, in recruiting stout and honest farm boys. The lure of distant islands is strong, even if they can only be seen through a porthole.

Voyages were long. A clipper ship took almost three months to reach San Francisco from New York—the famous clipper *Flying Cloud* set the record in 1851. It was far faster at that time for the Navy to send its dispatches to Chagres, in Panama, have them carried by hand across the Isthmus, and then forwarded by another ship.

It wasn't until 1861, when the first transcontinental telegraph line was completed, that communications were speeded up.

[*ii*] Some of the Navy's role in explorations—particularly the very successful expeditions of Rear Admiral Richard E. Byrd and Rear Admiral George J. Dufek, of Operation Deepfreeze fame, have been well publicized. There were earlier explorations, however, which are little known.

For example, in 1848, Lieutenant William Francis Lynch undertook an expedition to explore the River Jordan and the Dead Sea. He took small boats inland on the backs of camels, which was quite a feat in itself. This led, later, to the Navy's supplying some camels to the Army, for use in the Southwestern deserts.

In 1851 and 1852, Lieutenant William Lewis Herndon again took a Navy outfit overland, and went from Lima over the Andes, and then down the mighty Amazon River; one of the amusing highlights of this trip was that he encountered an American traveling circus on the headwaters of the Amazon, in Peru. In 1853, Lieutenant Thomas Jefferson Page, in U.S.S. *Waterwitch*, charted the headwaters of the Paraguay River.

But the Antarctic intrigued early naval explorers most of all: it had been long suspected that there was land lying around and above the South Pole. The first sailor who attempted to go deep into these uncharted seas was England's famous navigator, Captain James Cook. He sailed two ships there in 1773, searching for new seal colonies. The expanding and brutal trade of the seal fishery had virtually exterminated the seals on most islands. Seal hides were sold to the Chinese, who converted them into fashionable fur coats, and it was a very profitable industry. Millions of the friendly, harmless, and lovable creatures were clubbed to death within a few years.

Cook's ships were the first ever to penetrate the Antarctic Circle. Icebergs turned him back. The following year he cruised again, and went past latitude 71 degrees south, farther than anyone else had ever been. On a third cruise in 1775 Cook finally found islands heavily populated by seals—and the sealing ships moved in for the bloody slaughter.

Beyond these small islands, Captain Cook saw nothing but icebergs. It was the sealers, pressing on in their greediness, who thought they might have seen something that looked like a continental land mass. The actual discoverer may have been an English naval officer, Edward Bransfield, or a very young American captain, Nat Palmer. Both sailed the frozen sea in 1820.

[*iii*] About this time, a former American Army man named John Symmes came up with a very odd-ball theory that the earth was made up of hollow, concentric shells. He lectured and wrote pamphlets and tracts on this subject. At the North and South Poles, he said, there were openings thousands of miles in diameter. Ships, according to Symmes, could sail into these polar holes, enter the next shell, and find themselves in warmer waters. Indeed, he declared, some of our Indian tribes had emerged from the shells below.

It is too bad that John Symmes is a man hard to track down. Was he a sort of advance agent for the medicine shows that were soon to become very popular, or was he really a scientific and professorial type? The more solid citizenry snorted in derision at his theses. But, after all, the polar regions were unknown, and

My Love Affair with the Navy

many people are likely to believe anything about the mysterious. Symmes's lectures and broadsides won many supporters, and a great number of his disciples wrote to their Congressmen.

In the long run, Symmes was at least partially responsible for a naval expedition, to be sent "to the Pacific Ocean and the South Seas, to examine the coasts, islands, harbors, shoals and reefs in those seas, and to ascertain their true situation and description."

The stage was then set for thirty-year-old Charles Wilkes, a Navy lieutenant who also was a surveyor and an astronomer. He had been a boy prodigy, first going to sea in a merchant vessel in 1815 when he was only seventeen. He studied hard, paying particular attention to mathematics, navigation, languages, and sciences. By the time he was commissioned as a Navy lieutenant in 1826, he had become a somewhat strange sort of naval officer for that day—he was really more of a scientist than an officer of the line. Still, he proved very capable of command, and was quite strict and severe—in fact, he was a rather harsh disciplinarian.

Much of this harshness likely was due to the fact that he was taking a command that had been refused by several much more senior officers, who very justifiably thought that their lives and their careers could suffer from heading up an expedition of frail wooden ships into such perilous waters.

Wilkes took the job. It was highly unusual for a mere lieutenant to command other lieutenants in a task force of several ships. The command was rejected by Captain William B. Shubrick, Captain Lawrence Kearney, Captain F. H. Gregory—and even by Captain Matthew Calbraith Perry, who later would win undying fame as a gun-point diplomat, by opening the hermit kingdom of Japan to the western world. Wilkes asked President Van Buren for the temporary rank of Captain. Van Buren reportedly promised this, but it did not materialize.

So, in the summer of 1838, Charles Wilkes—after years of hassling and haggling in the Navy Department to get what he wanted in the way of vessels—took command of six small ships. They carried a large number of chronometers and other magnetic devices which he had personally bought in Europe with $20,000

210

the Navy allowed him. These instruments were very precious to him. He broke the code of naval etiquette by not allowing his ships to answer any gun salutes; instead, he had his crews man the rigging and the yards, and respond with hearty cheers. Gunfire, he said, would wreck his chronometers. This unorthodox practice got him into trouble with superior officers more than once, but Wilkes did not mind. He was a single-purposed man.

To fly his squadron flag, Wilkes chose the sloop *Vincennes,* of 780 tons. The other ships were the sloop *Peacock,* 650 tons; the supply ship *Relief;* the *Porpoise,* a brig of 230 tons which Wilkes had already used in Atlantic coast surveys, and two tiny pilot boats, the *Sea Gull* and the *Flying Fish.*

Nine civilian scientists, whittled down from some thirty applicants by Wilkes, accompanied the expedition. They covered such fields as zoology, conchology, botany, and anthropology, and included two artists. It was a measure of young Wilkes's supreme self-confidence, and his stubbornness, that he turned down Nathaniel Hawthorne, who wanted to go along as historian. Wilkes said he would personally write the history of the cruise. He also personally delegated to himself the departments of physics, surveying, astronomy, and nautical science.

At the last minute, Secretary of the Navy Paulding dealt a final blow to already low morale by ordering what amounted to a very strict censorship. Nobody in the squadron could release information of any kind concerning the objects or the proceedings of the expedition. All specimens of natural history would be preserved, but would become the property of the Navy.

This discouraged the scientists, each of whom had hoped that he could announce important discoveries in his field, and write about them for publication. It discouraged all officers and crewmen who had planned to come back with at least some shells, as souvenirs of the cruise. (It took the Navy many years to learn that the by-line of a well-known scientist or newspaperman was worth a hundred stereotyped news releases made by the Navy Department.)

The squadron touched at Madeira. The supply ship, *Relief,*

had shown herself so slow that Wilkes ordered her to skip *Madeira,* and join up at the Cape Verde Islands, the next port of call. She barely made that rendezvous. A storm blew—it was the hurricane season—and Wilkes did not see the *Peacock* or the *Flying Fish* for some twenty days. Ships' pumps rusted and broke down; the holds were awash; the drinking water turned green and stank and crawled with bugs; the quarters assigned to the scientists were cramped, poorly lighted, and hardly ventilated at all: they brought forth much criticism.

Wilkes put out an order to all his ships: the scientists could wear officers' undress uniform, but all officers and civilians must be clean shaven.

In 1838, an era of luxuriant sideburns and sweeping mustaches, this was another blow at morale. It helped establish Wilkes, a lowly lieutenant, as a petty tyrant. He later bore out the image by flogging a couple of men much beyond the limit authorized other than by a court martial.

Now, when Wilkes entered the harbor of Rio de Janeiro, he found the *U.S.S. Independence,* with Commodore John B. Nicholson aboard. Nicholson had a band, as well as fifty-four guns. He fired a salute, and struck up "Hail Columbia."

He got no answer. Wilkes explained to him later that his chronometers would not stand gunfire, but the Commodore was aggrieved. To make matters worse, Commodore Nicholson later came aboard *Vincennes,* to repay a courtesy call. He wore his medals and his sword—and now young Wilkes really stuck his neck out. He refused to allow Nicholson to come anywhere near his chronometers while wearing that blade of metal. He wrote, later, that the Commodore "was vexed."

Then the supply of bread aboard the expedition's supply ship, *Relief,* became rife with weevils. Commodore Nicholson inspected this, and said that the bread looked good enough for his own people. So Wilkes had all the weevilly bread sent to Nicholson's ship, the *Independence,* and in his own mind, at least, had the last laugh.

[*iv*] After ship repairs in Rio de Janeiro, Wilkes sailed south. It was February 1839—the last month of summer in those latitudes. The voyage had become stormy in more ways than one. Wilkes had bestowed the title of Captain upon Lieutenant Hudson of the *Peacock,* just as he had taken it for himself. Serving under Hudson was Lieutenant Samuel Phillips Lee, a hotheaded and rebellious Virginian, aged twenty-seven.

Lee refused to address Hudson as anything but "Mister"—the proper title for a lieutenant. Wilkes asked Hudson, "Why did you not cut him down?" Then Wilkes moved Lee to the supply ship *Relief,* which was to have little enough glory in the expedition, and shifted ten other officers in the squadron. Later, he had to deal with a mutinous plot in his own ship.

But Lee did all right. He went on to a long and distinguished career in the Navy, remained loyal to the Union, fought bravely at New Orleans and Vicksburg, and was promoted to Rear Admiral in 1870. His crowning glory came posthumously. A destroyer was named for him.

The ships of Wilkes's little squadron fared badly. The *Sea Gull,* with eleven men, was lost on this first brief dash into the ice. The *Flying Fish* was sold in Singapore three years later, and became the opium smuggler *Spec.* Just two years after the Antarctic cruiser, the *Peacock* was wrecked off the Columbia River. *Porpoise* was lost in the China Sea in 1854; *Relief* was sold about 1865, and *Vincennes* was sold at Boston on October 5, 1867, forty-one years after her launching. At least *Vincennes* and *Porpoise* got to serve in the Ringgold expedition to the North Pacific in 1853.

Wilkes's first dash into the Antarctic was short and frustrating. It was too late in the season. He left *Vincennes* at Tierra del Fuego because he felt she was too big to navigate the ice; he went aboard the *Porpoise* as an observer.

The ships got separated in the storms and had to turn back. Hudson took the *Peacock* on around the Horn to Valparaiso, where they were to rendezvous. The store ship *Relief* was missing when Wilkes got back to Tierra del Fuego—but he found her later at Valparaiso, and had five of his original six ships not exactly intact, but at least assembled.

After a month in Valparaiso, Wilkes sailed for Callao, and then to the South Pacific islands. There were still storms not of the weather: at Callao Wilkes flogged two deserters with thirty-six and forty-one lashes respectively, and whipped several other men who got drunk while unloading liquor from the *Relief*, giving these twenty-four lashes. Regulations required that only a court martial could order a flogging of more than twelve lashes, and Wilkes did not convene a court martial. He was to hear about this later.

But if Wilkes was commanding his ships with an iron hand, he was also getting them around. He spent four months in the islands, where a few of the men succumbed to the lure of the tropics and deserted. Then he sailed for Sydney, to outfit for the second trip into the ice. It was on this voyage that one of the scientists tried to persuade the officers to mutiny. Wilkes promptly threatened to maroon the scientists on a desert island, and that ended that.

The ships reached Sydney unannounced, which alarmed the Australians because an enemy could have done the same. But the citizens of the town were very hospitable, and Wilkes and his crews greatly enjoyed their stay while they once more repaired their flimsy vessels. Still, Wilkes was eager to get back to the Antarctic—this time before the summer season ran out. December was the height of summer at the bottom of the world.

They hoisted anchor and sailed the day after Christmas, 1839.

Wilkes had learned that ships were likely to be separated in bad weather, so he wisely established a number of points for rendezvous. Sure enough, a few days later the *Flying Fish* vanished astern. Then the *Peacock* disappeared—and next, the *Porpoise*.

Wilkes finally sighted the *Porpoise* after a heavy fog lifted, only to find that their position was well beyond Macquarie Island, the first rendezvous point. Like Columbus, he sailed on for the next place of rendezvous—Emerald Island.

What a blessing it would have been to have radio! How helpful to have had reliable charts! As far as Wilkes could determine, there was no Emerald Island. The ship Captain who had charted it may have sighted a green iceberg. Icebergs came in various hues.

It was characteristic of the man's courage and determination that he decided to go on toward the ice barrier, although now he had only two ships. On January 11, the *Vincennes* and the *Porpoise* were among huge icebergs, some a mile long, and soon they found themselves hemmed in by ice in what appeared to be large bay.

Wilkes was discouraged. Observations to fix his position showed that he still had not penetrated as far south as Captain Cook. He lost *Porpoise* again in bad weather, and felt very much alone.

But miracles happen more often on the sea than on the land. *Porpoise* was actually not far away, and both ships were hunting for an open lead in the ice that would take them south. Neither had given up. On January 15, *Porpoise* sighted a sail; it was the *Peacock*, missing for nearly two weeks.

The thrill of discovery came to *Peacock* and *Porpoise* at about the same time. It also happened to Wilkes, apart from them. All three ships sighted what appeared to be mountains: dark masses, in contrast to the light-colored icebergs. There were three of them, but they were a long way across the ice barrier. Under date of January 16, Wilkes charted the mountains, claimed the discovery of the land, and loyally named the mountains for officers in his squadron—Reynolds' Peak, Eld's Peak, and Ringgold's Knoll.

There was still another miracle in the form of tricky atmospherics. Next day, Wilkes plainly sighted a ship not far away, and fired a gun that brought no response. The other vessel disappeared. It was found later that *Peacock* had been nowhere near the *Vincennes,* but that Wilkes had seen her reflection on a cloud!

[*v*]   *Peacock*, which had always been the least seaworthy of the group, was hammered by floating masses of ice that damaged her rudder. Out of control, she rammed an iceberg and barely escaped being sunk by a huge mass of ice and snow that broke away from the top of the berg: only her own recoil from the collison saved her by a few yards.

Lieutenant Hudson showed, then, that he deserved the title of Captain. He made full sail, while his men worked on the rudder; he found a channel, and drove the almost unmanageable ship through it to the open sea. Then he headed for Sydney again. The *Peacock*'s Antarctic explorations were over.

Wilkes did not know about this. He was still sighting land, but could not reach it. He named Disappointment Bay. A gale struck, with driving snow; the entire weather decks of the ship were soon top-heavy with ice, and she was in great peril. Next day, the weather cleared, and Wilkes came within a half-mile of the land.

Wilkes wrote in his log: "I make this bay in longitude 140 degrees two minutes and 30 seconds E., latitude 66 degrees, 45 minutes S., and now that all were convinced of its existence, I gave the land the name of the Antarctic Continent."

This was his hour of triumph. He had proved what he set out to prove—that there was a vast land mass in the Antarctic. The French later disputed his claim to discovery, and argued that their d'Urville expedition had sighted the land first. An amusing anachronism had occurred, comparable to what happens when one fails to set back the clock for the switch from daylight saving time to standard time; d'Urville had failed to change his calendar by a day when he crossed the International Date Line.

Wilkes was first. He wanted to push on, but he had many men on the sick list, and so he reluctantly steered a course for Sydney.

Meanwhile, the *Porpoise* made her way out of the ice and reached the Bay of Islands, in New Zealand. There, to the delight of her crew, they found the *Flying Fish*, which gallantly enough had taken her solitary way into the ice after being separated from the other ships. She had many adventures, and much trouble; when the *Porpoise* found her, only four able-bodied men were aboard.

On March 30, 1840, the entire expedition joined up at the Bay of Islands, except for *Peacock*, which was being repaired at Sydney. They sailed seven days later for milder climes—up through the Pacific islands to Hawaii. The epic was ended.

Wilkes went on to extensive explorations in the Pacific. He attained the rank of Commodore in 1862, and was advanced to that of Rear Admiral after his retirement. Wilkes Land, in the Antarctic, commemorates his accomplishments there.

But, being Navy, he probably would have liked his final honors best of all. The first *Wilkes*, named for him, was Torpedo Boat 35. The second was an early destroyer, DD 67. The third was a modern destroyer, DD 441.

_17._ COMMODORE PERRY
AND THE
BAMBOO CURTAIN

> We pray God that our present attempt to
> bring a singular and isolated people into the
> family of civilized nations may succeed without
> resort to bloodshed.
> —_Perry's_ Journal, _9 July, 1853_

MATTHEW CALBRAITH PERRY was a man of parts. He
began his naval career under the handicap of being the younger
and undistinguished brother of Oliver Hazard Perry, the hero of
Lake Erie in 1812. But he went on stubbornly (stubbornness was
one of his principal traits) until he had finally outdistanced
Oliver Hazard in all but combat action, and had become even
more famous—mainly in the field of international diplomacy.

Before this happened, young Perry had already made a name
for himself by being a gadfly in the hide of the somewhat com-
placent Navy Department. He was a good man with a pen, and
as early as 1824 he wrote letters to the Navy Department suggesting that the Navy recruiting methods were all wrong, and urging
that an apprentice program be set up to get boys into the Navy,
and then train them. He thought every ship of the line should
take 300 apprentices—aged fourteen and up—to sea.

Also in 1824, Perry, who was then First Lieutenant of the
U.S.S. _North Carolina_, spelled out some cardinal rules for first

lieutenants which are still applicable today. The *North Carolina* was quite a ship: she had 102 guns, her main truck was 225 feet above the water line, and she carried 832 men. Perry's rules for the first lieutenant were:

A prompt, cheerful and unconditional obedience to all lawful orders.

An equal determination to enforce obedience from juniors.

A perfect command of temper, and a kind of respectful deportment to all, whether senior or junior.

A parental interest and regard for the improvement and welfare of the Midshipmen; and an equal regard for the health comfort and cheerfulness of the Crew.

A patient and unevinced industry; and, last of all, a disinclination to leave the Ship.

Perry was also to become known as the father of the steamship Navy, because of his insistence that sailing vessels be replaced by steamships. Before he went on to his historic voyage to open Japan, he was severely tried because of what happened aboard a ship in his squadron—the U.S.S. *Somers.*

Somers was a brig, and a beautiful ship that could outsail almost anything on the sea in 1842. Perhaps unfortunately, her captain, Alexander Slidell Mackenzie, was Perry's brother-in-law. Perry's son, Lieutenant Matthew C. Perry, Jr., was aboard as Acting Master; he was only twenty-one, but had already been in the Navy for eight years. Another son, Oliver H. Perry II, seventeen, named after his distinguished uncle, was also in *Somers* as the captain's clerk.

The *Somers* was the scene of an attempted mutiny. The case was severely complicated by the fact that the author of the mutinous plot was Midshipman Philip Spencer, nineteen, who happened to be the son of the Secretary of War, then John Canfield Spencer.

Midshipman Spencer had obtained his appointment through political connections, and not through any qualifications—and this was the thing Perry had just begun fighting. In addition, Spencer seems to have been a punk. Quite understandably, he had been given kid-glove treatment, because nobody wanted bad reports about the Navy going back to the Secretary of War.

My Love Affair with the Navy

Spencer had been thrown out of Hobart College; there they remembered that he was fond of reading books on piracy, and that he said he was going to become a pirate.

Well, now was his chance . . .

Commodore Perry had just spent several years putting down pirates and slave ships, and was not inclined to deal kindly with either. Spencer got into trouble several times during his first years in the Navy, but always used his father's influence to get out of it. When he was ordered to the *Somers* after a bad record in a couple of other ships, Captain Mackenzie refused him. Then, characteristically, Spencer went over Mackenzie's head and appealed to Perry. Perry put Spencer on board, hoping that discipline would straighten him out, and not wanting to incur the displeasure of Washington.

This was a mistake, indeed. Young Spencer began plotting to commit one of the most bloodthirsty crimes in all history. He had everything figured out in the minutest detail. In his favor was the fact that 70 per cent of the crew of *Somers*—Commodore Perry's first cadet ship—was made up of young men or boys. There were seventy-four apprentice boys aboard, many of them only fourteen.

Spencer selected his associates with an expertise that indicated he could have gone far in a trade less dangerous than piracy. His first tentative, joking whispers were with Samuel Cromwell, a boatswain's mate, past thirty. And then with Elisha Small, about the same age, the captain of the main top. Both Cromwell and Small had served in the slave trade before joining the Navy, and therefore knew considerable about piracy. How Spencer learned this has not been revealed. With these two, Spencer ultimately cut in on the plot the purser's steward, James W. Wales.

This proved his undoing. Spencer thought Wales would go along with the mutiny, because he had had some trouble with Captain Mackenzie. But Wales remained loyal, and tipped the Captain off as soon as he could get a private hearing—which wasn't easy.

But for Wales, the plot might well have succeeded. It was simple and murderous, and based on the pirate thesis that dead men tell no tales. When the *Somers* was nearing St. Thomas, with the Captain below and Spencer on watch, Cromwell and Small would start a mock fight on the foc'sle. Spencer would then go below and kill Mackenzie. With the help of Cromwell and Small, he would then invade the wardroom, catch the other officers off guard, and murder them. Then he would muster all hands on deck, choose a few men who could be counted upon to go along with him, and throw the others—including all the boys—over the side.

Then the *Somers* would be sailed to the Isle of Pines, a notorious pirates' rendezvous, would recruit more men, and enter the piracy trade to plunder and sink merchant vessels. Spencer even spelled out what was to happen to the merchant crews: all would be killed. Any women aboard would be put into the *Somers'* brig for the officers and men to use as long as they wanted—and then they, too, would be silenced by death.

[*ii*] Once in possession of Wales's story, Mackenzie had Spencer up on the quarterdeck. Spencer admitted having talked to Wales, but said it was all a joke. Mackenzie told him that such a joke could cost him his life, and that "it will be necessary for me to confine you, sir." (The "sir" to a young punk of warped and disordered mentality seems to have been laying on naval courtesy a bit thick, but Mackenzie was a stickler for that sort of thing.)

Spencer was put in irons, chained to the bulwarks, and handcuffed. Officers of the deck were ordered to shoot him if he tried to get any word to the crew.

They searched Spencer's sea chest and found some very incriminating papers, written in Greek. Midshipman Henry Rodgers (*Rodgers* is one of the most famous names in the Navy!) translated these easily enough. They listed the names of more than thirty men who probably would go along with the plot. That meant that something over eighty had to be killed.

Cromwell and Small were next arrested. Later, four more men were ironed. Mackenzie found that there was an increasing insubordination on the part of his crew, and began to fear that he could not make port unless decisive action were taken.

There was no court martial. Instead, Mackenzie asked a board of officers to take evidence, and study the case. The answer was unanimous: Spencer, Cromwell, and Small were guilty of having determined to commit mutiny. There was no ship to deliver them to the United States for trial: it was not known how many others in the crew were disaffected, and mutiny was punishable by death.

Mackenzie acted promptly. The three men had time for prayers and Bible reading. Spencer fell on his knees and wept; Cromwell tried to jump over the side; Small went to his death bravely, and said "God bless that flag! . . . Now, fellow topmen, give me a quick death." An execution gun was fired, the colors were lowered, Mackenzie read the burial service for the dead at sea—and three bodies were hanging dark against the sky from the yardarms.

Mackenzie was later tried—and acquitted—for what seemed to some people very highhanded action. The worst effects of the incident were suffered by Commodore Perry. It set back the cadet and training program he had advocated by about a dozen years.

Meanwhile he had another job to do.

[*iii*] In 1852, Perry was fifty-eight years old. He had heavy jowls, was inclined toward corpulence, and walked with a deep-sea roll, not unlike a bear. This, and his bellowing voice, had earned him the sobriquet of "Old Bruin," a name used fully as much in affection as in derision.

In the years since the *Somers* incident, he had added greatly to his fame, first by exploits against pirates and slavers as commander of the African Squadron, and then by brilliant victories in the war with Mexico.

He wanted command of the Navy's Mediterranean Squadron,

and perhaps he did not want to go to the Pacific, which he had never seen. But his penchant for writing letters now got him on the hook: in 1851 he had written the Secretary of the Navy suggesting that an expedition should be sent to Japan to open commercial relations with that country, self-isolated for more than two hundred years against the "western barbarians."

Perry wrote the letter, and Perry got the job, which he didn't want.

No naval commander in his right mind would have wanted to lead the expedition. Perry's task would have been far more simple if he had been ordered to bombard and invade the Japanese island. As it was, he had to use diplomacy, tact, and persuasion, and while he had to do this at gunpoint, no blood was shed. He also had to put on a virtual three-ring circus for the edification of his Japanese audiences.

Observers of the highly industrialized complex that is Japan today find it difficult to picture the Japan of some 115 years ago. Now, the Japanese lead the world in production of such small technical marvels as cameras, optical instruments, and transistor radios. They go on up the scale to motorcycles, and to the new Honda automobile—it carries four persons, has a top speed of seventy-two miles per hour, and gets sixty-five miles on a single gallon of gasoline! Still farther up the scale, in size, not quantity, Japanese shipyards have launched ships much bigger than those built in the United States, or anywhere else.

As this is written, the Japanese-built *Universe Ireland,* a tanker, has sailed from Yokohama to Kuwait, on her maiden voyage. This is the largest ship in the world: she is a staggering 312,000 deadweight tons. (Remember that our huge battleships displaced only 60,000 tons.) It cost $20,000,000 to build her at the shipyard of Ishikawajima-Harima Heavy Industries.

It is not too much to say that Matthew Calbraith Perry started all this, and not only started it, but prophesied that the time would come when Japan would actively compete with America for the world's trade. It is not too much to say, either, that Perry unwittingly sowed the seeds that eventually produced the attack on Pearl Harbor.

Therefore, the Perry expedition remains the most historically important bit of exploration the Navy has ever undertaken, up to its present scientific onslaughts on space and the great depths of the seas.

In 1853, the Japanese knew nothing about the electric telegraph. They had not a single steam engine, stationary or mobile. None of their ships were larger than the fifty-foot fishing junks. They could not forge steel to make any kind of modern firearms; their earthen forts were armed with ancient iron guns. The Bamboo Curtain was so complete that no Japanese ship was permitted to have any communication with vessels from the outside world. When a Japanese junk was wrecked on any alien shore, its crew was forbidden to return to Japan, for fear that they might bring in new thoughts.

Therefore, Perry's main problem was not in reaching Japan, but in reaching the Oriental mind, with its concern about "saving face," or "losing face."

It was a fantastic situation, the same kind that led to an amusing incident later, in the days when Navy gunboats patrolled the Yangtze River. An American warship was sent to a Chinese port to obtain redress and apology for some outrage that had been committee against American citizens. The ship's Commander—he was probably a lieutenant—sent a boat ashore with the word that his instructions were in two parts.

The first part was that he was to give the Chinese authorities twenty-four hours in which to make the required reparation. He waited twenty-three hours. Nothing happened. Then he sent another boat ashore with the word that since the time limit was almost up, and nothing had been done, in another hour he would regretfully be compelled to comply with the second portion of his orders.

Immediately, a Chinese boat came out with the local mandarin, and the stipulated reparations were paid on the spot. As the mandarin was leaving the ship, he stopped at the gangway, and said: "By the way, Captain, what was the second portion of your orders?"

"Oh," the Captain said, "if my demands were not complied with in twenty-four hours, I was to depart and take no further action in the matter."

This was a splendid example of the perfect poker face, in the international card game called diplomacy . . .

[iv] It took time and money to organize and equip the Perry Expedition. He was ordered to command what was called the East India Squadron, early in 1852. He was told he could pick his own officers, and that he would be provided funds to buy presents for the Japanese. He was promised twelve ships, but the Navy was running short of cash, and it didn't turn out that way.

Perry flew his Commodore's pendant in the barque-rigged side-wheeler *Susquehanna;* her sister ship *Powhatan* was also in his squadron. Originally, he set out with two other steamers, *Princeton* and *Allegheny,* but they developed engine trouble, and had to be left behind. This was too bad, because the Japanese had never seen steamships before, and were very much impressed with what they called the "Black Ships." Perry had four sailing ships, sloops of war: *Macedonian, Saratoga, Plymouth,* and *Vandalia.*

The problem of making a peaceful approach to Japan in those days was exactly the same as that of making a hostile approach in World War II, although a little—but not too much—safer. The approach had to be made from island to island, so that bases could be set up. One of the main objectives of the expedition was to establish coaling stations on these island, which would be of great value to merchant ships cruising to China. In opening Japan, Perry would in effect be opening China as well.

Someone understood the Oriental mind well enough to know that the Greeks should come bearing gifts. Perry took along Audubon's folios of *Birds of America,* and his *Quadrupeds of America*—a wise choice, indeed. The folios cost $1000 each. He took a barrel of whiskey and cases of champagne; he carried

French perfume for the ladies, and a set of pistols donated by Mr. Samuel Colt, himself. Thus Colt helped open another frontier, besides the American West, with his Peacemaker.

Preparations took months. At last, Perry was ready to sail. He had been given full powers to negotiate, conclude, and sign a convention or treaty. He had with him a letter to the Emperor, signed, "Your good friend, Millard Fillmore." It called for humane treatment of American whaleships' crews that might be shipwrecked on Japanese islands, and asked for the right for ships to buy coal or water. (A little earlier, Daniel Webster had helped spark the expedition by saying the coal was "a gift of Providence deposited by the Creator . . . in the depths of the Japanese islands for the benefit of the human family.")

Perry's job was to deliver President Fillmore's letter, in an inlaid rosewood casket, to the Emperor. He showed his stubbornness again when he declared he would not deliver it to any minor official. This was very wise.

[*v*] Perry showed excellent judgment when he selected as one of his officers Lieutenant George Henry Preble, of the *Macedonian*. Preble, who went on to become a Rear Admiral, had a literary bent, and was enough of an individualist to ignore the order that no journals or diaries were to be written except that of Perry, himself. Preble faithfully kept a diary in the form of letters to his wife, and these, fortunately, have been preserved.

He was a good reporter, with an eye for the unusual. He chronicled, for instance, the case of the sailmaker's mate who turned into his hammock something more than half seas over, and swallowed some false teeth. He nearly choked to death, and was black in the face when the doctor was called. The surgeon managed to reach the bridgework with his finger—but dentures of that time being what they were, the teeth had become detached from it.

It was too bad that Preble was in *Macedonian*, and not in the flagship with Perry. Otherwise, we surely would have many more salty personal anecdotes about "Old Bruin." When Preble published the letters to his wife, a few years later, the twenty-one officers in *Macedonian* had met various fates: the Captain and his son were among five who died; three later fought for the Confederacy; two were "Lost in the Levant"; and one "Run at Manila, Aug., 1854"—in other words, deserted.

To the excited and frightened Japanese who lined the shores of what Preble calls "Jeddo Bay" (Yedo Bay), the visitors must have appeared like creatures from another planet. Their ships breathed smoke, and bristled with guns; their dress was nothing like the kimono. But everything was done to assure the Japanese that the mission was peaceful.

Perry delivered two personal messages to the envoys of the Emperor, the first on 7 July, 1853, requesting personal handling of President Fillmore's letter; the second, a week later, when he gave Fillmore's letter to two Japanese nobles, Lord Toda of Iwami and Lord Ito of Izu. Then, knowing that Oriental diplomatic negotiations were not accomplished in a hurry, he discreetly retired. His ships were scattered from Portuguese Macao to Whampoa, Hong Kong, and Shanghai.

He waited until March of 1854 to return, with his whole squadron, and get the answer.

When the ships came back next March, Perry anchored in the Bay of Tokyo, which he optimistically called "Treaty Bay." The squadron was not received with as much ceremony as it had been on the first visit, and this disturbed the Americans until the Japanese explained: on the first visit, the "Black Ships" were regarded as enemies . . . on the second visit, they were regarded as friends!

It turned out that the Japanese had a sense of humor, after all. They laughed gleefully as they told a story about the Russians, with whom they had just refused to sign a treaty. While the Russians were at Nagasaki, they built a fort, which was wrecked by a typhoon. Its big guns went floating out to sea—having been made of wood.

Perry's people now put on a show. They set up some railroad

track of very narrow gauge, and sent their miniature steam locomotive puffing along it, hauling delighted Japanese dignitaries. They sent and received telegraph messages, and subjected a few Japanese to minor and harmless electrical shocks. They entertained Japanese Commissioners aboard ship with banquets and band concerts.

One Commissioner was so delighted that he threw his arms around Commodore Perry's neck and hugged him. Somebody said to the Commodore that he shouldn't stand for that. But, according to Preble's diary, "Oh," said old Perry, "if he will only sign the Treaty, he may kiss me!"

Meanwhile, the Japanese reciprocated by putting on some shows of their own. They paraded troupes of *sumo* (pronounced s'mo) wrestlers, and it was the Americans' turn to be amazed. For a race of ordinarily small physical stature, the wrestlers were surprising. They weighed two hundred pounds or more, and were prodigiously strong. It was all the more surprising to be told that almost any Japanese lad could grow up to be a sumo wrestler, through what amounted to force feeding—he was required to eat, and eat, and then eat some more.

The Treaty Matthew Calbraith Perry was after was signed on 31 March, 1854. Preble wrote:

> Eureka! It is finished! The great agony is over! In vulgar parlance, the egg has hatched its chicken today. The Treaty of Amity and Friendship between Japan and the United States was signed today to the satisfaction of everybody. Even Old Bruin would smile if only he knew how to smile.

So it was done, and Japan was opened to the scientific and technological advances of the western world. And what happened?

A scant fifty years later, Teddy Roosevelt sent the Great White Fleet around the world. When the U.S. warships dropped anchor off Japan, a Japanese warship moved up to face each of them.

The Japanese had learned that fast. They moved on toward Pearl Harbor.

18. THE U.S. NAVY
KEEPS THE PEACE

Sea power is essential to the security of our
Nation. The mobility and versatility of our naval
forces manifested each day are a constant re-
minder to any aggressor that this country has the
means to act quickly and decisively to protect
the interests of the United States and the Free
World. Paradoxically, the powerful U.S. Navy is
a symbol of peace . . . The dedicated men serving in Navy Blue . . . safeguard the peace and
freedom of the world and the future of the American way of life.
—*President Lyndon B. Johnson, 1965*

PRESIDENT JOHNSON'S words are more true today than when
he spoke them. Even then the thought and the conviction were
not new. In 1776, stout Paul Jones wrote, "Without a Respectable
Navy—Alas America!"

But you can go back much farther than John Paul Jones.
Cicero, in his *Letters*, observed that "He who commands the sea
has command of everything."

A landsman may ask why sea power is so important. The answer is simply that the oceans of the world are broad and unlimited highways that never need repair or maintenance. The answer
today is that despite the marvelous improvement and growth of
air transport, surface vessels—Navy warships and Navy-protected
merchant ships—supply some 90 per cent of the need in Vietnam
for men, vehicles, beans, and bullets.

My Love Affair with the Navy

There have been many times in which the U.S. Navy kept the peace without having to fire a shot. It had only to show the American Flag, and let the belligerent know that there was plenty of force behind it.

John Paul Jones sailed the frigate *Ranger* into Quiberon Bay, France, away back on St. Valentine's Day in 1778, flying the new Stars and Stripes. Jones knew his protocol. He fired a 13-gun salute to the French warships present—the traditional salute for a monarchy. To his delight, the French squadron responded with nine guns—which was the top honors rendered to free republics. This was the first signal of recognition of American independence.

Tough times lay ahead, and our infant Republic learned the hard way. After the surrender of Cornwallis at Yorktown, America let her Navy dwindle, and then sold it. Soon afterward, the merchant ships upon which we depended so much were attacked and captured by privateers, and particularly by the Barbary corsairs. It became necessary, a few years later, to build another U.S. Navy. These new ships included the *Constellation* and the *Constitution,* both of glorious history . . . and both still proudly afloat.

After the War of 1812, there were pirates in the Caribbean, and buccaneers who sailed out of South American ports. They kept the small U.S. Navy busy from Florida to Cape Horn, protecting American merchantmen upon their lawful occasions. The Navy had to release American merchant crews that had been imprisoned in Chile and other countries. It accomplished this by a show of force, *but without using force,* which is diplomacy at its best and most dramatic. At the same time, it fought a fearful and tragic battle with the tropical fevers of those Caribbean islands and their mangrove swamps.

The Navy even established and supported a free nation in darkest Africa. It was the leader in helping to form Liberia, on the African coast. Slave ships were cruising busily around 1820. The U.S.S. *Cyane,* sailing the African coast that year, captured seven slave ships and freed their "passengers." For the next forty years, Navy ships patrolled the African trade routes, and seized more than a hundred ships carrying slaves.

This was indeed showing the American Flag in a good and noble light.

And the U.S. Navy was learning by doing. In its war with the pirates, it seems to have been the first Navy in the world to use a steam-propelled ship on combat duty: the converted harbor tug *Sea Gull* raised havoc with pirate ships that were becalmed, and paved the way for other steam vessels.

The Army is committed overseas only in years of war or occupation, but the Navy is committed all the time. In the 1880's—without a war—the Navy successfully confronted both Britain and Germany in Samoa, to protect American interests in those islands. All three countries sent warships. In the midst of this tense situation, the great Samoan hurricane of 1889 struck.

U.S.S. *Trenton,* our flagship, was among the vessels lost. The British *Calliope* narrowly made it out of the harbor, passing *Trenton.* The *Calliope's* captain wrote that as he passed *Trenton,*

which was lying helpless, with nothing to guard her from complete destruction, the American Admiral and his men gave us three such ringing cheers that they called forth tears from many of our eyes. They pierced deep into my heart, and I will ever remember that mighty outburst of fellow feeling which I felt came from the bottom of the hearts of the noble and gallant Admiral and her noble sailors. If the Americans stand as nobly to their guns, as they bravely faced that tremendous hurricane, the United States need fear nothing.

A case of "We who are about to die salute you." Few of the men, if any, survived.

The Navy had to get tough now and then, and it did. Soon after Commodore George Dewey whipped the Spanish fleet in Manila Bay, England, Germany, and Japan all sent warships there. The German Admiral had five ships. He chose to ignore the blockade Dewey had set up, and was trafficking with both Spaniards and Filipinos still fighting ashore. Dewey ignored the German's senior rank, and sent a message: "Does Admiral von Diedricks think he commands here or do I? Tell your Admiral if he wants war I am ready."

My Love Affair with the Navy

End of trouble. Years later, Theodore Roosevelt gave a beautiful thumbnail character sketch of George Dewey, when he said, "Dewey was the greatest possible provocative of peace."

A Navy in wartime is an acknowledged necessity. A Navy in peace time can do a great deal to promote and prolong the peace.

Our Navy sent sixteen battleships and some other vessels around the world late in 1907, to show the American Flag. This was popularly called The Great White Fleet, and it impressed people wherever it went. It was significant that talk of war died down.

The Navy was prompt in bringing aid to Japan after the devastating earthquake, fires, and tidal wave of 1923. Its help was so significant that it is still difficult to comprehend the switch in the Japanese attitude that produced Pearl Harbor. Nevertheless, I can personally testify that after the Japanese surrender in 1945, many individual Japanese remembered how "kindly" America was to them during the earthquake troubles.

Let's take a look at an official Navy Department summary of what the Navy has done in the past twenty years, all over the world, toward keeping the peace:

1946—The Navy task force, including carrier *Franklin D. Roosevelt*, went to Athens to bolster the Greek government and check Communism. The Greek Foreign Minister said, "The sea stands for freedom of every human soul; to us it stands for life itself."

1948–49—Twenty-four Navy planes participated in the famous Berlin Airlift, flying 45,990 hours, carrying 129,989 tons of supplies to the beleaguered city. Meanwhile, Navy ships transported enormous quantities of supplies and the fuel for the airlift.

1950–55—Large naval forces projected massed allied strength overseas to sustain South Korea, maintain control of the seas for assault or retirement, provide powerful air and gunfire bombardment and unrestricted logistic support, mobility, speed, and flexibility in combined operations—thus containing the war and ensuring the peace.

The U.S. Navy Keeps the Peace

1954—The U.S. Navy provided a "Passage to Freedom" for more than 300,000 refugees from North Vietnam to the south.

1955—At the request of the Republic of China, units of the Seventh Fleet evacuated troops, civilians, and tons of material from the Tachen Islands off the China mainland. The impressive power of the fleet discouraged any idea of Communist interference.

1956—When the Suez–Middle-East crisis became critical, Sixth Fleet ships evacuated American and allied nationals. An evacuee wrote: "We never realized how much the Flag meant to us until we saw it on the sterns of the landing craft."

1957—In April and May the Sixth Fleet deployed in the Eastern Mediterranean to support Jordan's King Hussein and avert world disaster. An official there said, "Jordan . . . has been saved for Western Civilization by Bedouin knives and the Sixth Fleet."

1958—At the request of the Lebanese government, the Sixth Fleet landed 1,800 Marines on a beach near Beirut, with ships' guns trained on shore targets and carrier planes overhead. Another grateful official said, "In the powerful gray diplomats of the Sixth Fleet, we see the guarantee of small peoples' independence."

1960—The governments of Guatamala and Nicaragua requested help against an expected invasion. Navy surface and air units were supplied. Their presence discouraged the would-be invaders, and another tense situation was eased.

1960–61—Violence erupted in the Congo. Atlantic Fleet units sped to the African Coast. They included the carrier Wasp, and transported both United Nations troops and supplies to prevent starvation. The Navy and United Nations mission balked Communist domination of this key African country.

1961—Navy task forces began a long-term buildup strength in South Vietnam.

1961—When the East German Communists erected the Berlin Wall, the Navy activated Reserve ships and men to meet any crisis.

1962—On October 24, air and surface units of the Atlantic

Fleet established the Quarantine of Cuba to force withdrawal of Soviet Ballistic missiles. (This was probably the most dramatic eyeball-to-eyeball confrontation we have ever had with Russia.) Power afloat succeeded: the missiles were withdrawn.

1963—The Dominican Republic threatened to invade Haiti. The U.S. Navy promptly went to the scene, and the crisis subsided.

1964—There was a political crisis in Zanzibar. U.S.S. *Manley* guarded American citizens and interests, and evacuated American and allied nationals.

1964—U.S.S. *Maddox* and U.S.S. *Turner Joy,* are destroyed attacking North Vietnamese PT boats in the Gulf of Tonkin. Planes from U.S.S. *Ticonderoga* and U.S.S. *Constellation* hit North Vietnamese bases, destroying many of their PT boats.

1965—Dominican Republic revolutionaries ran wild. Ships of the Second Fleet, including the carrier *Boxer,* landed both Marines and Army forces in Santo Domingo. These evacuated U.S. nationals, kept law and order, and prevented a Communist coup.

1967—War erupts again in the Middle East, the third time since World War II. The Sixth Fleet still exerts a strong and stabilizing influence against Soviet aims in this strategic area.

1968—You name it, and read your newspapers. The Navy is always ready, and on hand . . . .

19. VIETNAM—WAR ON
THE RIVERS

Seapower's first advantage to the United
States is that it keeps the enemy's main forces
overseas. It controls the oceans for our use, de-
nies them to the foe, and makes his coasts the
frontier of war rather than those of America.

Nor does seapower stop at the hostile coastline; it projects the Nation's total power in a re-
sistless tide inland beyond the coast. The long
arm of seapower reaches inland with guns, with
planes, with missiles like Polaris, and wherever
water will float a boat. * * * Operations inland
on restricted waters have come to be called "riverine warfare."

—*Rear Admiral E. M. Eller, U.S. Navy (retired),*
Director of Naval History

SALT-WATER SAILORS hate fresh water, especially in the
warm rivers of such places as Vietnam. Marine growths flourish,
and all kinds of organisms attach themselves to the hull. The bottom becomes foul much sooner than if the ship were cruising in
the cold salt sea.

But war is war, and the U.S. Navy is nothing if not versatile.
Therefore we have "riverine warfare" in Vietnam today.

Not many Americans have heard the term "riverine warfare,"
and yet it is far from being new. Benedict Arnold practiced it on
Lake Champlain in 1775. (Arnold was a good man until, in the
words of a Texas history student, he "sold his saddle.") Oliver
Hazard Perry's battle on Lake Erie in 1813 was riverine warfare;

235

so was Commodore Joshua Barney's defense of Chesapeake Bay a year later. And so was David Glasgow Farragut's transit of some 110 miles of the Mississippi River, in 1862, to capture New Orleans.

Riverine warfare is beset with navigational hazards. The charts do not cover the shallow waters, there are shifting currents and unknown rapids. Always there is the danger of ambush and attack from enemy guns hidden somewhere along the banks.

For riverine warfare to be successful in the first place, the fleet using it must control the high seas adjacent to the mouths of the rivers: otherwise, the riverine force could easily be bottled up, cut off from supplies, and made to surrender.

There is something terribly romantic about rivers, and perhaps this romanticism can extend to the inland lakes of America, where decisive naval engagements were fought in the Revolutionary War. It was remarkable that the British were able to build a fleet of twenty-nine vessels at St. John's, Newfoundland. This may have been the first use of prefabrication; some of the ships had been built in England, then knocked down and reassembled at St. John's.

Benedict Arnold was a sailor before he turned soldier. At the southern end of Lake Champlain, he had a new type of gondola built, a small craft that would be fast under either sail or oar. The timber was green and was still weeping pine pitch when Arnold led fifteen of these American ships into battle west of Valcour Island.

It was fifteen against twenty-nine, and the British ships were heavier, with considerably more fire power. Nevertheless, the fight was close. It raged all afternoon on 11 October, 1776. Arnold had wisely positioned his ships where they had the advantage of the wind gauge. He inflicted a great deal of damage on the enemy, but superior weight of metal told, and his ships were pretty badly cut up. That night was foggy with a north wind; Arnold took advantage of the weather and made a daring escape through the anchored British squadron.

The British gave chase next day, and began to overhaul Arnold's force, capturing the ships or running them aground. Arnold got back to Ticonderoga on 14 October with only six ships out of fifteen, and some eighty men killed. It was a temporary victory. The battle served to delay the British southward advance for a year, giving America time to build up an army strong enough to whip Burgoyne at Saratoga.

In 1813, Commodore Oliver Hazard Perry fought a little riverine warfare on Lake Erie. Another shipbuilding race ensured before the battle—and before Perry's immortal message: "We have met the enemy and they are ours . . ."

[*ii*] Joshua Barney, the lad who took command of a merchant ship at fifteen, was about to be heard from again in that war. Barney came up with a plan to defend the river approaches to Washington, and it was quickly adopted. There was more hasty construction. In April 1814, Barney was able to sail on a shakedown cruise from Baltimore, with 550 men in ten barges, the cutter *Scorpion,* and gunboat No. 138. On 1 June, he attacked and routed a British scouting force. He fought like a fox against the superior enemy force, striking and then retreating up rivers and inlets.

In the long run, despite some brilliant delaying actions and despite his personal gallantry and efficiency, Joshua Barney was whipped and had to blow up his little ships. The British came on in and burned Washington.

There was other riverine fighting in that War of 1812, in the waterways around New Orleans—and with happier results. There followed a great deal of riverine warfare against the pirates of the 1820's and later. The Navy learned things in riverine operations in the swampy waters of the Everglades, more than a hundred years ago, that stand it in good stead today in Vietnam. The similarity of methods is striking.

Let me quote from the Naval History Division's essay on Riverine Warfare:

> The similarity of seapower in a riverine environment in the Seminole Wars and Vietnam is vivid. First, the fundamental goal

was control of waterways to reestablish internal order and restore normal activity. Secondly, the waterways were not only restricted waters in every sense, but they criscrossed the soil so completely that land transportation was totally inadequate and the character of the neighboring terrain became paramount. The absolute dependence of Navy upon Army and Army upon Navy gave the whole force a homogeneous character of a single tactical entity closely integrated and interdependent. . . .

The Civil War, as fought afloat, was almost entirely a riverine war—with the exception of such Confederate commerce raiders as Raphael Semmes' C.S.S. *Alabama,* which sailed in all oceans to destroy Union ships. The North instituted a 3000-mile blockade of Southern ports, from the Chesapeake around the Florida peninsula, and on to Brownsville, Texas. Northern warships went up the Mississippi to split the South in two; they went as far as the junction of the Ohio and Mississippi rivers . . . to Cairo, Illinois, and Belmont, Missouri. In the latter place their fire support enabled Ulysses S. Grant to reembark his outnumbered troops and withdraw. They assaulted Fort Henry, on the Tennessee River.

The historic sea battle between *Merrimac* and *Monitor* was nothing compared to the fight on the rivers. It should be remembered that Farragut's victory in the Battle of Mobile Bay was won in inland waters, and that the year-long siege of Vicksburg was ended not by land, but by riverine warfare.

At the end of the war, Abraham Lincoln observed:

> Nor must Uncle Sam's web feet be forgotten. At all the watery margins they have been present. Not only on the deep sea, the broad bay, the rapid river, but also up the narrow muddy bayou, and wherever the ground was a little damp, they have been and made their tracks.

The Civil War is usually thought of in terms of Gettysburg and other land battles. Actually, it saw more amphibious warfare than any other conflict up to that time. It was one of the greatest amphibious wars in all history.

[*iii*] What about modern times? From the turn of the century, when there was fighting on the rivers both in the Philippine Insurrection and the Boxer Rebel-

lion, we went on to a fabled and fabulous operation known as the Yangtze Patrol.

Old-timers can tell you fascinating stories of the Yangtze Patrol. During the 1920's and 1930's, shallow draft gunboats went 1500 miles up that treacherous stream to guard American lives and property in revolution-torn China. Landing parties had to be readied at an instant's notice. The water level in the river fell as much as twenty-four feet in as many hours; navigation was difficult, and different classes of Chinese—from war lords to petty bandits—were always trigger happy. Still, the bluejackets got ashore on occasion for liberty, and a story persists that two of them sold their ship, one alcoholic evening, to an ambitious war lord—and collected good Hong Kong gold for it. There is no evidence that the story is true.

Even World War II saw some highly important riverine warfare, which has been overshadowed by more momentous affairs. In March 1945, five U.S. Armies crossed the Rhine in a spectacular riverine operation staged by the Navy. Some fifty thousand troops, thousands of vehicles, and pieces of ordnance were put over the river in seventy-two hours. Nothing in this operation gave any visual credit to the Navy: the men all wore Army field uniforms, the boats had all been painted olive drab. Even the soldiers did not know the Navy was assisting them, and most correspondents missed a good story.

In some ways, we are an innocent, trusting, unsophisticated nation, wide-eyed and ready to believe the best of anybody. Hence we first went to Vietnam thinking that we were merely supporting the liberty of South Vietnam against the encroachment of North Vietnam. It would seem that we did not at first know that we were facing the entire Communist world.

As it is today, unfortunately enough, the Communists retain the initiative. Until we destroy that initiative, and seize it for ourselves, the Vietnam war can go on indefinitely.

We have control of the sea around Vietnamese inland waters. Inland, on the rivers, a guerrilla warfare is being waged. The late President Kennedy described it as:

> . . . another type of warfare—new in intensity, ancient in its origin . . . war by guerrillas, subversives, insurgents, assassins . . . war by ambush instead of aggression . . . seeking victory by eroding and exhausting the enemy instead of engaging him. . . .

What the Navy has to do today in Vietnam is to isolate the enemy by cutting off his supply lines. All Vietnam is a system of shallow waterways, and so riverine warfare comes once more to the fore. The newly re-commissioned battleship *New Jersey* can supplant a large number of bombing planes by shelling supply depots and troop-concentration centers. But in the long run the river boats have to go in and ferret out the enemy.

The Navy has four major groups committed to coastal and riverine warfare in Vietnam. They are the Coastal Surveillance Force, the Naval Advisory Group, the River Patrol, and the Mobile Riverine Forces.

The Coastal Surveillance Force guards more than one thousand miles of rugged coastline to deny Viet Cong supply ships the use of the rivers. It has radar picket escort ships, Coast Guard cutters, minesweepers, and patrol aircarft. In 1967, this force boarded or inspected more than 500,000 watercraft, mostly small boats.

There was a large-scale infiltration attempt by the Viet Cong on the morning of 14 March, 1967. It was detected by the Coastal Surveillance Force, which moved in immediately and blew up a 100-foot steel-hulled trawler on the beach at Quang Nagai. A large amount of ammunition, rifles, and medical supplies was seized.

The Vietnamese Navy is small, but it is being coached by its big brother. It is only natural that jealousies occur, and the Vietnam Navy wants more independence of command, having begun to feel its muscle. Most naval observers believe it would be a tragic mistake for the U.S. Navy to turn over the whole operation to the South Vietnamese: this is a case where we have to work together.

The Navy has developed several types of small war craft for the River Defense Force. The larger vessels are called PGM gunboats; they range on down to the small PBR, river patrol boats. Use of aluminum hulls and fiber glass deckhouses have made possible such things as a draft of only five feet, and only a few feet more showing up above the waterline to be detected upon enemy radar. The PGM is 165 feet long, carries a crew of twenty-four, and is armed with one three-inch .50-caliber mount, one 40-millimeter and two .50-caliber machine-gun mounts. With its speed and maneuverability, this is quite a bit of fire power.

Our riverine patrol in Vietnam runs into dangers of mines and always intense small-arms fire from the jungled shores. They have to land Marines in mangrove swamps, and pick them up again. There is no eight- or twelve-hour working day for these lads: they have to be awake and alert as long as the patrol lasts. Which reminds me of a true story from World War II:

Cruiser U.S.S. *Honolulu* returned to Tulagi, fresh out of fuel and ammunition after strenuous operations in the famed "Slot." This exchange of signals followed:

Commander Naval Advanced Base, Captain "Scrappy" Kessing: "What are your requirements?"

Captain of *Honolulu*, Robert Ward Hayler (later a vice admiral):

"Sleep."

Naval operations in Vietnam are a tough, dangerous, and exacting job. The observer cannot help but feel that we are wasting our sustenance there: in one of the most famous search and destroy operations, given the high-sounding title of Overlord II, we sought to clean out a Viet Cong stronghold on an island fifteen miles south of Saigon. Navy River Assault Groups and other Navy craft supported the 199th Infantry Brigade and other Army troops.

What happened? We took the island. We killed all of 15 Viet Cong, captured 16, and rounded up 101 suspects. Those are not very impressive figures, considering the millions of Viet Cong still at large.

Again: you cannot fight a war a little.

20. "CAN DO!"—
THE NAVY'S
FANTASTIC SEABEES

We're the Seabees of the Navy—
We can build and we can fight—
We'll pave a way to victory
And guard it day and night.
—Official Seabee song

JUST A COUPLE of years ago, when the Seabees were celebrating their twenty-fifth anniversary, they were literally paving a way to what we hope will be eventual victory in Vietnam by building a road through the jungle near the top of Monkey Mountain. This is a 2000-foot green elevation named for the many huge baboons found there. At the time, the baboons were likely outnumbered by Viet Cong prowlers.

Nobody has more fun with his work than a Seabee. The construction was being done in steamy 130-degrees temperature, and the crew had placed a sign against a rock crusher. It said: YOUR TAX DOLLARS AT WORK. THIS ROAD BUILT BY THE SEABEES FOR THE CONVENIENCE AND COMFORT OF THE UNITED STATES MARINES.

The love affair between the Navy Seabees and the U.S. Marines is based upon mutual respect, and goes back through the entire history of the Seabees. Until their advent, the Marine Corps proudly boasted for more than a century that it was the "first to fight, on land or sea." But when the first Marines landed on Japanese-held New Georgia, in World War II, Seabees had arrived several days earlier. The first thing the Marines saw was a Seabee sign saying:

WELCOME TO THE U.S. MARINES.

The average age of men in the Navy Construction Battalions in that conflict was thirty-seven, making them considerably senior to the youthful Marines. Both outfits were very "Gung ho!" and soon were kidding each other. (It is notable that you never kid anyone you do not like.) The Marines came up with a saying. It was, "Be kind to the Seabee—he may be some Marine's grandfather."

When the Monkey Mountain road was being built, a helicopter landed, and out stepped Lieutenant General Victor H. Krulak, commander of Fleet Marine Force Pacific. General Krulak is always explosive, in combat or not. He is a small man, about as safe to be around as a hand grenade that has been armed. He is so charged with dynamite and TNT as to have become affectionately known as "The Brute," and there is no doubt that he could whip several times his weight in wildcats.

Krulak looked around. Baboons everywhere. Also barebacked, sunburned, hairy-chested men, sweating profusely. After his briefing, the General picked out a young sailor and ask, pokerfaced, "How can you tell the Seabees from the baboons?"

"No problem, sir," the lad answered brightly. "The Seabees are the ones who are smoking cigars."

Krulak took another look. Sure enough, every Seabee had a cigar stuck into his mouth . . .

The motto of the Seabees is "*Construimus, Batuimus*," or, "We Build, We Fight." The unofficial slogan is simply "Can Do." The truth of both modest assertions has been proved all over the world.

Not all the wonderful accomplishments of the Seabees have been related to warfare. On Samoa, their ingenuity replaced a condenser with wax paper, tinfoil from cigarette packages, and an empty beer can. They salvaged automobile tires that would no longer hold an inner tube—tires were in short supply—by filling them with palm tree sawdust and cement. The Seabees in the South Pacific at that time would have chortled at a headline that appeared on the front page of the *San Francisco Chronicle*. It said: "Rubber Shortage: Petting Parties and Joy Rides Over for the Duration."

Seabees replaced broken watch crystals by using plexiglass from wrecked planes. They repaired dental plates with a mixture of ground rubber and cement.

Today, in Vietnam, we have thirty thousand Navy men operating ashore, and have had more than twice that number offshore. Reserve Seabee components have been called up, each to serve some eight months in the fighting zone. There are some eight thousand of them at this writing. They build landing fields, helicopter pads, deep water ports on the rivers, camps of all kinds, water, sewage, and electrical systems, as well as roads in a very difficult terrain. When working with bulldozers, shovels, hammers, and pickaxes, their rifles are always handy—they do, indeed, protect what they build.

It should be pointed out that doctors and hospital corpsmen serve with both the Seabees and the Marines, often under the most arduous and heroic circumstances.

[*ii*] The Navy's Civil Engineer Corps was a hundred years old when the Seabees observed their twenty-fifth anniversary. Of course the Civil Engineer Corps really fathered the Construction Battalions.

The Civils Engineer Corps had plenty of reasons for being proud of its own seventy-five year record of accomplishments. The need for civil engineers in the Navy was recognized as early as the 1790's, even before the Navy Department was established. By 1800 the Washington Navy Yard and other shore facilities were in operation. In 1801, Thomas Jefferson appointed Benjamin Henry Latrobe as the Navy's first civil engineer. Latrobe worked on plans for a drydock that would hold twelve 44-gun frigates. Congress turned down his plans, and he died before seeing his work completed by other men.

Expansion of shore bases began in earnest in 1826, when the Navy selected Loammi Baldwin as a civil engineer. Some seven years later, there were Navy yards in both Boston and Norfolk. By 1842, the new Bureau of Navy Yards and Docks had control of seven yards, four hospitals, some ammunition magazines, and some recruiting offices, as well as timber lands in which the Navy was interested. In 1854, the important Mare Island Navy Yard on San Francisco Bay was established.

The Navy's civil engineers were civilians until 1867. It took another four years before they were given relative rank with line officers, and were authorized to wear line officer uniforms. They performed splendidly in the Spanish-American war.

One thing was wrong. The officers were civil engineers, with technical training and know-how. The enlisted men they had to work with were seamen, who didn't know a thing about civil engineering. This is why establishment of the Seabees was such a wonderful boon—suddenly the C.E.C. had men who could run a bulldozer and operate a transit, and do other technical things.

In the Pacific, in World War II, the Seabees built 111 major air strips, 441 piers, 2,558 ammunition magazines, 700 square blocks of warehouse, tanks for storage of 100 million gallons of gasoline, hospitals for 70,000 patients, and housing for 1,500,000 men.

Some very famous men have been connected with the C.E.C. Captain Peter C. Asserson was the Navy's senior Civil Engineer from 1881 to 1898, and did much to build Norfolk Navy Yard and raise a number of ships sunk in the Civil War. Rear Admiral M. T. Endicott succeeded him and built the famous Dewey floating drydock. Rear Admiral H. H. Rousseau then took over—he made flag rank at the age of thirty-six, and his honors included having his photo used on a postage stamp, and the award of the Navy Cross: he had been responsible for Navy building in the Panama Canal Zone.

Others of equal renown followed in the job: In 1937, another man who was to become the youngest ever to hold the rank of

Vice Admiral headed up the Corps, and became the father of the Seabees. This was the colorful and capable Admiral Ben Moreell. In 1941, when he was forty-nine, he formed the Seabees as part of the C.E.C. with 3,300 men. Before the war was over, more than 350,000 men had served as Seabees.

The Seabees fought in more than four hundred actions in World War II. When you open recruiting to a group with an average age of thirty-seven, you are bound to assemble a rather motley crew. There were Seabees who were already famous, and some who would shortly be so. Nobody could accuse these enlistees of draft-dodging, because service in the Seabees was about as dangerous as anything you could get.

The Third Marine Division, Second Raider Regiment, erected a sign in the South Pacific. It said:

> So when we reach the "Isle of Japan"
> With our caps at a jaunty tilt
> We'll enter the city of Tokyo
> On the roads the Seabees built.

The Seabees were not yet six months old when they were bloodied at Guadalcanal, where they built Henderson Field while Japanese bombs and shells kept tearing holes into the concrete. At one point, Japanese troops pushed the Marine line to within 150 feet of the landing field, and in a forty-eight–hour period blasted fifty-three bomb and shell holes into the airfield.

They went on. One of the best known stories of Seabee daring and ingenuity is that of a first class petty officer, Aurelio Tassone. In the Treasury Island fighting, Tassone was landed with his bulldozer. He came under enemy fire from a pillbox. While a Seabee lieutenant provided covering fire with a carbine, Tassone raised his bulldozer's blade as a shield against bullets, and advanced on the pillbox. With wonderful timing, he dropped the blade, demolished the pillbox, and killed its inmates.

In addition to the Pacific, the Seabees were building in Newfoundland, Iceland, Scotland, Northern Ireland and England, France and Germany—and they were fighting wherever there was fighting to do. When a German air strike on an English village set off a fuel dump and sent a stream of flaming gasoline downhill toward the village, Seabee Philip Bishop quickly bull-dozed a dam that diverted the river of fire and saved the town. He was awarded the British Empire Medal (Military) for this act.

During the Allied landings in Normandy in 1944, in the vil-lage of St. Marie du Mont, a very excitable Frenchman appeared before the Seabees and informed them that fighting or no fight-ing, his wife was having a baby. A Seabee doctor, Richard D. An-derson, offered aid. The baby, a girl, was born during shot and shell, liberation and death. Her parents named her "Seabee."

Intriguing. Today, Mademoiselle Seabee Paule Fouchard would be about twenty-five years old. Where is she?

[*iii*] Author James Michener gave the Seabees a tremendous plug when he wrote his best-seller, *Tales of the South Pacific*. And the stories were true. The actual experiences of Seabees were as vivid as the stories.

Seabee officer Bradford Bowker stepped ashore at Guiuan, in the Philippines, and was mistaken for General Douglas Mac-Arthur. Everybody on the beach thought that "I shall return!" had been fulfilled, and there was quite a celebration.

Seabee Raymond Armstrong raised the tarp cover off the en-gine of his crane, and flushed a Japanese soldier. Armstrong threw rocks, and the Japanese surrendered.

H. D. (Pop) Niday, veteran of two World Wars and four Pacific landings, was hit on the chest by a Japanese grenade. He picked up the grenade and hurled it into the sea. Then he took a souvenir sword that had belonged to a Japanese officer on Gua-dalcanal, and neatly cut off his attacker's head.

Seabees knew judo. They knew it very well. Oddly enough, away back in 1932, the Japanese had hired Roy H. Moore to coach their judo teams for the Olympics. When war came, Moore joined the Seabees, and taught *them*.

There were some tragic and humorous interludes. At Momote airstrip in the Admiralty Islands, nineteen-year-old Edward

O'Brien killed sixteen Japanese attackers before he was shot to death. And then the ten-man detachment of defenders repulsed the assault, and killed 320 of the enemy.

You always wonder, considering language difficulties, just what the enemy is saying. Seabee John Hunter studied both Aleut and Russian to see what an aged Aleut Indian shouted at him every time he came near the old man's house. He was finally rewarded. The old man was yelling: "Keep away from my daughter, you young scoundrel!"

There were characters in the Seabees. A Seabee lieutenant, John Volpe, became Governor of Massachusetts. A Seabee musician in the South Pacific became a popular entertainer on radio and TV. His name was George Liberace.

The emblem of the Seabees, showing a bee with a machine gun in one pair of hands and tools of various kinds in the others, was drawn by Frank J. Iafrate, a civilian employee at Quonset Point Naval Air Station, Rhode Island, in 1942. Iafrate did not remain a civilian for very long—he became so enamored of his subject that he joined the Seabees. By now his symbol has been seen all over the world.

Renowned military leaders were quick to express their appreciation of the more than 350,000 Seabees who served in World War II. But when a news reporter enthusiastically labeled them as heroes, the Seabees modestly retorted that they were just construction men.

General Douglas MacArthur said, "The only trouble with the Seabees is that we don't have enough of them." General Bankson Taylor, Jr., of the Marine Corps, said "Wherever Marines have gone, they have seen their Seabee comrades performing miracles of construction and repair, often under heavy fire." James Forrestal congratulated the Seabees on their work, and so did Harry Truman. President Franklin D. Roosevelt told them, "You have come forward more quickly than any branch of the service, and I want you to know that we are all mighty proud of you."

So it went, with accolades from all over. But such praise never turned the Seabees' heads. They remained, at heart, not heroes but just "construction men."

Not long ago, the Grecian towns of Iklaini and Sgrapa named the road connecting them *"O Ektos Americanos Stolos,"* or Road of the American Sixth Fleet. It had been built by a Seabee detachment. After finishing the road, the Seabees threw in a soccer field for each town.

When the Korean War came along, the active force of Navy Seabees had dwindled to 3,300 men—in that way of false economy we have of allowing our defenses to shrink in times of peace, only to have to spend much more money later, in times of national emergency. Fortunately, however, there were more than 11,000 men in the Seabee Naval Reserve. These were called up to active duty, and the Seabees were back at their old stand. Despite strong tides and a continuous enemy fire, they built pontoon causeways during the Inchon landings of September 1950.

Following these landings, the Marines were pushing inland when a locomotive chugged toward them from enemy territory. They aimed rifles and bazookas at the engine until they saw familiar green uniforms in the cab, and a veteran sergeant said, "Hell—it's just them damn Seabees, at it again!" And it was. Ten Seabees had gone about ten miles behind the enemy lines, and had liberated the locomotive. What else to do but drive it back in triumph, probably singing "Casey Jones"?

In peace time—if there has been a so-called time of peace since the Korean War—the Seabees have acted as the Navy's Peace Corps. They have been operating in Haiti, Santo Domingo, Liberia, the Republic of Chad, the Central African Republic, Ethiopia, Chile, Costa Rica, Thailand, South Vietnam, and other countries.

In these areas, they work in teams of one officer, thirteen construction men, and one hospital corpsman. Before such a task force goes out on a job, it is given a course of "sprouts" on the country's history, geography, religion, politics, economics, and traditions. The team has bulldozers, a grader, a dump truck, and medical supplies.

As an example of the importance of the Seabees' work, one

has only to cite the task performed by the hospital corpsman. He handles as many as one hundred civilian cases per day.

[*iv*] The first Navy man to be awarded the Congressional Medal of Honor (posthumously) in the Vietnam fighting was a Seabee—Marvin G. Shields. His, indeed, was a heroic story.

The Seabees landed along with the first Marine Corps troops at Chu Lai, and immediately became heavily committed in the fighting at Da Nang and other places in the area. The Viet Cong, in great force, attacked an Army Special Forces camp at Dong Xoai, and a Seabee team of only nine men held them off for two days before support arrived. In this action, two Seabees were killed, the other seven were wounded, and all were decorated for bravery.

Marvin G. Shields got the Congressional Medal after he died.

He was a Construction Mechanic, Third Class. Wounded while supplying his fellow troops at Dong Xoai, he continued to serve them with ammunition, and kept returning the enemy's fire for some three hours. Then the Viet Cong launched a massive attack with flame throwers, hand grenades, and small-arms fire. Wounded a second time, Shields still assisted a more critically wounded man to safety, and then resumed shooting at the enemy for four more hours. He was bleeding critically all the time.

When the commanding officer asked for someone to accompany him on a desperate mission to knock out an enemy machine-gun emplacement, Shields—still bleeding—unhesitatingly volunteered. The two moved on their objective with a 3.5-inch rocket launcher, and destroyed the enemy position. But Shields was killed by enemy fire while returning to his defensive position.

It has been that way, all too frequently, in the history of the Navy's Seabees. They build well; they fight gloriously.

The Seabees are now doing things which the ordinary mind cannot understand. For instance, they are studying radiostope power, with a radiostope generator powering an automated telemetering station for oceanographic studies in Bering Straits. A five-year plan will be developed.

Radiostope? It isn't even in the dictionary. It's so new, I cannot explain or enlarge upon it here . . . but if the Seabees are involved, I will go along with the project, and expect great things from it.

21. WHO OWNS THE OCEAN FLOOR?

"None of us would sleep nights," a deeply informed congressional administrator told me, . . . "if we knew how far ahead of us Russia has pulled." Well, we do know that in Space, in the combination of defensive-offensive nuclear weapons, in merchant marine, in many phases of advanced industrialization the Soviet Union has made the United States a second-class power . . . our scientific community, unhappy for various reasons, is not delivering the goods . . . our vaunted Labor force is giving us sloppy workmanship. . . .

—*Holmes Alexander, syndicated newspaper columnist, 1 October, 1968*

MR. ALEXANDER'S COLUMN deplored the resignation of top-flight scientists in the Defense Department who could not go along with the war in Vietnam—or with Robert McNamara.

I have known some Admirals and Generals who felt exactly the same as the scientists, but, being in uniform and being career officers duty-bound to carry out orders from higher authority, there was nothing they could do about it. Some day before long, somebody will write another book to prove just how costly the Vietnamese war has been to America. He will show, as I have suggested before, that while getting nowhere fighting a piddling war a little in Vietnam, the United States has lost much of its leadership in Europe and the rest of the world.

And we are being bled by degrees. As I write this early in 1969, I find that in the eight years since January 1, 1961, the Marine Corps has had 9,691 men killed in Vietnam. The Navy has lost 905 men in combat action there; the Coast Guard lost one. The Army, more heavily involved, had nearly 18,000 men killed; the Air Force lost 598. The Vietnam war now ranks fourth in its toll of American lives.

Every thinking American will ask himself, "For what purpose were these fighting men sacrificed? What have we accomplished beyond gaining time, which is to say a stalemate? Would there not have been far fewer casualties if we had gone into North Vietnam with a powerful and decisive blow, and cleaned up the situation for all time? If we are so apprehensive about Russia and Red China, we have paved the way to be much more apprehensive in future . . ."

But in the scientific field, I believe it would reassure Mr. Alexander a great deal if he could be briefed on some things the Navy, General Dynamics, and some other people are currently doing. First, however, let's go back just a week before Mr. Alexander's remarks, and consider what happened in the United Nations General Assembly.

The Assembly was reminded that, a year before, the tiny country of Malta had submitted a proposal for ". . . the reservation exclusively for peaceful purposes of the seabed and the ocean floor." Gold, antimony, magnesium, and other precious minerals lie on the bottom of the ocean for the taking. Also, petroleum is there, and with new drilling techniques oil wells can be successfully sunk a long way from tidewater.

The certain promise is enormous, the possibilities are staggering. Our land resources are dwindling. Now we may well find them bolstered for many years by the wealth at the bottom of the sea.

Several things now going on in the Navy are pertinent to this. The U.S. Naval Ship *Kane*, carrying more than thirty top-flight oceanographers, has just completed the second leg of a voyage to chart a very deep scar on the bottom of the Atlantic. U.S.N.S.

vessels are under the Navy's Military Sea Transportation Service, with civilian crews and a Navy military officer aboard. The chief scientist in *Kane* is Professor Bruce C. Heezen, of the staff of the Geology Department of Columbia University, and of the Lamont Geological University in the Palisades.

In magazine articles current with this writing, Dr. Heezen has excited a great deal of interest among oceanographers by describing that scar on the Atlantic floor as a veritable Grand Canyon. He believes this break on the bottom of the sea definitely proves that at one time—many millions of years ago—there was only one great land mass. It broke up and drifted apart; it formed the continents, and created the oceans between.

This brings up an intriguing thought to a nonscientific mind. Are the continents still drifting? Does every major earthquake mean that the land masses have moved a few inches? In the centuries to come, will this cause a slow but drastic change of climates, so that man may have to migrate?

At any rate, the studies being done by scientists in the *Kane* will contribute greatly to our knowledge of what has been going on for millions of years at the bottom of the sea. They will help immeasurably when we begin trying to tap the wealth that lies there. Minerals sink to the lowest depths: therefore a good deal of the wealth will likely be found in this Grand Canyon that cuts across the Atlantic floor.

Jules Verne has been outmoded and outdone. For more than three years, now, the Navy has been actively engaged in some marvelous experiments known as SEALAB I, SEALAB II, and now SEALAB III. By the time this book is published, it could well be undertaking SEALAB IV.

SEALAB I was called a Man-in-the-Sea experiment. It and the ones following were so technical as to be difficult of comprehension, but, in simple terms, they have tested the ability of man to survive for extended periods at the bottom of the sea—not only to survive, but to be able to live, breathe comfortably, and do creative work despite the terrible pressures.

This has not been undertaken lightly. Preparations and advance training are elaborate, indeed. The Navy's Experimental Diving Unit (EDU) puts men through nine months of aquanaut training, and duplicates the pressures the divers will encounter in the open ocean. This training begins with simulated 450-foot dives—the dives may be simulated, but the pressure on the diver's body is very real. It goes on to depths of 1,000 feet and more, and involves two pressure chambers—a wet diving tank, and a recompression chamber that is very much like an igloo.

A man can stay down several days, living and breathing and working in the recompression chamber and out of it. But he is being subjected to pressure of about 100 pounds to the square inch of his body surface—or some seven times what you are breathing as you read this.

By 1970, the Navy hopes its Man-in-the-Sea program can keep men on the ocean floor, healthy, happy, and working efficiently, for indefinite periods. There will be nothing then to prevent them from harvesting the great treasures of the sea.

A great deal of this is due to what Navy Captain George F. Bond calls "the fallout of laboratory experiments." Captain Bond is a most unusual and dedicated man. He was educated at the University of Florida, where he majored in psychology and literature and took a pre-med course. Later he received his M.D. degree, and practiced medicine for a time in North Carolina. The Navy had him during World War II, and called him back to active duty in 1953.

It is obvious that Captain Bond loves the Navy, and that his affection is reciprocated. He began his deep-sea experiments very cautiously, using rats and guinea pigs in tests to develop a proper mixture of air to be breathed under pressure. Some of the old beliefs, such as those about pure oxygen, went by the boards.

The lessons learned from dives in deep-sea diving suits, and escapes from submarines with Momsen lungs, were helpful, but needed more intensive study. A man can go under deep-sea pressure very quickly, with no harmful effects: it is later, when he is coming back to the surface, that his whole body is surcharged with pinpoint bubbles like a bottle of carbonated soda, and an ascent too abrupt will rupture his lungs and kill him.

Captain Bond first tried normal air on his subjects, at seven atmospheres of pressure. It didn't work. All the rats were dead within thirty-five hours. He then used pure oxygen at the same simulated depth of 200 feet, and the same thing happened.

Then he tried 3 per cent oxygen and 97 per cent nitrogen. His guinea pigs and rats survived fourteen days of pressurized living, but developed some significant histological alterations that were revealed by autopsies, including pneumonia and changes to their adrenal glands.

Genius, it has been said, is an infinite capacity for taking pains. Captain Bond went on taking pains, and replaced his nitrogen with helium. This time, in a two-week testing period, there were no adverse physiological reactions and no histological changes. He moved up the scale and tested monkeys, and then a pair of goats. All survived, and thrived. Then, in 1962, he was given permission to use men as his subjects.

The men suffered no "bends," no decompression sickness. On the contrary, they reported that breathing the helium mixture was better than "even fresh sea breezes."

To understand how the tank or chamber works on the bottom, turn an empty glass upside down in a pan of water. It will capture a bit of air—pressurized—at the top of the glass. Now, figure that if you had lateral entrance and escape locks—tunnels, in effect—which entered the glass, and in which the pressure could be equalized, you could duck below the water level, enter the glass, and then stand erect with your head above water, and breathe.

That, in a very oversimplified way, is how it is done.

[*ii*] The use of helium and the pressure did present SEALAB I with a couple of problems. One was that human speech traveled much faster in the lighter atmosphere, and came out sounding like Donald Duck at his angriest. The other was that helium conducts heat much more readily than the earth's atmosphere does on a Saturday afternoon when you

are pushing the lawn mower. A temperature of 88 degrees had to be maintained to keep the "patients" comfortable. This was not the worst: a speech-translating device had to be developed to translate the Donald Duck quackings into intelligible English.

It is no wonder that Captain Bond was awarded the Legion of Merit for heading up SEALAB I.

In SEALAB II, three ten-man teams spent fifteen days under water, carrying on scientific studies of the ocean's bottom and its currents. It seemed odd that the Navy was involved in plankton sampling, bioluminescence studies, marine-life censuses, and the like. But, then, I have heard somewhere that mankind could very well survive on plankton.

Now, in SEALAB III, one hesitates to predict what will happen, or what will be learned. But it is certain that in future years, teams of Navy aquanauts will be under water during most of their working hours. By the end of 1970, Captain Bond expects to have provided the Navy with the means and techniques so that men can live for indefinite periods at depths of at least 600 feet.

This will do a lot toward the time when we begin to mine the ocean floor.

SEALAB III's goal of 600 feet is hardly more than wading depth compared to recent accomplishments of small research submarines which are equipped with underwater floodlights and very ingenious mechanical arms or "hands" that have picked potato-sized chunks of magnesium off the sea bottom to show the wealth that lies there waiting to be mined.

There are a number of such boats, which are expensive to build. Most were constructed by privately owned corporations— Electric Boat Division of General Dynamics, Reynolds International, General Motors, the Scripps Institution, the American Submarine Company, Lockheed, the Litton Industries' Woods Hole Oceanographic Institute, and the like. John H. Perry, a former scuba diver, built the Cubmarines, and saw them become famous through the "Flipper" television shows.

The Navy owns two boats outright, and has leased most of the others. Operators, who are called "drivers," are mainly former

Navy officers who have had experience in submarines.

Bathyscaphes, which are in effect hollow steel balls weighted down with tons of lead shot, have gone deeper than any other craft. In 1960, the Navy's bathyscaphe *Trieste* took Jacques Piccard and Navy Lieutenant Commander Don Walsh to a depth of 35,800 feet, or nearly seven miles. This record, sixty times as deep as World War II submarines could go, still stands.

But bathyscaphes can only go straight down, stay on the bottom for a limited time, then jettison their lead shot ballast to attain positive buoyancy, and come straight up. They cannot cruise the ocean floor or pick up samples of rocks and minerals from it.

Experiments with the deep-diving boats began early in the 1960s, and amazing progress has been made since that time. On 28 February, 1968, Larry Shumaker drove the *Deep Quest*—shaped like a shark and nearly forty feet long—to the unprecedented depth of 8,310 feet in the Pacific. In doing this, he broke his own world's record of 6,300 feet, established less than two months before.

Shumaker planted an American Flag on the bottom. Nobody is likely to see it, but this was fully as significant and historical as the famous flag-raising on Iwo Jima during World War II. It marked a victory and symbolically staked America's claim to her share of the wealth waiting on the ocean floor.

Shumaker had a considerable pay load aboard *Deep Quest*, in the persons of two other divers, Don Saner and Glenn Minard, and Rear Admiral P. E. "Pete" Summers, U.S. Navy, retired. Admiral Summers, commander of a submarine flotilla in World War II, helped design and build *Deep Quest*, and is her program manager. A graduate of Annapolis in 1936, he has the Navy Cross with star, with fourteen campaign ribbons. It is a standing joke around the Lockheed Missiles and Space Company's plant that wherever Pete Summers goes, a man has to follow him carrying a chest that contains his medals.

Summers knows the depths of the Pacific from long acquaintance, but his wartime dives were blind. Now, in *Deep Quest*, he saw strange fish and plantlike animals that looked like lilies which have not yet been classified. Oceanographers have said they may well be an animal thought to be extinct.

Deep Quest sighted tremendous quantities of plankton in her more than eight hours under water. It is known that these passive organisms are extremely nutritious and could someday do much to enhance the world's diminishing food supply.

Shumaker's dive, while the deepest, was only one of many made in the last several years. Gene Rodgers, thirty-nine, was inspecting a deep-sea cable for a telephone company. He took *Star III* down 1,800 feet off Cape May, New Jersey, turned on his lights, and saw the same kind of half-plant, half-animal life, with red fish and lobsters that were two and a half feet long and appeared to weigh twenty pounds.

America's famous moon-orbiting astronauts certainly deserve all the glory that has been heaped upon them. They explored a new frontier—outer space. Just as important, perhaps, are the accomplishments of American aquanauts in what might be called inner space. For a very thorough and readable account of their explorations, too extensive to be detailed here, I recommend a book called *Undersea Frontiers,* by Gardner Soule (Rand McNally).

22. OUR AMERICAN LIFE LINES

> To ensure our national security and to sustain the economic vitality of 200,000,000 American citizens, it is of critical importance that:
>
> 1. Raw materials from throughout the world be fed into the U.S. industrial machine by waterborne commerce;
>
> 2. Manufactured products be moved into the world marketplace by ocean shipping; and
>
> 3. Sea lanes be kept open and secure in time of peace, and denied to our enemy in case of war.
>
> Keeping the sea lanes open is a vital mission of the United States Navy. These sea lanes are the *life lines* of America!
>
> —*Admiral Horacio Rivero, U.S. Navy, Vice Chief of Naval Operations, 1966*

THERE WAS A TIME in our history, when the plows were breaking the western plains—and even later—when this country was self-sufficient. Its farms, mines, oil wells, and timberlands and fisheries turned out more raw materials than American industries could use.

There was a time when we owned no far-flung and overseas States, Territories, or Dependencies such as Alaska, Hawaii, Guam, and American Samoa. We had no need, then, for defense bases overseas. We sat between two mighty oceans, not completely secure—as was proven by the War of 1812—but much more secure than we would be today if we did not have a strong

Navy.

Those days are forever gone. They began going out shortly after the turn of this century; they were gone in World War I when we had to fight overseas, and when German submarines were sinking American shipping. Today, American manufactories and allied industries not only lead the world, but are mutually dependent upon the free world for sales, and for the raw materials that alone can keep the wheels turning and the labor force drawing paychecks. Industry, economy, jobs and security are one and indivisible.

As a young and vigorous growing nation, we squandered our national resources in a fearful way. In the meat department, we virtually exterminated the buffalo and the antelope: conserved, these could be great assets today. As late as the 1930's, we wasted petroleum and natural gas in a disgraceful way.

Look at what happened. The famed East Texas oil field, in 1939, had nearly 29,000 producing wells. They pumped millions of gallons of oil every day. It was a time of depression, and oil went down to ten cents and less per barrel.

No owner of an oil well dared stop pumping, because just a short distance away his neighbor's pumps were working, and helping to drain the same pool. There was no adequate storage. Tanks could not be built big enough. The Texans tried tanks dug into the earth, or behind dams that were thrown up in canyons. The rains came, the dams broke, and crude oil by the millions of gallons went down the rivers to the sea, killing fish and birds, ruining trees. It was a terrible waste. Finally, oil production was put under federal control.

Wells and whole oil fields are not inexhaustible, and eventually both run dry. Production falls off, but meanwhile the demand steadily increases. We have multiplied our industries by many times, and have added untold more millions of automobiles to our highways. The smog problem alone testifies to how much oil and gasoline is being burned.

America now consumes one-third of the entire world's supply of petroleum every year. In 1965, the United States used the amazing total of 3,300,554,000 barrels of oil—and we had no oil at all in the government stockpile. (Figures for 1969 will be even more impressive.)

A great deal of the more than three billion barrels came from Sumatra, Canada, Colombia, Venezuela, Kuwait, Iran, and Saudi Arabia.

The important thing to remember is that it had to be brought into this country by tankers, over the sea.

[*ii*] The list of our essential raw materials covers the range of the alphabet, and is an eye opener. It begins with Antimony and Asbestos, and ranges on through to Zinc and Zircon. In between are bauxite, beryl, chromite, and cobalt; copper, lead, and lumber; manganese, mica, and nickel; ribber, sugar, thorium, tin, and tungsten. And that vitally important substance that can save the day when the world's oil supply dwindles—uranium.

Offshore drilling already exists. Deep-sea drilling for oil and other mining of the ocean floors will receive a tremendous boost from the Navy's SEALAB III and continuing experiments in submerged living. But no matter what degree of success crowns the deep-sea drilling efforts, it cannot replace the tanker or the cargo ship.

"Freedom of the Seas," Heaven forbid, has sometimes been in danger of becoming a trite phrase that was not really understood by John Q. Public. We will always need a strong Merchant Marine, and should encourage the building of merchant ships by other nations: they carry world trade, in which America has a large and vital interest. But in time of war or peril they cannot carry it unless the sea lanes are protected by the Navy. Few ships are so vulnerable to submarine torpedoes or aerial bombs as are the squat, sluggish, unarmed merchantmen.

The world's merchant marine now faces certain problems. That short cut known as the Suez Canal is currently obsolete, especially insofar as the transport of oil is concerned. Modern tankers are simply too wide of beam for this historic waterway, and the ships have to take the longer way around.

The Suez has been inoperative since June of 1967, when the six-day war between Israel and the Arab States closed it. Tankers carrying oil made up about three-fourths of its traffic at that time, and now nobody knows when the Canal will resume business. Its continued disuse is very serious to the Egyptian economy, to which it was an importance source of revenue.

There are two sides to the coin, and one is Progress. Six tankers of 276,000 tons displacement are being launched. It is claimed that these huge ships can use the Cape routes from the Persian Gulf to European ports, and to America, at lower costs than transiting the Suez Canal.

Other times, other stations. The Suez would have to be widened and perhaps deepened before it could accommodate such ships. The cost of such alterations would be tremendous. Great Britain, having pulled back to her tight little island, might not wish to underwrite much or any of this expense: things have changed since the days of Kipling, when the Suez was known as "The Ditch." There is also the competitive threat of oil pipelines: a project is under development for a pipeline from the Gulf of Aqaba to the Mediterranean. This would bypass the Canal, and would amount to a deep-sea filling station.

At any rate, the big tankers are coming. In 1967, more than forty million tons of new tankers were ordered—almost twice the amount of the previous year. At the end of 1967, with 294 ships on blueprint or already on the ways, 115 of them were tankers of over 200,000 tons.

The world's merchant marine is growing in size and importance. Between the middle of 1966 and the middle of 1967, construction rose more than ten million tons to a total of 178 million tons. Japan is now building almost half of the world's merchant marine tonnage. The significance of this should not be lost on Americans.

We have never exactly been a "have not" nation, although we now approach that status in a number of important materials necessary to our industrial complex. But Japan, from before the time when the Perry Expedition opened it to the rest of the world, has always been a "have not" country.

However, she had manpower and skills. She overcame the handicap by importing what her industries needed, and then, with low-cost labor, producing vast quantities of her products. She tied this in with a big and active Merchant Marine. "Made in Japan" was soon known all over the world.

It would behoove us to profit by this example. Our Merchant Marine, unfortunately, has dwindled since World War II, and has fallen into low estate. That of Soviet Russia bids fair to surpass ours within the next three years. The Norwegians also have been engaged in some formidable shipbuilding.

We can pride ourselves on having launched N.S. *Savannah,* the world's first nuclear-powered cargo ship, which began operating in August 1965. She completed two years of service, and traveled more than 90,000 miles—and used only thirty-three pounds of enriched uranium fuel. The experts say that some 17,000 tons of fossil fuel would have been required to drive a conventionally powered ship of the same size, for the same distance.

What we need is more *Savannahs,* flying the Stars and Stripes. What we need is more uranium. It is discouraging to report that the world produced 31,000 tons of uranium in 1963, 26,700 tons in 1964, and only 20,800 tons in 1965. The United States has used from 74 to 63 per cent of this production. Whether or not we have a government stockpile is classified.

[*iii*] In 1894, Rudyard Kipling wrote:

> *The Liner she's a lady, and she never looks nor 'eeds—*
> *The Man-o-War's 'er 'usband, an' 'e gives 'er all she needs . . .*

The poem is as true today as when it was written. No liner or cargo ship sailing the seas can be safe from sudden, crazy, unprovoked attack, unless it is protected by warships within easy range. Piracy has not been ended: some recent acts of anti-Castro

Cubans prove that. There may be times when we will have to have warships guarding all liners, and all commercial ships ploughing the sea. We have already come pretty close to that with our wartime convoys.

We should remember that in World War II we fought a bitter battle to keep the sea lanes open so that we could transport men and materials to Europe, despite the German submarines. We won because we devised the Hunter-Killer groups and made the Atlantic unsafe for U–Boat operations.

We could have the same problem—somewhere—tomorrow.

We have six thousand miles of continental coast line to defend.

Seventy per cent of the earth is covered by salt water.

Most of the supplies that feed our industries are brought in by sea.

It follows, then, that we must maintain a strong Navy, to protect the Life Lines of America. I cannot say it as well as the Navy itself has said it, in what amounts to an official creed:

THIS, THE NAVY BELIEVES—

THE UNITED STATES NAVY
Guardian of Our Country

The United States Navy is responsible for maintaining freedom of the sea and is a ready force on watch at home and overseas, capable of strong action to preserve the peace or of instant offensive action to win in war.

It is upon the maintenance of this freedom that our country's glorious future depends; the United States Navy exists to make it so.

WE SERVE WITH HONOR

Tradition, valor and victory are the Navy's heritage from the past. To these may be added dedication, discipline and vigilance as the watchwords of the present and the future.

At home or on distant stations we serve with pride, confident in the respect of our country, our shipmates, and our families.

Our responsibilities sober us; our adversities strengthen us.

Service to God and Country is our special privilege. We serve with honor.

THE FUTURE OF THE NAVY

The Navy will always employ new weapons, new techniques,

and greater power to protect and defend the United States on the sea, under the sea, and in the air.

Now and in the future, freedom of the sea gives the United States her greatest advantage for the maintenance of peace and for victory in war.

Mobility, surprise, dispersal, and offensive power are the keynotes of the New Navy. The roots of the Navy lie in a strong belief in the future, in continued dedication to our tasks, and in reflection on our heritage from the past.

Never have our opportunities and our responsibilities been greater.

(Written for and by the U.S. Navy. Office of Armed Forces Information and Education, Department of Defense.)

ENVOI

STATEMENT before Court of Inquiry, 13 March, 1969, of E. Miles Harvey, attorney for Commander Lloyd M. "Pete" Bucher, of U.S.S. *Pueblo:*

The commanding officer . . . did *not* surrender his ship. He never struck his colors nor gave any manifest indication to the North Koreans that he was delivering either the ship or the crew to them. The search of the ship—the act prohibited by the first part of 0730 [Naval Regulations]—was done at gunpoint, and the record contains ample testimony on this fact. Certainly the commanding officer did not permit his command to be searched by any person representing a foreign state . . . *so long as he has the power to resist* (author's italics). . . . The Pueblo was simply not a combatant ship. . . . We submit [the commanding officer] did not have the power to resist.

John H. Chafee, secretary of the Navy:

I am convinced . . . that neither individual discipline, nor the state of discipline or morale in the Navy, nor any other interest requires further legal proceedings with respect to any personnel involved in the Pueblo incident.

It is my opinion that . . . they have suffered enough, and further punishment would not be justified. . . . The Court was of the opinion that, during his internment, Commander Bucher upheld morale in a superior manner; that he provided leadership by insisting that command structure be maintained and providing guidance for conduct; and that he contributed to the ability of the crew to hold together and withstand the trials of detention until repatriation could be effected.

Editorial, the *San Diego Union,* 18 April, 1969:

The United States is stunned, shocked and sick at heart over the wanton shooting down of an unarmed Navy aircraft in international air space by North Korea, with the loss of 31 lives.

It is an attack upon the United States which bears out the

prophecy of those who warned after the capture of the U.S.S. Pueblo that there would be future Communist piracy if the United States did not show strength. . . .

The alternatives are clear and their effectiveness is recorded in history. We lose battles of words with Communists. They understand and respect only our strength and our will to use it properly. . . .

We have had enough. We should teach North Korea the biblical lesson of an eye for an eye and a tooth for a tooth—promptly and decisively before no American ship is safe on the seas, or airplane in the skies.

An envoi is ordinarily a short stanza appended to a ballade, dedicating the prefatory verses and repeating the last line of each, summing up the usually amorous and tender message. While this one appears at the end of a love letter to the Navy, there will be a great deal more anger than tenderness in it—all directed toward our unprincipled North Korean enemy.

Before we get into history, let us consider the kind of people who were involved. What are the North Korean people like? No doubt many are kind and worthy of trust, but there are some of them fiendish enough to enjoy picking up baby birds that have fallen from their nests, and pulling their legs off while they are still alive. (Several Americans who had witnessed this cruelty told me about it when I was in Korea and Japan. I note that Bernard Weinraub cited it in a recent article in The *New York Times Sunday Magazine,* and quoted Commander Bucher's testimony that he had seen it. I am inclined to think, therefore, that whether representative or not, it was no single, isolated incident. Such an act would hardly be done by a civilized person.)

On 23 January, 1968, U.S.S. *Pueblo* was captured *in international waters,* by North Korean gangsters. It was an act of sheer piracy, and required no courage at all—no more than does pulling off the legs of baby birds. The fact that North Korea was allowed to get away with this infamous deed, without retaliation, undoubtedly encouraged and brought about the recent shooting down of the unarmed Navy plane, with the loss of thirty-one American lives.

The *Pueblo* was the first U.S. Navy ship taken in 160 proud years. The *Pueblo* was a warship, just as a Navy hospital ship, although a noncombatant, is a warship. (All Navy ships are warships.)

Who was to blame? Not Commander Lloyd M. "Pete" Bucher, captain of the *Pueblo*. Was it bureaucracy of high Navy brass? This is unlikely, because the Navy naturally wants more and better guns on *all* its ships. The reduced naval appropriations effected under Defense Secretary Robert McNamara? Possibly. If you blame the latter, you may as well go all the way to the White House and blame the policies of Lyndon B. Johnson.

Nobody can say. Bucher, after taking command, repeatedly asked for heavier armament and did not get it. But more than the usual and very necessary principles of economy dictated this refusal. There has been a feeling that it would be bad psychology to arm Navy reconnaissance ships—call them "spy" ships if you like—because it would tend to make them aggressors. We operate quite a number of them, and they sail openly, *in international waters*. The Russians have a large number of such vessels, mostly in the guise of fishing trawlers, with high-frequency radios. The short, ugly term *spy ships* is quite correct. But remember that if we had had a number of such vessels in the Pacific before 7 December, 1941, the holocaust of Pearl Harbor might have been averted, or at least diminished.

The real culpability for what happened to the *Pueblo* lies in the fact that the U.S. did not think any nation would violate the freedom of the seas. We learned the hard way. Secretary of State William P. Rogers summed up things at their philosophical best when he observed, "The weak can be rash; the powerful must be more restrained." But there is small comfort in this.

The *Pueblo* was a small former Army transport, of the type the Navy slangily calls a "spitkid." (A spitkid is a small box filled with sand, to receive cigarette butts and tobacco juice.) She was all of 176 feet long, had a beam of under 33 feet, and displaced 935 tons with a full load. She was commissioned 13 May 1967, with Commander Bucher in command, and was designated an environmental research vessel (AGER-2). Other such ships, including U.S.S. *Banner* and U.S.S. *Palm Beach,* were already operating.

U.S.S. *Banner* had been subjected to a series of harrassments by North Korean vessels, but nothing came of them. U.S. authorities were probably lulled into a false sense of security. The *Pueblo* sailed, to operate nearer the North Korean coast than the *Banner* had done. And she went out virtually unarmed.

A North Korean S-O (submarine chaser) challenged the *Pueblo,* more than fifteen miles off the coast. The *Pueblo* hoisted the American flag, and signaled that she was in international waters but would withdraw. Three other patrol boats then joined the North Korean vessel, all with armament superior to *Pueblo's* fore and aft .50-caliber machine guns and a few pistols. *Pueblo* had orders to keep her machine guns covered. At the moment, this was hardly necessary because the canvas housings were covered with several inches of ice, making the guns so difficult of access as to render them useless. Both guns were so completely exposed that men firing them would have been slaughtered in a minute.

Bucher broke radio silence to ask for American assistance, saying, "These guys mean business." But darkness was closing in, and all available help was too far away. MIG planes were still circling overhead.

It has recently been revealed that the Navy actually did launch a rescue mission very quickly after the capture. Two destroyers, U.S.S. *Truxton* and U.S.S. *Higbee,* were ordered to get under weigh. The U.S. would send an ultimatum to North Korea; Higbee would make speed to Wonsan harbor under air cover, and bring *Pueblo* out.

But the operation was called off by "higher authority." History students and Navy buffs likely will argue about this for years. The "higher authority" was Lyndon B. Johnson, who conferred in the White House with leading military aides and foreign affairs advisors. It appears that these people were unanimous in counseling the President to do nothing, and that LBJ said with a sigh of relief, "I don't want another war." There was no horror in this decision for him, or anybody else, except that it was based on the belief that any rescue attempt would have meant the deaths of Pete Bucher and all his men.

Courageous as he was, Bucher was unable to do anything but comply with the North Korean orders. He had had one man killed, and was himself suffering from shrapnel wounds in the legs and buttocks. The North Koreans paraded a stretcher past his room and halted long enough to let him see a wounded man with his intestines hanging out. This casualty was not treated for several days; the wound suppurated, and the stench from it was so bad that another man in the same compartment continually vomited.

So, six officers, seventy-five enlisted men, and two civilian technicians of the *Pueblo* became prisoners of the North Koreans, in total violation of international law.

You may be sure that Bucher and all his crew knew what they were doing, and knew that they were gathering intelligence, i.e., spying. But everybody else was doing the same thing. It was supposed to be quite proper to do this on the high seas.

The North Koreans had acted in haste and hot anger, and now they realized they would have to defend a case of piracy in international waters. They started at once to force Pete Bucher to sign a confession that his ship had been guilty of spying. Bucher held out for a period of incredible torture. He and his men were subjected to starvation, beatings, kickings, and other cruelties. Bucher's normal weight was 195 pounds, and he lost an even 100 pounds of that. He and his people were blindfolded and kicked and beaten; they were forced to kneel with sticks behind their knees and their hands clasped behind their heads while being whipped with two-by-fours until the boards were shattered —and then they were whipped with the splintered remainders. Some of these attacks were so vicious that afterwards the men could neither stand nor walk. They urinated blood.

The only glorious chapter of the inglorious proceedings is that the spirit of American defiance did not fail, and there was even a bit of typical American humor. The crew posed for group photographs which were to show Americans that they were well and being cared for . . . and the photos showed that every Navy man was making an obscene gesture with his middle finger upraised and erect. These photos had already been released for propaganda purposes when the North Koreans finally caught on to the idea that such a gesture is not the "Hawaiian good-luck sign" after all. The crew was beaten again, but they were gleeful: they had put their idea across.

They got away with other things which proved that starvation and harsh treatment had not broken them down. They were ordered to write letters home to the President, to their congressmen and their parents, telling how they had been guilty of espionage and how very generously they had been treated by the forgiving North Koreans.

This was, indeed a laugh.

The North Korean order plainly shows that the North Koreans realized they had committed an act of piracy. They had no feeling of guilt about having seized the *Pueblo,* but now there was a nagging fear about repercussions from the United Nations.

So it was important to them that Pete Bucher confess.

To put it as kindly as possible, the North Koreans are stupid. Very, very stupid.

Pete Bucher wrote a "confession" which sent the North Koreans to the English dictionary—but they didn't look hard enough. This is what he said in doubletalk:

"We are extremely grateful to the Korean people for having forgiven us. The rosy finger of dawn is now replacing the fickle finger of fate upon which we have been rotating so long.

"Not only do we wish to paean the Korean people, but we want to paean the whole country."

Well, the dictionary says that a *paean* is a song of praise. It says nothing about any vulgar connotation having to do with the way the word is pronounced. And Bucher got away with it!

Similarly, the letters the crewmen were forced to write were filled with doubletalk to make the homefolks see they were fakes. There were instances of nonexistent relatives, such as, "Give my love to Uncle Ben and Aunt Jemima," which got past the Koreans. So did "Garba Gefollows," which translates easily into "Garbage Follows." As one *Pueblo* crew member said in an understatement, "The North Koreans were not very clever."

Malnutrition was the order of the day. Quartermaster First Class Charles B. Law suffered so much from starvation that he sustained permanent damage to his eyesight. He also was beaten for an eight-hour period with fists and sticks.

Electrician's Mate Second Class Stephen E. Woelk was critically injured in the initial shelling of the *Pueblo*. He was then carried off the ship to prison . . . and it was three agonizing days later before the North Koreans performed surgery upon him. When they did, they worked without an anesthetic of any kind.

There is little use of detailing the *Pueblo* crew's sufferings any more, because the account becomes repetitive and thus loses force. It suffices to say that at no time in history were men ever subjected to greater cruelties or worse torture. It should be noted that neither Law nor Woelk broke down when they testified before the Naval Court of Inquiry—the things that had happened to them were in the past.

But Commander Bucher broke down frequently, and wept, although he testified he had not been very much mistreated after the first few days and after he signed his "confession." When this had been extorted from him, his captors brought him a big plate of food containing eggs and "other goodies." Bucher could not eat it.

He considered himself responsible for the treatment of his crew, and keenly felt every blow given to his people. He had been told that unless he confessed to the spy mission, all his crew would be shot—beginning with the youngest—before his eyes.

The members of the Court of Inquiry probably were unanimous in their feeling of sympathy for Pete Bucher and his men, but they did not do a whitewash job. After all, a Navy ship had been lost. The Court recommended that Bucher be brought to trial by general court-martial for the following five alleged offenses:

1. Permitting his ship to be searched while he had the power to resist.

2. Failing to take immediate and progressive protective measures when his ship was attacked by North Korean forces.

3. Complying with the orders of the North Korean forces to follow them into port.

4. Negligently failing to complete destruction of classified material aboard U.S.S. *Pueblo* and permitting such material to fall into the hands of the North Koreans.

5. Negligently failing to ensure, before departure for sea, that his officers and crew were properly organized, stationed, and trained in preparation for emergency destruction of classified material.

Three largely similar charges were brought against Lieutenant Stephen R. Harris, U.S. Naval Reserve, the officer in charge of the *Pueblo*'s research department. The Court further recommended that *Pueblo*'s executive officer be given an official letter of admonition.

The Court could do no less. But it was brought out that the devices carried aboard the *Pueblo* to destroy her highly secret electronic gear consisted of a few sledgehammers, that her incinerator for the burning of codes and classified messages was so tiny as to be utterly inadequate, and that she had only a pitifully small supply of weighted bags in which things could have been thrown over the side. Even if they had been jettisoned in such a manner, the sea's depth in that area was shallow enough to permit them all to be recovered.

The Navy has a heart. The Commander-in-Chief of the Pacific Fleet, who was convening authority for the Court of Inquiry, refused to accept the recommendations for general courts-martial when he reviewed the Court's findings. The Chief of Naval Operations agreed with him. And then came the heart-lifting dismissal of all charges by the Secretary of the Navy.

Some good has come out of it all. The Secretary of the Navy says: "Every feasible effort is being made to correct any Navy deficiencies which may have contributed to *Pueblo*'s seizure. The Navy's leaders are determined that the lessons learned from this tragedy shall be translated into effective action."

The major lesson learned, of course, has nothing to do with armament or operating procedures. It is simply that we cannot trust the gangster nation of North Korea to abide by any laws, international or otherwise.

And Commander Bucher? He made a statement that was released by his civilian attorney, E. Miles Harvey. It said:

> Commander Bucher is extremely relieved that the proceedings have been completed and the matter has become final. It has been fifteen agonizing months for the officers, the crew and their families, as it has been for Commander and Mrs. Bucher.
>
> He is satisfied with the final outcome and is looking forward to his next duty assignment—whatever it may be.
>
> Commander Bucher understands the philosophy with which the members of the Court of Inquiry viewed the matter, and the reasoning process that they went through. He has no personal feeling toward any member of the Court, and feels that counsel to the Court did a commendable job.
>
> He continues to have the highest praise for the overall conduct of his officers and crew, and hopes there will be commendations for some of them. Commander Bucher is pleased that certain corrective measures have been instituted.
>
> The expressions of interest and concern received and the many courtesies extended by so many people are sincerely appreciated.
>
> We are satisfied that the news media has acted in a responsible manner, but fervently hope that this appearance will be the final one.

Most likely the personal appearances are over as a result of the action of the Secretary of the Navy, but the *Pueblo* story will be debated and written about for a long time. Accounts published thus far have praised Bucher highly. But the June, 1969, issue of *Reader's Digest* (which went to press before the Court of Inquiry had finished its hearings) had some gloomy thoughts: "No matter what happens . . . none of the participants can emerge whole. Bucher will be stained in the eyes of a service not known to forgive and forget. *Pueblo* will go down as a ship not equipped for its job. The Navy, no matter how lengthy the explanations, will go down as allowing a tactical situation to get out of hand. And the United States will have to bear the overall responsibility for the ship's capture."

There may be some hotheads who maintain that the *Pueblo* and her crew should have been sacrificed on the altar of tradition, and gone down firing the puny .50-caliber guns to the last. I am not one of them. As an old Navy hand, I believe Pete Bucher's decision to save the lives of his men took a higher degree of courage than would have been required to engage in hopeless battle. All honor to him.

BIBLIOGRAPHY

PRIMARY SOURCES

Interviews and correspondence with scores of Navy men, ranging from enlisted personnel to Admirals. The author's own recollections of thirty-eight years of association with the Navy, including twenty years of active duty.

Official documents in the Library of Congress, the National Archives, the Naval History Division, and the Navy Department Library.

Docustats of material supplied by the U.S. Naval Historical Display Center, Washington Navy Yard.

OFFICIAL PUBLICATIONS

Naval Documents of the American Revolution. 2 vols. U.S. Government Printing Office, 1964–1966.

Naval Documents, Quasi-war with France. 6 vols. U.S. Government Printing Office, 1935–1938.

Naval Documents, Barbary Wars. 6 vols. U.S. Government Printing Office, 1940–1944.

U.S. Naval Institute Proceedings. Files covering several years. A monthly magazine devoted to professional and historical articles about the Navy.

U.S. Submarine Losses in World War II. Naval History Division, 1949.

Command Decisions. Prepared by the Office of the Chief of Military History, Department of the Army. Published by Methuen, 1960.

Such official handbooks as *The Naval Officer's Guide, The Watch Officer's Guide, The Bluejacket's Manual, Naval Terms Dictionary, Almanac of Naval Facts,* etc.

SECONDARY SOURCES

Colonel Hans Christian Adamson and Captain Francis Kosco, *Halsey's Typhoons.* Crown, 1967.

Saul Braun, *Seven Heroes.* Putnam, 1965.

Fred J. Buenzle, *Bluejacket.* W. W. Norton & Co., 1939.

Captain Robert J. Bulkley, Jr., *At Close Quarters; P.T. Boats in the*

My Love Affair with the Navy

U.S. Navy. U.S. Naval Institute, 1962.

Captain Edmund L. Castillo, *Midway, the Battle for the Pacific.* Random House, 1968.

Howard I. Chapelle. *History of the American Sailing Navy.* W. W. Norton, 1949.

Admiral J. J. "Jocko" Clark, *Carrier Admiral.* McKay, 1967.

Rear Admiral W. Scott Cunningham and Lydel Sims, *Wake Island Command.* Little, Brown, & Co., 1961.

Rear Admiral George J. Dufek, *Operation Deepfreeze.* Harcourt, Brace & Co., 1957.

James C. Fahey, *Ships and Aircraft, U.S. Fleet.* Naval Institute.

Donovan Fitzpatrick and Saul Saphire, *Navy Maverick: Uriah Phillips Levy.* Doubleday, 1963.

John Foster, *Rebel Sea Raider.* Morrow, 1965.

Captain Daniel J. Garrison, *The Navy from Wood to Steel.* Watts, 1965.

Commander Herbert Gimpel, *Navy Men and What They Do.* Watts, 1963.

D. S. Halacy, Jr., *The Shipbuilders.* Lippincott, 1966.

Lieutenant Commander Brayton Harris, *The Age of the Battleship.* Watts, 1965.

Jim Dan Hill, *The Texas Navy.* Barnes, 1937.

Captain Walter Karig, *Battle Report.* 4 vols. Rinehart, 1946–1952.

Professor Harold D. Langley, *Social Reform in the United States Navy, 1798–1862.* University of Illinois Press, 1967.

Vice Admiral Charles A. Lockwood and Colonel Hans Christian Adamson, *Battles of the Philippine Sea.* Crowell, 1967.

Walter Lord, *Incredible Victory.* Harper & Row, 1967.

Vice Admiral Leland P. Lovette, *Naval Customs, Tradition, and Usage.* 4th edition. U.S. Naval Institute, 1967.

Peter Maas, *The Rescuer.* Harper & Row, 1967.

James M. Merrill (editor), *Quarterdeck and Foc'sle.* Rand McNally, 1963.

Admiral Samuel Eliot Morison, all his works pertaining to the Navy. Little, Brown & Co.

Howard P. Nash, Jr., *The Forgotten Wars.* Barnes, 1968.

Richard F. Newcomb, *Iwo Jima.* Holt, Rinehart, & Winston, 1965.

Theodore Roscoe, *Destroyer Operations in World War II* (1953), and *Submarine Operations in World War II.* U.S. Naval Institute, 1949.

Captain W. G. Schofield, *Destroyers—60 Years.* Bonanza, 1962.

Karl Schuon, *U.S. Navy Biographical Dictionary.* Watts, 1964.

Robert Silverberg, *Stormy Voyager; the Story of Charles Wilkes.* Lippincott, 1968.

S. E. Smith (editor), *The United States Navy in World War II.* Morrow, 1966.

Gardner Soule, *Undersea Frontiers.* Rand McNally, 1968.

Boleslaw Szczesniak (editor), *The Opening of Japan*. University of Oklahoma Press, 1962.

Captain John M. Waters, U.S. Coast Guard, *Bloody Winter*. Van Nostrand, 1967.

INDEX

Index

Index

Index

Index

Index